Pacific Northwest

John Doerper
Photography by Greg Vaughn

COMPASS AMERICAN GUIDES
An Imprint of Fodor's Travel Publications

Compass American Guides: Pacific Northwest

Editors: Sarah Felchlin, Chris Culwell
Photo Editors: Christopher Burt, Jolie Novak
Archival Research: Melanie Marin
Map Design: Mark Stroud, Moon Street Cartography; Eureka Cartography
Production House: Twin Age Ltd., Hong Kong

Third Edition

ISBN 0-676-90496-3
ISSN 1539-3275

Although all prices, opening times, and other details in this book are based on information supplied
to us at press time, changes occur all the time in the travel world, and the publisher cannot accept
responsibility for facts that become outdated or for inadvertent errors or omissions.

COMPASS AMERICAN GUIDES gratefully acknowledges the following institutions and individuals for the
use of their photographs, illustrations, or both: **American Museum of Natural History,** pp. 22, 95; **B.C.
Archives and Records Service,** p. 81, neg. A-04656; **James Chatters,** p. 19; **City of Vancouver Archives,** p. 44
neg BU.P. 403.N.387, p. 60, neg MI.P. 43.N.33; **Columbia River Maritime Museum,** p. 329; **Ken Straiton,**
p. 11; **Museum of History and Industry,** pp. 167, 168, 178; **Puget Sound Maritime Historical Society,** p. 173;
Royal B.C. Museum, p. 16 neg 7376, p. 99 neg 4606; **University of Washington Libraries,** p. 25; **Vancouver
Public Library,** p. 33 neg. 1091; **Washington State Historical Society, Tacoma,** pp. 188, 200. We also wish to
thank John Ciavarella for copy-editing the book and Ellen Klages for proofreading it.

Compass American Guides, 280 Park Avenue, New York, NY 10017
PRINTED IN CHINA
10 9 8 7 6 5 4 3 2 1

To Victoria
who loves the Pacific Northwest more than her native California

AUTHOR'S ACKNOWLEDGMENTS

A book is more than a product of a single mind. I would therefore like to thank the many people who have made the original edition of this guide possible: Christopher Burt, Kit Duane, Julia Dillon, and Debi Dunn of Compass American Guides for asking me to write this book, and for making me feel like I could do it, and for welcoming me so graciously when I dropped by the office. I would especially like to thank Kit Duane for her truly inspired editorial guidance. I must also show my appreciation for the splendid Thai meals Ben Burt has created for our get-togethers. Special thanks go to Deborah Wakefield of Portland and Irene Hoadley of Salem, Oregon; to Eileen Mintz and Norma Rosenthal of Mercer Island, Washington; to Tamara Wilson; and to the Eclipse Bookstore and Village Books in Bellingham, Washington, for the splendid variety of books on the Northwest they carry. I would also like to thank Rising Sun Motors in Bellingham for keeping my car going as I burned up the miles.

C O N T E N T S

Topical Essays and Literary Extracts

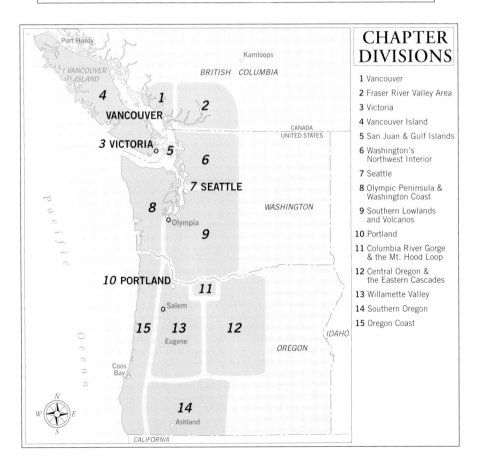

CHAPTER DIVISIONS

1 Vancouver
2 Fraser River Valley Area
3 Victoria
4 Vancouver Island
5 San Juan & Gulf Islands
6 Washington's Northwest Interior
7 Seattle
8 Olympic Peninsula & Washington Coast
9 Southern Lowlands and Volcanos
10 Portland
11 Columbia River Gorge & the Mt. Hood Loop
12 Central Oregon & the Eastern Cascades
13 Willamette Valley
14 Southern Oregon
15 Oregon Coast

Maps

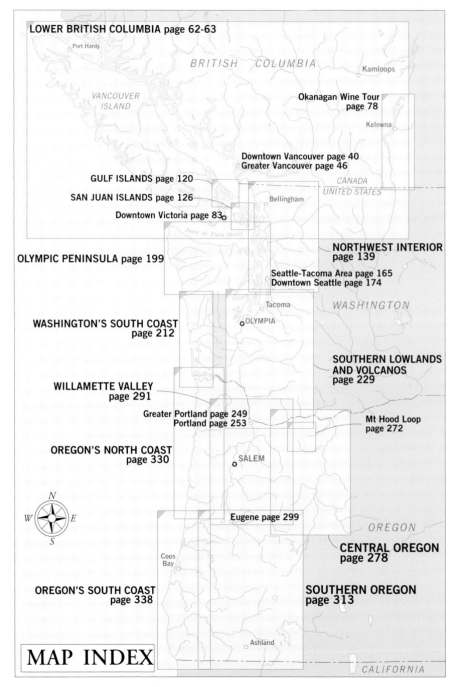

MAP INDEX

CALIFORNIA

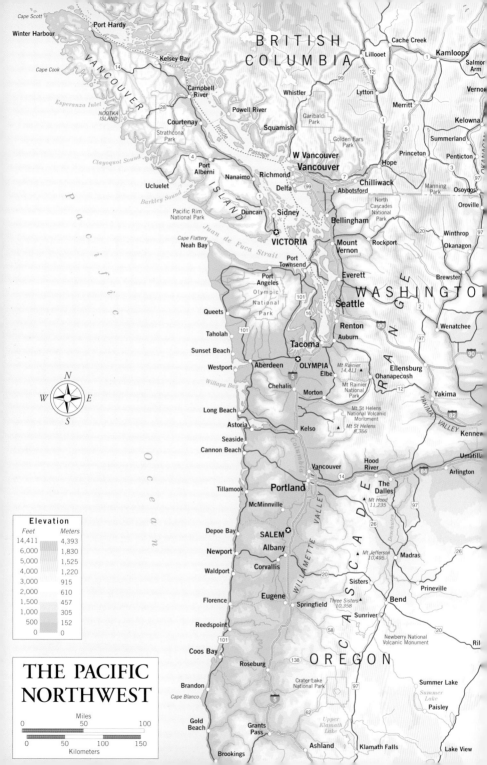

THE PACIFIC NORTHWEST

Elevation

Feet	Meters
14,411	4,393
6,000	1,830
5,000	1,525
4,000	1,220
3,000	915
2,000	610
1,500	457
1,000	305
500	152
0	0

Miles
0   50   100

0   50   100   150
Kilometers

OVERVIEW

THE PACIFIC NORTHWEST'S coastline is one of quiet river estuaries, sand dunes, and rock-walled fjords. Dense forests border the shore and tall alpine peaks rise above the horizon. The beauty of the landscape and the quality of the cuisine in sophisticated Vancouver, Seattle, and Portland attract an ever greater number of visitors. But the spaces are so vast, no one feels crowded.

1 V A N C O U V E R   *pages 30–55*

2 F R A S E R   R I V E R   V A L L E Y   *pages 56–79*

Bordered by saltwater fjords, towered over by alpine peaks, Vancouver truly is one of the most beautiful cities in the world. Here you can sail in the morning and ski in the afternoon. But the city has other attractions as well: excellent accommodations, theaters, art galleries, museums, sports arenas, and restaurants, including some of the best Chinese restaurants this side of Hong Kong.

KEN STRAITON

The Fraser River rises in the Rocky Mountains and cuts a swath across the wilds of central British Columbia before it descends to tidewater in a deep, rocky gorge. Before reaching salt water, it flows through a beautiful pastoral valley bounded by tall mountain ranges to the north, east, and southeast.

3 **VICTORIA** *pages 80–93*

4 **VANCOUVER ISLAND** *pages 94–115*
Enjoy Victoria's lovely English colonial architecture and views of its beautiful harbor. Sip
afternoon tea in the lobby of the Empress
Hotel or in the tropical lushness of the Crystal
Gardens. And relax. Victoria is a laid-back
city, just made for taking it easy.

Beyond the city lies the misty west coast of
Vancouver Island, a wonderland of deep
fjords, rocky islands, and remote sandy
beaches where the only noise you hear is the
roar of the surf, the lonely croak of a raven, or
the splash of a gray whale. There are few
towns here and even fewer roads, making this
a great region to explore by kayak or canoe.
The rain-sheltered east coast of the island has coves and beaches warm enough for
taking a summer swim.

5 **ISLANDS**
pages 116–137
Incredibly beautiful and
rugged, the San Juan and
Gulf Islands are but a
short boat or plane ride
from the major metropoli-
tan cities of the Pacific
Northwest. Rocky cliffs
and sandy beaches alter-
nate along the maze of
tidal waterways that
resemble white-water rivers at the change of the tide. Here mountains rise straight
from the sea. In quiet bays, the flexible boughs of red cedar hang out over the
water and catch eelgrass at low tide.

6 **N O R T H W E S T   I N T E R I O R** *pages 138–163*
With its jagged, razor-sharp peaks flanked by glaciers that glow with an inner blue-green light, the North Cascades are among the most beautiful mountains found anywhere. Rocky islands and reedy shores attract bird-watchers; rivers and lakes attract fishermen.

7 **S E A T T L E** *pages 164–197*
A vibrant, modern city, facing the blue waters of Puget Sound, Seattle has more restaurants and museums than any other Washington city. To see the city at its best, take a harbor tour, which will also take you into the Ship Canal and through the locks connecting Lake Washington to Elliott Bay, or grab a window table in a waterfront restaurant just at sunset.

8 **O L Y M P I C   P E N I N S U L A   &   W A S H I N G T O N   C O A S T**
pages 198–227
The lichen-, moss-, and fern-bedecked trees of the Olympic rain forest are about as close as a temperate forest can come to being a true jungle. Elk and black bear amble through these forests, and eagles fly overhead. On lonely beaches tall sea

stacks rise from the surf, and there are windswept headlands, white-water rivers, and alpine peaks covered with wildflowers. Along the southern coast, oysters thrive in estuaries. Taste them fresh from the shell or smoked, or stop at a local restaurant for barbecued, fried, or stewed oysters.

9 SOUTHERN LOWLANDS

pages 228–247

On hazy days, when the sun hits them just right, the tall volcanic peaks rising above the low, rolling southern Washington Cascades seem to float in the air, separated from the earth by their own shadows. They can be seen from the cities of southern Puget Sound, or visited. Observe the devastation caused by the 1980 eruption of Mount St. Helens, or stroll through wildflower meadows on the flanks of Mount Rainier.

10 PORTLAND *pages 248–263*

The City of Roses is a beautiful river city with many parks and a casual, cosmopolitan air. Enjoy the amenities of some of the region's finest hotels, sample the exquisite meals prepared by local chefs, watch a play, visit a museum, cruise on the river, enjoy the music scene, or just take a long walk.

11 COLUMBIA GORGE & MOUNT HOOD *pages 264–275*

Beautiful snowcapped peaks towering over a picture-perfect river gorge—what more can you ask for? The region has hiking trails through rugged canyons, quiet forests, and wildflower meadows by tall waterfalls. If you want to learn about the recreation possibilities, look at the cars: many carry both sailboards and skis on their rooftop racks. You might, on the other hand, just sit quietly and watch the river flow by or dangle your feet in the pool beneath a waterfall.

12 **C E N T R A L   O R E G O N** *pages 276–289*
This sunny country of open woods, of tall ponderosa pines, of rock-bound whitewater rivers running through lush meadows, of sagebrush flats and volcanic flows is a prime vacation destination. Hike across lava flows, visit the Warm Springs Indian Reservation, or sip a microbrew at a Bend pub. If you hear Indian drums and chanting on your car radio, you're not hallucinating: the Warm Springs radio station airs a program called *Drums and Talk*.

13 **W I L L A M E T T E   V A L L E Y &**
W E S T E R N   C A S C A D E S *pages 290–311*
Forests of tall oaks alternate with a quilted pattern of fields, orchards, and vineyards in this pastoral valley, which was among the first in the West to be settled. The Willamette River runs through it, and tall volcanic peaks rise to the east; the forest-clad ridges of the Coast Range protect the valley from the chilly drizzle of the Pacific Coast. Visit wineries and covered bridges, stock up on berries at fruit stands, or hang out with the locals in a sidewalk cafe.

14 **S O U T H E R N**
O R E G O N *pages 312–327*
15 **O R E G O N   C O A S T**
pages 328–343
The lovely small town of Ashland and its Shakespeare Festival attract most visitors to this region, but there are many more attractions to explore, including white-water rivers and Crater Lake. To the west lies the wild Oregon coast, its headlands sculpted by wind and surf. Most of the towns along this coast are quiet but have excellent restaurants and interesting shops.

H I S T O R Y

Landscape and climate are the keys to the natural and human history of the Northwest Coast. On clear days, the mountains seem close enough to touch; on foggy or drizzly days, you can't see them at all. Even east of the Cascades, where the weather is generally dry, storm clouds, dust storms, or the bright glare of the sun can obscure the landscape: near trees seem far away, and distant mountains appear close. This explains why early navigators often missed prominent landmarks obscured by fogs or mists, and why overland travelers became disoriented in the wide-open spaces.

■ INDIAN CULTURES

During the perhaps 25,000 years that migrations of hunting peoples from Asia crossed into North America, tribes with very different origins and traditions washed back and forth across the face of the Pacific Northwest. We assume this because the tribes living in this area spoke languages deriving from all of America's major native language groups. The history of the ebb and flow of these tribes, their chiefs, battles, and traditions, has been for the most part lost, but we have some remains and artifacts that help us piece the story together. Sandals woven from sagebrush 13,000 years ago have been discovered in a cave near Fort Rock in Central Oregon. And 4,000-year-old settlements have been uncovered on Vancouver Island. The oldest house foundations from Ozette Village on the Olympic coast of Washington State date back 3,100 years.

When Europeans arrived in the area about 200 years ago, they found two distinct native ways of life had evolved in the Pacific Northwest, based on its natural geographic divisions. Those people living along the Pacific coast and on the wooded western side of the Cascade Mountains developed a culture geared to the sea and the forest; those living in the high dry plains of the plateaus to the east lived as horsemen and traders.

A classic portrait of a Kwakiutl Native American taken by photographer Edward Curtis in 1914. (Royal British Columbia Museum)

■ PEOPLE OF THE COAST

The original inhabitants of the coast lived off the bounty of the sea, mostly on salmon, and on any other marine creature they could catch, dig up, or gather. They carved sleek canoes from single logs of giant cedar, and they traveled far and wide hunting seals, sea lions, and even the mighty whale.

Native houses were windowless longhouses, huge dwellings some 60 feet wide and 100 feet long, their frames constructed from beams 2.5 to 3.5 feet in diameter and covered with thick cedar planks. Entrance was through a small hole at one end, which made the house more defensible during attack. From central Vancouver Island north, this hole might be carved into the lower end of a totem pole, which rose high above the gable and proclaimed the owner of the house and his status through the animals carved on the pole's face. More "crest" designs, as well as depictions of family myths or honors, might be painted on the face of the house.

In 1803, after visiting a plank house near the falls of the Columbia, American explorers Lewis and Clark noted that these structures were "the first wooden buildings we have seen since leaving the Illinois country."

The insides of these houses might be decorated with painted screens and painted or carved house posts. Several related families would live together, their living quarters partitioned off by screens. In the early 19th century, after raids on native Puget Sound villages by Tlinkit, Haida, and Kwakiutl warriors increased, houses were protected by tall palisades of cedar planks. Villages on Whidbey Island were unfortified when British navigator George Vancouver visited the region in 1792, but were enclosed by 30-foot-high palisades when the Wilkes Expedition visited the island in 1841.

Warfare among tribes was brutal. As Chief Martin Sampson wrote in his history of the Skagit tribe, "Heads were taken as trophies, villages were burned, and captives became slaves of the victors." In his mid-19th-century essay *Almost Out of the World*, schoolteacher James Swan describes one such raid that happened when he worked on the Makah Reservation:

> Imagine yourself in the centre of a circle of wild and excited savages, standing beside two trunkless heads—a most shocking and revolting spectacle of itself— and knowing that these very dancers are a portion of a band of miscreants whose name has henceforth been a terror on the Straits of Juan de Fuca....

A PREHISTORIC MYSTERY

Columbia Park in Kennewick, Washington, has one of the prettiest riverfronts in the Northwest, and it's not at all the kind of place where you'd expect to discover the victim of a homicide. But that is what two college students thought they had found when they literally stumbled over a human skull half-buried in the shallows of the Columbia River. They called the police, who called the county coroner, who in turn called in James Chatters, a forensic anthropologist often consulted to identify recent murder victims and distinguish modern skeletons from the bones of an Indian burial.

Chatters quickly determined that the skull was not Native American in origin and that it had too many "Caucasoid" features. These are structural features shared by such diverse people as Europeans, Persians, and the Ainu of Japan, but not necessarily meaning "white" or "European." He went down to the river to look for additional bones, and came away with a nearly complete skeleton. Determining the deceased was male, between 40 and 55 years old, about 5 feet 9 inches—much taller than most prehistoric Native Americans of the Northwest—and well-nourished, he deduced he had the remains of a 19th-century trapper or pioneer. Then he noticed a gray object embedded in the hip bone strongly resembling a Cascade projectile point used widely between 4,500 and 9,000 years ago. Radiocarbon dating performed at a university confirmed the bones in his lab were some 9,300 years old. Despite the age, Chatters and other anthropologists maintain he is not of a typical Native American origin. (The local Umatilla tribe believes otherwise, and, under the Native American

Reconstruction of Kennewick Man's face, courtesy of James Chatters.

Graves Protection and Repatriation Act, wants to halt further study and bury the remains.)

Anthropologists believe this prehistoric man might have been part of a nomadic group that wandered about hunting, fishing, and gathering plants. Isotopic-carbon studies show he ate a lot of seafood, and might have fished for salmon on the Columbia. Chatters believes Kennewick Man, with his Caucasoid features, could have moved through the streets of contemporary Seattle without standing out. Whatever he was—or whoever his remains belong to—his discovery, when added to the six other similarly dated Caucasoid-like skeletons found on the continent, creates a fascinating and mysterious twist to the complex puzzle concerning human migration to North America.

Afterward, the heads were taken to other villages, where the dances were repeated. They were finally "stuck on two poles and will remain till time or the crows knock them down."

■ COASTAL ART AND CULTURE

During the dark nights of winter, villages resounded with the telling of stories, the singing of songs, and the performance of plays recounting the exploits of mythical beings. Elaborately carved dance masks and totem poles, painted screens and house fronts, bowls, even spoons, are part of Northwest Indian art—their forceful, symbolic abstractions of real and supernatural beings, drawn in fluid lines and cut in ovoid shapes. Each of the different peoples of the Northwest Coast—the Coast Salish, Nootka, Kwakiutl, Tsimshian, Haida, and Tlinkit—shared a similar cultural, economic, and environmental background, as well as the basic forms of artistic expression.

Yet there were tribal differences that are obvious to the expert eye. Nootka and Tsimshian used a more flexible, flowing line than the more formal style of Kwakiutl and Tlinkit tribes. The Haida, perhaps the greatest artists on the Coast, combined the best elements of both in highly expressive artworks. The Coast Salish had their own more free-form abstract expression (though they have, in recent decades, adopted elements from the art of the northern tribes).

Contact with white fur traders gave the native tribes access to iron, and some of the most magnificent totem poles were carved after native artists of the coast began using iron tools. Carved totem poles found their highest (and tallest) expression among the Kwakiutl, Haida, and Tlinkit. The mythical beings depicted in masks, totem poles, screens, and house paintings were more than family crests: they were the actual *property* of families or powerful individuals. Owners had rights not only to the characters themselves, but to design features and the right to tell stories associated with these characters. These rights were jealously guarded, for their acquisition was a tedious—and expensive—process. It was possible to inherit them, but the prospective heir had to validate his inheritance by giving a potlatch, a very expensive proposition at best.

■ POTLATCH

A potlatch was an elaborate affair, requiring long preparation, formal invitations, observation of a strict ritual, and the giving away of valuable property by the host,

GIVEAWAY PARTY

One celebrated potlatch was held in 1922 by Kwakiutl chief Dan Cranmer on Village Island, off the northern coast of Vancouver Island. "I started giving out the property," he recalled. "First the canoes," twenty-four of them, "some big ones." He gave pool tables to two chiefs. Such large gifts cast high honor upon Cranmer and incurred a deep obligation upon the recipients to match the gesture in the future. "It really hurt them," said Cranmer. "They said it was the same as breaking a copper," another display of unsparing wealth. Chief Assu received a gas boat and $50 cash. Three more gas boats were given away and another pool table. Dresses, shawls, and bracelets went to the women, sweaters and shirts to the young people. For the children, small change: "I threw it away for the kids to get," Cranmer remembered. Then came blankets, gaslights, violins, guitars, basins, glasses, washtubs, teapots, boxes, three hundred oak trunks, sewing machines, a gramophone, bedsteads, bureaus, and more cash. Finally, on Christmas Day, the fifth and last day of the ceremony, came the sacks of flour....

Potlatches were accompanied by dances and feasts. Chief Charles Jones of the Pacheenaht tribe described a cooking vessel used at a potlatch in the early 1900s:

> One day...a large steel buoy was found ashore. My father and other
> members of the tribe tried to cut the buoy in half. Axes and sledge
> hammers were used to cut through the half-inch steel and nine of the
> axes were worn out. A lot of tools were ruined but the men managed
> to split it in half. It was then decided to use it as a cooking pot. At
> one potlatch, we cooked an elk and thirty-one harbour seals in the
> pot—it was so big.

Potlatches might deteriorate from peaceful "fighting with property" to actual warfare, especially since war and raids on other villages were also a means of acquiring property, slaves, and status. The vessels of war were giant canoes carved from a single cedar log. They might be more than 50 feet long and up to 8 feet wide—the size of a small Viking ship—and carry a considerable number of warriors. According to ethnographer Philip Drucker, the elegantly shaped canoes of the Nootka "inspired the New England designers of that queen of the seas, the American clipper ship, whose racy bow lines were nearly identical."

a man of high caste in a strictly stratified society. Gifts eventually had to be returned in kind, with exorbitant interest. If this "gift" was not repaid within a reasonable time, the recipient would lose status, which is why the potlatch has also been referred to as "fighting with property." These notions of giving pervaded the everyday lives of the natives of the Northwest Coast—the reason why Lewis and Clark quickly decided not to accept gifts from native chiefs.

Before the arrival of white traders and their goods, the objects given away included canoes, hand-woven blankets, or valuable shield-like sheets of scarce copper. To show off his wealth, the host might break a sheet of copper or kill slaves along the beach where visiting canoes pulled up. As the Indians of the coast began to work as commercial fishermen or sealers, they acquired—and gave away—many of the new consumer goods introduced by white traders.

Kwakiutls prepare for a potlatch at Fort Rupert in 1898. Photographs of potlatches are rare since the practice was banned by the government. (American Museum of Natural History)

The Painted Hills of north-central Oregon are at the southern end of the Columbia Plateau, once the domain of the Nez Percé, Cayuse, and Yakama tribal groups.

■ HORSEMEN OF THE COLUMBIA PLATEAU

Tribes living east of the Cascade Mountains on the high and dry plateaus were traders, desert wanderers, and by the early 19th century, when some tribes acquired horses from the Utes of Utah, accomplished horsemen who followed game as it migrated from the lowlands to summer forage in the mountains. These people counted their wealth in horses and on them traveled through their hunting lands to the greenest pastures, digging camas and other bulbs as staple food, and gathering by the rivers in July when salmon (before the construction of dams) still ran hundreds of miles inland to spawn. They brought with them teepees or built long lodges covered with rush mats or buffalo hides.

Confident and well traveled, these people braved dangerous warrior tribes to the east when they hunted in the Plains for buffalo, which had become extinct west of the Rocky Mountains by the early 19th century. The Nez Percé, Cayuse, and the Yakama were only a little impressed by the pale-skinned newcomers who began first to visit, then to invade their territories. When too many whites poured in, the tribes fought brave battles, but lost because of inferior weaponry. Eventually, they were moved to reservations, small remnants of their original lands. Here, deprived of hunting land and dependent on government handouts to eat, they suffered, despaired, and tried to preserve their ancient customs and myths.

The tribes living between the warrior cultures of the coast and horse-herding tribes of the east were great traders. These middlemen lived along rivers: the Columbia, Fraser, Skeena, and Stikine, controlling both the catching of salmon at the rapids and the movement of goods from the coast to the plateaus and the trade routes of the interior to the sea.

■ EUROPEANS ARRIVE

Three great expansionist powers sent navigators along the north coast of the American continent in the 16th, 17th, and 18th centuries: England, Spain, and Russia. The nations themselves were seeking power, conquest, gold, and new trade routes. The men who manned their ships were a uniquely courageous and curious breed, taking small wooden ships through unchartered waters to fulfill visions of glory and adventure, or perhaps to satisfy an incurable wanderlust. The writing in the logbooks of these ships possesses a courtly formality and grace; their records indicate that encounters with mariners from rival nations were for the most part cordial.

These explorers were the first Europeans to encounter the native people of the Pacific. England's Captain Cook, a great admirer of both the Hawaiians and the Eskimos, recorded that he was nonplussed by the Indians of Nootka Sound, especially after these natives expected him to pay for the wood and water his crew took. Captain George Vancouver found the natives of Puget Sound gentle and friendly. Russian fur traders, who had pushed east across Siberia to the Bering Sea, made alliances with the Aleut people of the Aleutian Islands. Establishing Sitka early in the 19th century, Russians sent kayak flotillas of Aleut hunters south along the Northwest coast to northern California and hunted the sea otter until it was close to extinct. Then, at the beginning of the 19th century, a new player entered the scene: the fledgling United States of America.

■ ONE REGION, TWO COUNTRIES

Less than 30 years after the American colonies fought the Revolutionary War with Britain, President Thomas Jefferson ensured that his country, rather than any

European power, would dominate North America when he acquired the Louisiana Territory from France. Knowing little of what these vast tracts of land encompassed, Jefferson sent explorers Meriwether Lewis and William Clark to chart a route to the Pacific and to open the area up for American trade and settlers.

All of these people—explorers, navigators, adventurers, and merchants—unwittingly brought diseases to the Pacific Northwest that killed tribal people. But the greatest changes came after Russia and Spain pulled back from the northern Pacific Coast, and American and British settlers began moving into the region.

In 1846, Britain and the United States divided their territories in the Pacific Northwest along the 49th parallel. British Columbia joined the Canadian Federation in 1871 and became a member of the British Commonwealth. The Americans of Washington and Oregon maintained a paradoxical attitude toward England. They spoke its language and its pioneers read the King James Bible and

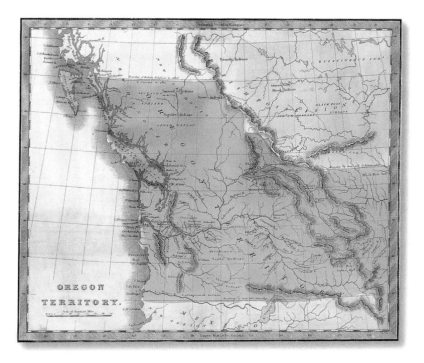

A map of the Oregon Territory before the settlement of U.S.–Canadian border claims in 1846. (University of Washington Libraries)

Gray Discovers the Columbia River

The year 1792 was now come, and it was a great year in the annals of Oregon, three hundred years from Columbus, two hundred from Juan de Fuca. The struggle between England and Spain over conflicting rights at Nootka, which at one time threatened war, had been settled with a measure of amicability. As a commissioner to represent Great Britain, Captain George Vancouver was sent out, while Bodega y Quadra was empowered to act in like capacity for Spain. Spaniards and Britons alike realised that, whatever the Nootka treaty may have been, possession was nine points of the law, and both redoubled their efforts to push discovery, and especially to make the first complete exploration of the Straits of Fuca and the supposed Great River.

Two days later the lookout reported a sail, and as the ships drew together, the newcomer was seen to be flying the Stars and Stripes. It was the *Columbia Rediviva,* Captain Robert Gray, of Boston. In response to Vancouver's rather patronizing queries, the Yankee skipper gave a summary of his log for some months past. Among other things he states that he had passed what seemed to be a powerful river in latitude 46 degrees 10 minutes, which for nine days he had tried in vain to enter, being repelled by the strength of the current. He now proposed returning to that point and renewing his efforts. Vancouver declined to reconsider his previous decision that there could be no large river, and passed on to make his very elaborate exploration of the Straits of Fuca and their connected waters, and to discover to his great chagrin, that the Spaniards had forestalled him in point of time.

The vessels parted. Gray sailed south and on May 10, 1792, paused abreast of the same reflex of water where before for nine days he had tried vainly to enter. The morning of the 11th dawned clear and favourable, light wind, gentle sea, a broad, clear channel, plainly of sufficient depth. The time was now come. The man and the occasion met. Gray seems from the first to have been ready to take some chances for the sake of some great success…. So, as he laconically stated in his log-book, he ran in with all sail set, and at ten o'clock found himself in a large river of fresh water, at a point about twenty miles from the ocean.

—William Denison Lyman, *The Columbia River,* 1909

British Camp on San Juan Island was the site of occupation by British forces. The island was also inhabited by American citizens, and a dispute over the island's national status was not resolved until 1872, when San Juan became U.S. territory.

the plays of Shakespeare. But their American identity was infused with pride at having thrown off a great power and having established the first democracy in modern times. The Pacific Northwest was thus split, and yet its settlers maintained a civility that is still a pleasurable part of life in the Northwest.

■ PLUCK IN HARD TIMES

In 1893, the economy of the Pacific Northwest collapsed in the wake of the failure of banks back east. People had scarcely enough to eat. Tacoma pioneer Thomas Emerson Ripley wrote in *Green Timber*:

> We quickly learned the trick of the clambake—the underlayer of dry wood, the seaweed, the clams, and then more seaweed. The long summer twilight was lighted up by the fires of the clambakers, and it was a heartening sight. What would have happened to the dwindling population of Tacoma without clams, I don't know.

The clams were immortalized by Congressman George Cushman in a speech before the House of Representatives. After telling his fellow lawmakers how hard the depression had hit the Puget Sound country, he concluded: "When the tide was out, our table was set. Our stomachs rose and fell with the tide."

This depression ended in 1897, when the steamer *Portland* arrived in Seattle carrying "a ton of gold" from the Klondike. The mayor was so excited, he jumped on a ship and went north himself. During the gold rush excitement, Seattle set itself up as the economic capital of Alaska—a distinction it still holds a hundred years later. Vancouver, Tacoma, and Portland also benefited. By the time the last miner had been outfitted, the economy had rebounded. The mainstays of the Pacific Northwest economy were its lumber harvests and its fishing.

■ MODERN TIMES

In the U.S. portion of the region, the great public works projects of Franklin Delano Roosevelt's administration—the Grand Coulee and Bonneville Dams—opened up eastern Washington and Oregon to farming by providing water for irrigation. The dams made the Columbia River navigable, while they generated the cheap electric power that fueled the aluminum industry and large companies, such as Boeing. At the same time, the salmon runs were destroyed, a loss that served as a warning of the potential dangers of unchecked timber harvest and fishing along the coast, and prodded locals and environmentalists to fight for regulation of logging and fishing. Controversy continues, but so do natural beauty, a fine lifestyle, clean cities, and thriving businesses—such as Washington's Microsoft and Oregon's Nike, which spurred economic growth in the 1980s and 1990s.

By the end of the 20th century, the province that had changed most dramatically was British Columbia, where 40 percent of the residents of Vancouver and its suburbs were Chinese. The province had welcomed citizens of Hong Kong who left the island as the British were pulling out. After the mainland takeover, the Hong Kong economy did not decline as some had expected, and many heads of families returned to China.

(opposite) Gold fever strikes Seattle on July 17, 1897. The city's mayor resigned to join the exodus northward.

V A N C O U V E R

■ Highlights

■ Overview

You're driving along under a low, overcast sky, past gray buildings brightened by colorful Chinese shop signs. Fallen petals of cherry blossoms swirl in the breeze and cling to curbs, sidewalks, and concrete walls, making you reflect on the brevity of spring. But, short as the floral splendor may be, you see how truly spectacular the streets of Vancouver are this spring afternoon. More than 40,000 flowering cherry trees line the streets of the city, and when they burst into full bloom, the pale pink blossoms are augmented by the deeper colors of 9,500 flowering plum trees, 4,500 flowering crabapple trees, 2,000 magnolias, and 2,000 dogwoods. As you admire the flowers, set off by the gray sky, the clouds part and the sun pours out, painting the waters of Burrard Inlet to the north a burnished gold. And there, right in front of you—looking close enough to touch—rise snow-covered peaks, straight from the water. Awestruck, you park your car and gaze at the scenery. Vancouver, you declare, is the most beautiful city on the west coast.

The city sprawls at the edge of the wild, over a peninsula delineated to the south by the north arm of the Fraser River, and to the north by Burrard Inlet, the southernmost of the deeply glaciated fjords that cut into the coast at frequent intervals from here all the way to southeast Alaska.

(opposite) The gardens in Queen Elizabeth Park.

■ HISTORY

As a European settlement, Vancouver is a young city even for the Northwest, where most cities are less than 150 years old. Spanish mariners were the first Europeans to visit the region, followed by British explorer George Vancouver in 1792. Vancouver, who had been exploring the coast in small boats, was heading south, back to his ships, when he spotted Spanish vessels, only 15 meters (50 feet) long. He boarded the one of Captain Dionisio Galiano. In June 1792, he reported in his journal that the captain spoke a little English. This eased communications considerably:

> Their conduct was replete with that politeness and friendship which characterizes the Spanish nation; every kind of useful information they cheerfully communicated…having partaken with them of a very hearty breakfast, bad [sic] them farewell, not less pleased with their hospitality and attention, than astonished at the vessels in which they were employed.

■ SETTLERS ARRIVE

The northern boundary of the present city of Vancouver experienced no great initial influx of settlers because its shores were covered by dense stands of tall timber, which made it unsuitable for agriculture. The less densely wooded banks of the Fraser River, to the south of Vancouver, were settled first, since the river offered the additional benefit of a water route up the Fraser Valley. But the pioneers soon learned that the river would freeze in severe winters, as it did in 1861–62, when it was covered with ice from the mountains to its mouth. That year, steamers ran into Burrard Inlet to deliver the mail, which was hauled by sleigh to New Westminster, the capital of the new province.

Coal and clay for bricks were discovered in the heart of present-day Vancouver in 1862, and a lumber mill began operating in 1867. A company store catered to the domestic needs of loggers and millworkers, but it didn't sell liquor. That deficiency was remedied by John "Gassy Jack" Deighton, who opened a saloon just west of the lumber mill's property line. The village springing up around Deighton's saloon became known as "Gastown." Gassy Jack is considered Vancouver's founding father. The city's street-numbering system starts from the site of his saloon, in the middle of the present five-way intersection in the Gastown quarter.

■ Vancouver Booms

By the end of 1886, Gastown had been renamed Vancouver, and the town boasted a school, hospital, an opera house, a bank, and a two-story city hall, not to mention a church, roller-skating rink, two stables, nine saloons, 14 office blocks, 23 hotels, and 51 stores. Over the next few years, as the new city's population grew from about 1,000 in 1886 to 13,000 by 1891, Vancouver acquired the shops and terraced homes

On May 23, 1887, the first transcontinental train pulled into Vancouver, thus joining the city by rail with the east coast of Canada. (Vancouver Public Library)

that gave its streets such a "European" look. As the population was swelled by immigration from Europe—between 1901 and 1911 Vancouver's population jumped from 27,000 to more than 100,000—multistory office blocks, department stores, and hotels began to dominate the downtown business district.

This boom was fueled by the completion of the railway from eastern Canada. In May 1887, the first transcontinental train steamed into the little wooden depot just west of Granville Street. Vancouver had joined the modern world. In June of that year, the Canadian Pacific Railway steamer *Abyssinia* arrived from Yokohama, Japan, with a cargo of tea. The tea was shipped by rail via Montreal to New York, loaded aboard a fast steamship, and unloaded in London 29 days after leaving Japan. The Vancouver route was two weeks quicker than the old route through the Suez Canal.

Vancouver became a major seaport almost overnight, strengthening the city's new ties to the Pacific as well as reinforcing the bonds tying it to eastern Canada and Britain. This new status encouraged Vancouverites to see themselves as a vital link of the Empire, and it separated British Columbia's consciousness from that of the Americans just south of the 49th parallel.

■ THE PACIFIC CONNECTION

The port of Vancouver is larger than ever and contributes a major share to the city's prosperity. EXPO 86, a world's fair, celebrated Vancouver's 100th birthday as well as the city's coming of age. It also brought a stream of visitors that has not yet abated.

Vancouver is a place of change—if you go away for a year, you may not recognize a once familiar neighborhood on your return. That's because an influx of Hong Kong capital has led to major building projects in both commercial and residential sections of town. Some of these new buildings are attractive in a postmodern fashion; others reflect the waning powers of the International Style; yet others are simply large and cramped, designed to accommodate as many people as possible. This is especially true of some housing developments, where huge mansions are squeezed onto tiny lots.

Yet most of the old residential neighborhoods, which helped give Vancouver its relaxed atmosphere of British prosperity, are untouched. Though concrete and glass slowly replace clapboard houses and postage-stamp front lawns, Vancouver is still a city of gardens, where the scent of flowers mingles with the crispness of the sea breeze, and where on a warm day you can smell the conifers on nearby mountains.

Stanley Park on Vancouver's waterfront is a haven from the pressures of urban life.

■ CANADIAN IDENTITY

Canadian English is quite different from American English. In its intonation it is much closer to British English than, say, Australian is. And the Canadian government, aware of the forces threatening to tear the country apart, has made a conscious effort to promote "Canadian" things.

You'll notice the results of this initiative in the absence of U.S. books and magazines around town. And you'll definitely notice it when you switch on the TV set in your hotel room. There's even an all-Canadian country music channel—eat your heart out, Nashville.

But all is well in paradise. British Columbians take every opportunity to stream south of the border, despite the disparity in the exchange rate—the value of the Canadian dollar has fallen in relation to the U.S. dollar—and they flock to events in Washington State in ever increasing numbers, ignoring the attractions of their largest city. That may change, as British Columbians and Vancouverites develop an ever stronger pan-Pacific identity. In the meantime, they welcome visitors with open arms. Never in the 20-plus years I have visited Vancouver have I found the natives as friendly and welcoming as they are now.

■ EXPLORING VANCOUVER

Vancouver is by far the largest and most important city of the Canadian west. Most of British Columbia's population lives in the city, its suburbs, and the lower Fraser River Valley. What sets Vancouver apart from other West Coast ports is the way the waterfront has changed in the last decade. No Pacific waterfront is as user-friendly. Not only are there beaches for Vancouverites to frolic on, but there are bicycle paths and footpaths almost everywhere along the shores of Burrard Inlet and False Creek. A path even winds along the harbor front, past ship chandlers, boatyards, restaurants, pubs, moored boats, and floatplane docks, which makes it not only visually stimulating but also interesting for curious minds.

Vancouver is divided into several quarters or neighborhoods, the main ones being Stanley Park, downtown, Gastown, Chinatown, Yaletown, Granville Island, Kitsilano, and the section around the University of British Columbia. Farther out are Vancouver South, the north shore of Burrard Inlet, and the city of Burnaby. Each area has its own distinct character.

(following pages) False Creek Marina and the Vancouver skyline.

■ STANLEY PARK *map page 46, B/C-1*

Stanley Park has a shoreline promenade along the harbor, First Narrows, and English Bay shores. Lovely hiking trails wind through the woods. Scattered throughout the park are totem poles, cricket grounds, and the **Vancouver Aquarium** (845 Avison Way; 604-268-9900). This incredibly well-thought-out aquarium has it all: beluga whales, orcas, and sea otters, plus fish from local waters and exotic seas, a trek through a slice of Amazon jungle, and a wade in wetlands where a kid-size "swamp-bubble" lets you enjoy a "frog's eye view" of a freshwater pond.

Popular beaches line **English Bay** on the southern shore. A walk along the seawall to English Bay from Coal Harbour is 8 kilometers (5 miles) long and takes a minimum of two hours—if you're not distracted by bald eagles, nesting cormorants, or cruising sea lions. Near the Lumberman's Arch on the east shore is the site of Whoi-Whoi, one of the many native villages of the inlet.

The west end is an upscale residential area of high-rise condominiums and apartments, between Stanley Park and downtown, within walking distance of restaurants, shops, and beaches.

■ DOWNTOWN *map pages 40 and 46, B/C-1/2*

Downtown, the commercial heart of the city, sprawls across a peninsula north of False Creek, a tidal inlet. Here are most of Vancouver's fancy hotels, restaurants, and shops, plus office buildings to support them.

The heart of downtown is **the plaza**, which is located north of Robson Street, between Howe and Hornby and south of the **Vancouver Art Gallery** (750 Hornby Street; 604-662-4719). The gallery is housed in the old courthouse designed by Francis Rattenbury, architect of Victoria's Empress Hotel and Parliament buildings. The new courthouse to the south looks more like a parking garage that wants to be a greenhouse. A sunken plaza in the square is filled with water during freezing weather and serves as a municipal skating rink. The grand old **Orpheum Theatre** (601 Smithe Street) rounds out the picture. The 1927 vaudeville venue is home to the Vancouver Symphony Orchestra.

Howe Street north of Georgia is the city's financial heart, home to major banks and the Vancouver Stock Exchange, an institution known for arranging financing for mineral exploration and other risky investment schemes. **Granville Street** downtown is a pedestrian mall, but there's also an underground mall below the street and

department stores between Granville and Howe. **Robson Street** is one of the city's main shopping districts. Instead of sidewalk tables, many of the restaurants have terraces on the roof where you can dine al fresco.

Canada Place, west of Gastown on the shore of Burrard Inlet, is a cruise ship pier with a hotel, restaurant, and convention center. You can't miss the place: it's topped by huge, white, tentlike plastic sails. The best place from which to view the ships is the **Steamworks Brewing Co.** (The Landing, 375 Water Street) brewpub.

The nearby **Marine Building** (355 Burrard Street) is filled with terra-cotta detailing in a marine flora and fauna motif. It is the northernmost terminal of the SkyTrain, a high-tech commuter train that runs underground in the downtown area and on stilts

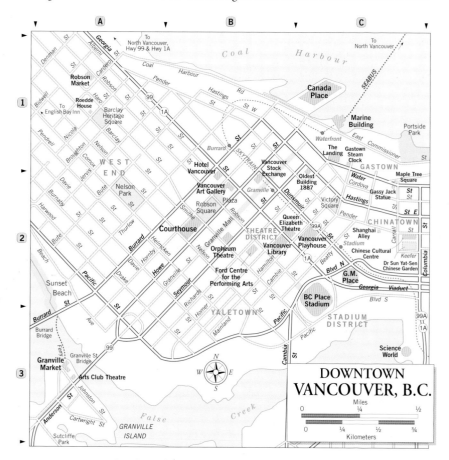

(opposite) The Art Deco Marine Building, reflected in the Daon Building.

to New Westminster and the southern suburbs. SeaBus is a fast passenger ferry that runs north from here to the Lonsdale Quai in North Vancouver. Tickets good for passage on SeaBus or SkyTrain are available from vending machines at all stations. A day pass is a great means of exploring other parts of town and the North Shore.

The **Hotel Vancouver** (900 West Georgia Street; 800-441-1414) downtown is one of Canada's grand old Canadian Pacific château-style hotels (like Victoria's Empress Hotel). A recent facelift has left the hotel as beautiful as ever and as up-to-date and comfortable as Vancouver's more modern hostelries. The **Park Royal Hotel** (540 Clyde Avenue; 604-926-5511) in West Vancouver, north of the Lion's Gate Bridge, has the air of a British country house. The romantic **English Bay Inn** (1968 Comox Street; 604-683-8002) is minutes from Stanley Park.

■ GASTOWN

map page 40, C-1/2

Vancouver started east of downtown in the shacks built near "Gassy Jack's" saloon. In the 1960s, the old buildings and cobbled streets were resurrected to attract tourists, but the locals liked Gastown so much that restaurants and shops now cater mostly to residents—which makes it even more fun to visit. The oldest part of the city, with late-Victorian buildings, Gastown stretches east from Canada Place to Maple Tree Square, which got its name from the tree that stood here and served as a municipal billboard. The Gastown Steam Clock at Water and Cambie Streets sounds the time with the Westminster chimes of Big Ben on the Houses of Parliament in London.

This steam-powered clock is a landmark in Gastown.

■ CHINATOWN *map page 40, C-2*

Chinatown, south of Hastings and Main Streets, and centered on Pender and Keefer Streets, has some of the oldest buildings in Vancouver, and the city's most beautiful garden. It is the most exciting place in Vancouver. Long billed as North America's second-largest Chinatown, after New York, it's rapidly on its way to becoming the largest, thanks to a great influx of immigrants from Hong Kong.

Hong Kong money is transforming Chinatown: the quarter is expanding beyond its borders; new shops and restaurants are springing up all over the place; the selection of artifacts and foods is greater and better than ever. Chinatown's clothing stores and shops sell some fancy Chinese silk robes, porcelain, and art objects. You will find many objects made from jade, since British Columbia is the world's main supplier of the gemstone.

The neighborhood's piece de resistance is the **Dr. Sun Yat-sen Classical Chinese Garden.** The only complete Chinese garden outside China, it was assembled by craftsmen from Suzhou, China's garden capital, in time for Vancouver's 100th anniversary. The walled garden, quite unlike those most Westerners are familiar

A pavilion in Dr. Sun Yat-sen's Classical Chinese Garden.

with, consists of ponds, pavilions with curved roofs of blue tile, covered walkways, and terraces. Accenting these are rocks, flowers and plants, and the water, which is kept deliberately murky to better reflect the buildings. A waterfall masks most of the city noise.

The garden changes with the seasons. It is as beautiful in spring, when a succession of blooms adds color, as it is in fall color, or on a snowy day in winter. The buildings are handcrafted in the

WAH CHONG
WASHING & IRONING

This pioneer family operated two of the city's first laundry services. Jennie Wah Chong (second from right) was the first Asian to attend public school in the city. (City of Vancouver Archives)

traditional Suzhou style with exquisite carving and lacy screens of honey-colored ginkgo wood. The best place for contemplation is the Scholar's Study, which has its own enclosed courtyard. Tea is served daily in the main hall. A gift shop stocks art books, Chinese porcelains, and other objets d'art. *578 Carrall Street; 604-689-7133.*

Dr. Sun Yat-sen Park, to the east, shares the pond with the garden but is not as elaborate and is open to the public free of charge. With its grove of black bamboo and island pavilion the park is a favorite lunchtime spot for local office workers. Canada geese have been known to nest among the rocks, and a great blue heron likes to hang out at the pond's edge between the garden and the park. *East of Yaletown and west of Chinatown at Pender, Carrall, and Keefer Streets.*

North of the classical garden is the **Chinese Cultural Centre,** which contains yet another garden, this one based on the style of the Ming Dynasty (from the 14th to the 17th century). Various facilities within the complex exhibit ancient and contemporary artworks and artifacts. A permanent display chronicles the history of the Chinese in Canada. *555 Columbia Street; 604-658-8880.*

■ YALETOWN AND THE THEATER DISTRICT
map page 40, B-2/3

Yaletown is a gentrified former warehouse district southeast of downtown that now houses offices, movie and video producers, furniture showrooms, fancy shops, and restaurants where the young and fashionable gather. There's even a microbrewery, the **Yaletown Brewing Company** (111 Mainland Street).

The loading ramps and docks leading to the former warehouses and the utilitarian brick building facades certainly give the district a unique atmosphere. The conversion of the warehouses began when EXPO 86 was held nearby. The district has been kept alive by its proximity to the Theater and Stadium Districts and high-rise condominium construction in a neighboring area dubbed "Downtown South."

East of Yaletown is the **Stadium District,** with the plastic-domed BC Place Stadium and GM Place, which also hosts concerts and other public events. Vancouver's **Theater District** is northeast of Yaletown, near the coliseum-shaped Vancouver Public Library. The **Queen Elizabeth Theatre** (Hamilton and Georgia Streets; 604-280-4444) presents ballet and Vancouver Opera performances. The **Vancouver Playhouse** (630 Hamilton Street; 604-280-3311) stages mainstream shows, musicals, and cabarets. Major musicals, such as *Phantom of the Opera* and *Riverdance,* are performed at the grand **Ford Centre for the Performing Arts** (777 Homer Street; 604-280-2222). One of the city's most popular theatrical venues, the two-stage **Arts Club Theatre** (Granville Island, 1585 Johnston Street; 604-687-1644) presents Canadian works in an intimate space.

■ GRANVILLE ISLAND *map page 40, A-3*

Granville Island, in False Creek (below the Granville Street Bridge), can be reached by car from the south shore or by passenger ferry from the downtown shore. The island was a sandbar until World War I, when the city dredged the inlet and used the dredged-up mud to create an island. After serving as a warehouse and industrial district for decades, the island is now mostly a collection of shops and restaurants. The **Granville Island Market,** which has fishmongers' and produce stalls that rival those at Seattle's Pike Place Market, is a great place to visit. It has its own brewery, which sells locally made unpasteurized lager beer. Artists' studios, galleries, theaters, and shops occupy former warehouses. A modern hotel, with room service for boats mooring out front, occupies the eastern tip; houseboats squeeze in along the north

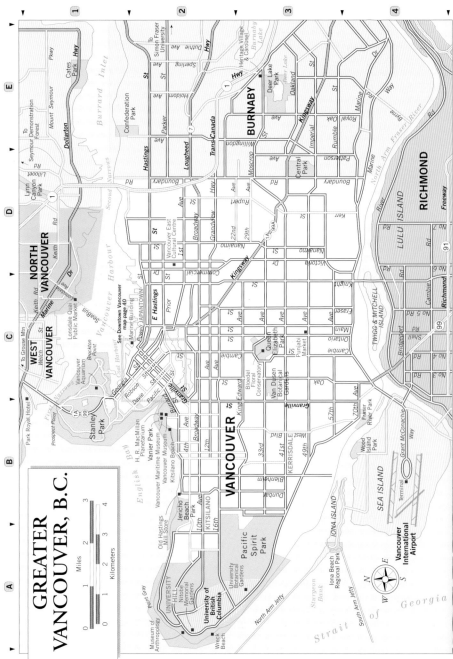

GREATER VANCOUVER, B.C.

See Downtown Vancouver map on page 40

Vancouver's diverse ethnic makeup is reflected in the variety of food markets scattered throughout the city.

shore; and a cement company yard survives from the industrial era. Walks lead along much of the island shore as well as along the north shore of False Creek. Where condominiums rise now, once stood Snauq village of the local Salish tribe.

■ KITSILANO AND UNIVERSITY AREA *map page 46, A/B-2/3*

Vancouver's Kitsilano District runs from Burrard Street and West Fourth Avenue west to the **University of British Columbia,** on Point Gray along the south side of False Creek. The area around West Fourth Avenue and Broadway has interesting shops, restaurants, and bookstores, and there is a small Greek district on Broadway. The university itself has one of the Northwest's most beautiful campuses.

West of Vanier Park are several popular beaches. South of Kitsilano, **Kerrisdale** is a genteel shopping and restaurant district at 41st Avenue and West Boulevard. The west side near the University of British Columbia and Point Gray is not to be confused with the West End or with West Vancouver. The area is popular for parks and beaches. **Wreck Beach** is the nudist beach—yes, it gets warm enough in summer to take your clothes off, and intrepid locals do it at all times of the year.

■ GARDENS

The **Bloedel Floral Conservatory** is in a triodetic dome with 1,490 Plexiglas bubbles protecting the plants from Vancouver's somewhat chilly weather. The conservatory has 500 species and varieties of plants native to a range of habitats—from jungles to deserts. A creeklike pond holds koi, colorful macaws perch on snags, and small tropical birds freely flit through the enclosure. The conservatory is the perfect place to alleviate the gloominess of a drab Vancouver winter afternoon. *Queen Elizabeth Park, 33rd Avenue and Cambie Street; 604-257-8570.*

Experts call the **Nitobe Memorial Garden** the most authentic Japanese garden outside Japan. *1903 West Mall, across from 6501 NW Marine Drive; 604-822-6038.*

The **University of British Columbia Botanical Gardens** was first planted in 1916 and is Canada's oldest university botanical garden. It has an alpine garden, a garden for native plants, a "Physick" garden, a winter garden, and an Asian garden. *6250 Stadium Road, just north of 16th Avenue and NW Marine Drive; 604-822-6038.*

VanDusen Botanical Gardens prove that old golf courses can be recycled—this one was turned into a first-rate arboretum with one of the largest collections of ornamental plants in North America. *37th Avenue and Oak Street; 604-878-9274.*

■ MUSEUMS

The University of British Columbia's **Museum of Anthropology** has one of world's finest collections of Northwest Indian art. *6393 NW Marine Drive; 604-822-5087.*

Old Hastings Mill Store Museum once stood east of Gastown on the Burrard Inlet shore. It survived the big fire of 1886 and was moved here in 1930. Indian artifacts and early Vancouver relics are on display. *1575 Alma Street; 604-734-1212.*

The small but well-appointed **Vancouver Maritime Museum** traces the history of shipping on Canada's west coast and the British Columbia fishing industry. The ship models are a delight. *1905 Ogden Avenue, at Cypress Street; 604-257-8300.*

The **Vancouver Museum,** Canada's largest civic museum, has a replica of a trading post, a Victorian parlor, an 1897 Canadian Pacific Railway car, and more. The ubiquitous Indian cedar canoe is on display, too. *1100 Chestnut Street; 604-736-4431.*

■ PLANETARIUM

At the **H. R. MacMillan Space Centre,** you can voyage into outer space via planetarium shows beamed onto a huge dome, ride a full-motion simulator, or take a peek at the night sky though a large telescope. *1100 Chestnut Street; 604-738-7827.*

■ Vancouver South and East   *map page 46, C/D-2/3*

Southeast of downtown, stretching along Main Street from 48th Avenue to 51st Avenue, is the **Punjabi Market,** an East Indian shopping district known for Indian silks, saris, and jewelry, as well as for shops selling uncommonly exotic foods. Farther north and east, closer to the downtown area, is the **Vancouver East** district, along Commercial Drive. It has long been known as Little Italy, because it used to be an enclave of Italian shops, but since EXPO 86 it has gone Latin-International and countercultural. One block away is **Vancouver East Cultural Centre** (1895 Venables Street; 604-254-9578), which often hosts ethnic performers.

If you don't want to park your car in the east—and occasionally dangerous—side of Vancouver, you can take the SkyTrain, which has a stop on Commercial Drive. Little remains of Vancouver's **Japantown** along Cordova and Powell Streets east of Main Street, but you can still find a shop or two selling exquisite kimonos.

A word of caution about shopping: In Vancouver, be careful when buying "genuine" Indian artifacts or art objects—some are made in factory workshops that don't employ native workers. Look out for a "Made in China" sticker, shop at a gallery that you trust, and ask leading questions.

An overview of Vancouver's ethnic groups would be incomplete without mentioning its large Scottish population. If you've been invited to a dress party but you forgot your tux, try to rent a kilt or buy the official British Columbia tartan.

■ North Shore of Burrard Inlet   *map page 46, C/E-1*

The north shore of Burrard Inlet has become a popular residential area in the last few decades, as you can tell by the ranks of houses rising up the slopes of the foothills. There's a good reason for this. As one resident said, "I used to live in a west end condo. But now I have my own house and garden, with one of the best views in the world. I have the wilderness on one side, but I can also take SeaBus to the city and be in my office in half an hour."

The SeaBus passenger ferries run between Vancouver's Marine Building and the **Lonsdale Quai Public Market** in North Vancouver. At the market, you can sit in a pub overlooking the inlet and watch the ships come in. Just east of the quai is a tugboat dock and shipyard. If you're lucky, you can watch one of the boats being hauled out. These stubby tugs are surprisingly powerful little machines. More likely, you'll see tugs cast off their mooring lines and, with a "bone in their teeth" and a large wake, rush out into the channel to lead a ship to moorage. Since Vancouver is a busy port, watching the ships come in is almost a spectator sport. (Before the market was built, I liked walking up the hill, to Pasparos Greek Taverna to watch the ships from the shade of the big fig tree in the courtyard out front.)

North of town, Lillooet Road leads to the **Seymour Demonstration Forest.** Here the Capilano Suspension Bridge spans a steep-walled canyon above the tumbling waters of the Capilano River. At the top of Capilano Road, the **Grouse Mountain SkyRide** (604-980-9311) aerial tram rises 1,100 meters (3,700 feet) to a great view of Vancouver and the Strait of Georgia; the Peak Chairlift to the summit whisks you to an even better view.

Where the rushing waters of the Capilano River enter tidewater just east of the First Narrows, the Coast Salish village of Homulcheson once stood. A pleasant, tree-shaded path leads upstream to **Capilano Regional Park.** A gently swaying suspension bridge 140 meters (450 feet) across and 72 meters (230 feet) above the Capilano River has been attracting visitors for over a century—and it's still as popular as it was on the first day it opened. There is a trout stream fed by mountain springs, trails meandering through a forest of tall trees, a 62-meter (200-foot)-long cantilevered observation deck, and much more.

From the Upper Level Highway (Trans-Canada Highway, Route 1, BC 99) in West Vancouver, Cypress Access Road leads uphill to **Cypress Provincial Park.** Like no other place, this mountain wilderness within easy driving distance of the city makes you aware of how young Vancouver is, and how recently the veneer of urban life spread out across the landscape.

■ **BURNABY** *map page 46, E-2/4*

Burnaby adjoins Vancouver to the east, stretching from Burrard Inlet to the north arm of the Fraser River. Though it is a major city, few visitors (or locals, for that matter) could tell where Vancouver ends and Burnaby begins, were it not for the conveniently named Boundary Road. Burnaby has an attractive green strip along the Fraser, with truck gardens where you can buy seasonal produce, and several very attractive parks. Near Burnaby Lake in Deer Lake Park, the **Burnaby Heritage Village & Carousel** (6501 Deer Lake Avenue; 604-293-6501) consists of buildings from the 1890s through 1925. Guides dressed in historical costumes demonstrate the everyday life of that period. The restored carousel dates from 1912 and has a chariot, four metal horses, and 36 wooden horses.

Vertiginous views from the Capilano Suspension Bridge.

■ **SUNSHINE COAST EXCURSION** *map pages 62–63, C/D-3/4*

The Sunshine Coast is a scenic stretch of land between the mountains and Georgia Strait north of Howe Sound. A narrow two-lane highway winds north between a rocky saltwater shore and the Coast Mountains, which here rise to heights of some 6,000 feet right from saltwater. It passes gnarled madrona trees, sandy beaches, and rocky headlands, where wildflowers spill down to the water. The views of the strait, islands, and mountains are breathtaking. Trails lead to hidden lakes and river gorges east of the highway. There are numerous campgrounds and lodges. The trip starts with a 45-minute ferry ride across **Howe Sound,** from Horseshoe Bay to Langdale. **Gibsons,** just west of the northern ferry terminal, is a quaint little town still living off the fame it gained in a popular TV series, "The Beachcombers." **Roberts Creek** is awiggle with painters and craftspeople; **Sechelt** is a rapidly growing retirement community.

The **Skookumchuck Rapids**, also known as the Sechelt Rapids, are an awesome sight. They more than live up to their Indian name, which means "strong waters." Rocks and islets restrict Sechelt Inlet near its junction with Jervis Inlet. In-flowing and out-flowing tidal waters turn the narrow channel into a churning white-water river. You can find the best viewing times listed in local newspapers and posted at the beginning of the 0.4-kilometer trail to the vista point.

Princess Louis Inlet is one of the most beautiful fjords on the Northwest coast. In the past, you could only visit if you had a boat of your own, but now there is a way to take a day trip with **Sunshine Coast Tours** at Lowe's Resort in Pender Harbour. *604-883-2456 or 800-870-9055.*

A 55-minute ferry ride takes you from Saltery Bay through Powell River to **Lund,** where the highway ends. North of here, no road reaches salt water until Bella Coola, and north of there the coast is roadless all the way to Prince Rupert. A ferry connects Powell River to Comox on Vancouver Island.

■ **EXCURSION TO WHISTLER** *map page 62–63, D-3*

Whistler, nestled in a beautiful alpine valley at the foot of two tall peaks in the British Columbia Coast Mountains, is considered to be North America's top ski resort. It is only a two-hour drive from Vancouver.

To get to Whistler, just follow Route 99, the road that has brought you north from the U.S. border, or take the daily train from North Vancouver, or take a ski-plane from Vancouver on Whistler Air. North of Horseshoe Bay, Route 99 winds about considerably, making the drive a bit adventuresome. But the scenery is grand. Don't rush. Turn out for the speed freaks on the highway and enjoy the views. The transition from maritime fjord to alpine creek is rather abrupt, and spectacular in late spring and summer when the wildflowers are in bloom.

This resort fulfills all it promises. The setting is incredibly beautiful, the skiing is magnificent, the restaurants are excellent, the lodging is luxurious, and the people are friendly. It's a perfect vacation spot in summer, too, with hiking trails leading to alpine meadows. *800-944-7853.*

■ **TRAVEL AND CLIMATE**

■ **GETTING THERE AND AROUND**

Located on the far southwestern shore of the Canadian mainland, Vancouver has high-speed road and rail connections to the other Canadian provinces to the east and to the United States to the south. Only a few winding roads lead into the rugged mountains to the north. Travel to the west, to Vancouver Island and the Gulf Islands, is by ferry or commuter plane.

Vancouver is a city made for walking. Major hotels, restaurants, shops, and attractions are close to downtown. The SkyTrain services outlying districts, like Chinatown and Commercial Drive, and the SeaBus heads to the shore. **Regular buses** run to Stanley Park, the University of British Columbia, and other parts of town. Small **passenger ferries** cross False Creek from the downtown shore to Granville Island. One of the delights of Vancouver is traveling on its surrounding waters.

By Air
Vancouver International Airport is located south of Vancouver in Richmond off Route 99. *YVR, 3211 Grant McConaghie Way; 604-207-7077, www.yvr.ca*

By Train
Amtrak (800-872-7245) links Vancouver to Seattle. **Via Rail** (800-561-8630) is the Canadian equivalent of Amtrak.

B.C. Rail operates trains to the Blackcomb area, past Howe Sound. *B.C. Rail Station, 1311 West First Street, North Vancouver; 800-663-8238 or 604-984-5246.*

Royal Hudson pulls excursion coaches along the scenic Howe Sound coastline from North Vancouver to the lumber town of Squamish at the head of the sound, a distance of 64 kilometers (40 miles). Trains depart from the B.C. Rail Station. Call B.C. Rail for information at 800-663-8238 or 604-984-5246. You can return by train or cruise one-way on the MV *Britannia*. The MV *Britannia* leaves from the northern foot of Denman Street. For information call Harbour Cruises at 604-687-9558.

SkyTrain is a nifty, fully computerized rapid transit train that runs from the Burrard Inlet waterfront downtown east to New Westminster and south to Surrey, with many stops en route. Downtown, the trains run underground, for the rest of the way on elevated tracks. On a clear day, the Fraser River crossing is spectacular.

By Car
If you arrive in Vancouver by car from the south, you will be crossing the U.S. border at Blaine, Washington. On busy weekends, you can expect delays of two hours or more. *(For border information, see page 348.)* Watch for directional signs as you arrive in Vancouver via the Route 99 freeway (directional signs in British Columbia tend to be small). North of the Fraser River Bridge, the freeway turns into Oak Street. Continue to 41st Street. Turn left (west), then right on Granville Street to the busy downtown area. North of the Granville Street Bridge over False Creek, take the off-ramp to attractive Seymour Street and continue north to downtown. The Trans-Canada Highway (TCH) Route 1 skirts the eastern edge of town before crossing

AUTHOR'S FAVORITES:
VANCOUVER FOOD AND LODGING

■ LODGINGS

Four Seasons. It's huge and fancy and right next to the stock exchange. The rooms tend to be on the small side, but the service is excellent. *791 Georgia Street; 604-689-9333. In Canada: 800-268-6282. In the U.S.: 800-332-3442.*

Granville Island Hotel. This small hotel, which is partly old stucco and partly modern high tech, sits at the eastern tip of Granville Island. Right in the heart of Vancouver, it's next to a marina and within easy walking distance of the island's restaurants, galleries, and theaters. *1253 Johnston Street; 604-683-7373.*

Pan Pacific Hotel. You can't get much closer to the water than this hotel, which rises above a cruise ship pier on Vancouver's waterfront. The three-story lobby has a totem pole and waterfall. *Suite 300-999 Canada Place; 604-662-8111. In Canada: 800-663-1515. In the U.S.: 800-937-1515.*

■ RESTAURANTS

Bishop's. This is a great restaurant where consistently fabulous food is served by an accomplished wait staff to the beautiful people who can afford it. *2183 West Fourth Avenue; 604-738-2025.*

The Fish House in Stanley Park. This Stanley Park restaurant serves up some of Vancouver's best seafood. Highlights include the fresh oyster bar and the signature flaming prawns. *8901 Stanley Park Drive; 604-681-7275.*

The Raincity Grill. The menu focuses on seafood, game and poultry, and organic vegetables from the Pacific Northwest. The extensive wine list, great food, and splendid views of the English Bay waterfront make this a popular restaurant. The atmosphere is relaxed and the service is professional. *1193 Denman Street; 604-685-7337.*

Sun Sui Wah Seafood Restaurant. Famous for seafood and roast squab, this is one of Vancouver's favorite Chinese restaurants. *3888 Main Street; 604-872-8822.*

Tojo's. This small sushi bar might be the best in Vancouver, if not the entire Pacific Northwest. Seats at the sushi counter are hard to get but are worth fighting over. *202-77 West Broadway; 604-872-8050.*

Burrard Inlet on the Second Narrows Bridge to North Vancouver. If you're coming in that way, turning west on Hastings Street will take you downtown.

By Bus

B.C. Transit buses run all over town. Deposit exact fare as you enter in front; free transfer slips on request for other buses, SeaBus, or SkyTrain. Partially wheelchair accessible. *604-521-0400.*

Pacific Central Station, at Main Street and Terminal, is Vancouver's long-distance bus depot. Greyhound Lines (604-482-8747); Maverick Coach Lines (604-662-8051); Pacific Coach Lines (604-662-8074). Wheelchair accessible.

West Vancouver's Blue Buses connect downtown with the Horseshoe Bay Ferry Terminal, departing from Homer and Georgia Streets. *604-985-7777.*

By Ferry

Aquabus runs between the Arts Club Theatre on Granville Island and the southern foot of Hornby Street. Ferries run from 7 A.M. to 8 P.M. daily. *604-689-5858.*

Harbour Cruises Boat-Train Daytrips leave daily from Vancouver, traveling up Howe Sound to Squamish. The return trip can be by water or by Royal Hudson train. Or you can take a motorcoach to Squamish and return to Vancouver by boat. *604-688-7246 or 800-663-1500.*

Granville Island Ferries stop at Bridges restaurant on Granville Island, at Stamps Landing, and at the Aquatic Centre at the northern foot of Burrard Street Bridge. Wheelchair accessible. *604-684-7781.*

SeaBus. Fast passenger-only catamarans run between Lonsdale Quai in North Vancouver and the SkyTrain Waterfront Station downtown. Bikes ride free. Partially wheelchair accessible. *604-521-0400.*

■ CLIMATE

Winter comes late and does not linger. In some years no snow falls, but even if it does, it stays only a week or two. Even at the height of the cold season, there are few days below 4.4 degrees centigrade (40 degrees F), and even fewer below minus-1 (30 degrees F). The warm rains melt the snow and turn the land green in spring. Summer is usually warm and sunny, with an occasional shower to keep lawns and flowers refreshed, but temperatures rarely rise above 26 degrees (80 degrees F). Fall is cool but sunny, with occasional rain or frost signaling the end of the balmy season.

FRASER RIVER VALLEY

■ HIGHLIGHTS

■ LANDSCAPE

THE LOWER FRASER RIVER VALLEY is unusually flat for a province where much of the landscape is vertical and where rivers always seem to be gushing over rocks. Once an arm of the sea, the Fraser Valley was turned into a mostly level plain as it was slowly filled by sand and silt carried downstream by the river and deposited here over millions of years.

The Fraser River rises in the Rocky Mountains in Mount Robson Provincial Park near the Alberta border, not far from the sources of the Columbia, and flows at first in a northwesterly direction through the Rocky Mountain Trench toward the Yukon and Alaska. After leaving this deep narrow valley a few miles north of Prince George, the river turns sharply to the south. As it collects waters from tributaries—the Nechako, Chilcotin, and West Road—the volume of the river increases. Below Quesnel, the river cuts a steep-walled canyon through the mountains. The Thompson River, flowing in from the east, almost doubles the Fraser's volume of water. Between Lytton and Yale—the stretch known as the Fraser River Canyon—the river flows through a deep, beautiful gorge above which tower craggy peaks rising to almost 3,050 meters (10,000 feet) to the west and 2,135 meters (7,000 feet) to the east.

South of Yale, the mountains recede. At Yale, the river turns west through the flat lower Fraser Valley, which was once a glaciated fjord, but has been filled with alluvial debris the river carried from the mountains. To the north, the valley is hemmed in by steep, deeply cut mountains; to the south it stretches across the border into northwest Washington's Nooksack Plain.

After skirting the southern city limits of New Westminster, Burnaby, and Vancouver, the Fraser empties into the Strait of Georgia through the two main channels of a delta, after having traveled 1,368 kilometers (850 miles). The bottomlands along the lower river and the islands of the delta are protected from seasonal floods by tall dikes—which are open to the public and make for some great walks above the marshy edge of river and tidewater.

Deepwater freighters ascend the river as far as New Westminster. Fishing boats and other commercial vessels with shallow draft can go farther upriver. Several species of salmon spawn in the Fraser and its tributaries, but stocks have been depleted in recent years, causing a virtual shutdown of the fisheries. Because of the importance of these salmon runs, the Fraser has no dams for generating hydroelectric power and is thus the Northwest's last major free-flowing river. Upriver settlements are dominated by logging and other forest industries; the lower Fraser Valley has highly productive dairies and farms.

■ HISTORY

The Fraser River is named for fur trader Simon Fraser, who explored much of it in 1808. The Hudson's Bay Company founded Fort Langley on the lower Fraser in 1827, anticipating a Fraser River route to the interior. Though that hope was dashed, the Hudson's Bay Company kept the profitable fort. (Today it has been restored and is a popular visitor attraction.) In March 1858, prospectors made a first big gold strike on the Fraser River, 10 miles north of Hope. Within weeks, gold seekers from adjacent Washington and from faraway California streamed into what was then the British territory of New Caledonia. The **Fraser River gold rush** was short but violent. In early summer of 1858, miners and Indians clashed at Spuzzum because the local Indians believed, quite reasonably, that any gold found in their river should belong to them. In retaliation, the miners destroyed an

(following pages) The dramatic Fraser River Valley is one of British Columbia's most fertile agricultural regions.

Indian village. The British government quickly established the new colony of British Columbia on the mainland and passed laws to govern its inhabitants.

Roads came late to the lower Fraser Valley because the lands bordering the river were covered by tall trees, swamps, and marshes. **New Westminster,** at the head of navigation for deepwater vessels, became the region's major port and served as the capital of British Columbia until 1868, when the provincial legislature moved to Victoria.

After the budding city of Vancouver, on ice-free Burrard Inlet, was chosen as the terminus of the transcontinental railway, the lower Fraser River became a rather polluted industrial zone of salmon canneries and lumber mills. The marshy

Vancouver's origins lay with the timber trade. Three lumber mills were established along Burrard Inlet during the early 1860s, supplying spars and masts for trading vessels and navies around the world. (City of Vancouver Archives)

north bank of the river in Burnaby and South Vancouver and the islands of the delta were diked by farmers, many of them Chinese, who raised produce for the Vancouver market as well as for railroad dining cars and ocean liner dining rooms. Today many of these farms survive, despite urban encroachment. The cupolas of *gundhwaras* (temples) are the heritage of Sikh immigrants, who came from India to work in logging camps and lumber mills.

■ RICHMOND   *map pages 62–63, D-4*

Richmond, on Lulu Island, is separated from Vancouver by the north arm of the Fraser River, but you'll see very little but fields and farms as you cross the island on Route 99. Until recently, much of Richmond was agricultural. During the glory years of salmon canning, when sockeye were incredibly plentiful, Japanese fishermen settled at Steveston Harbour. Situated at the southwestern tip of the island, the harbor is near the banks the salmon had to cross as they entered the south channel of the Fraser. Since the middle of the 1980s, Hong Kong money has thoroughly transformed Richmond. Large, and very fancy, homes now crowd into pastures where black-and-white cows grazed not so long ago, and high-rise condominiums are replacing barns and silos.

■ MALLS AND MARKETS

Aberdeen Centre in northwest Richmond was the first major Chinese mall outside Asia. Though it is somewhat "North-Americanized," with a bowling alley at its south end serving "fusion" fast food, it mostly has purely Chinese shops, from fishmongers to ginseng dealers, from news vendors to video outlets, with nary an English sign to be seen. A cash machine offers users a choice of written instructions in British Columbia's three "official" languages: English, French, and Chinese. During the Chinese New Year and at other important events, lion dancers invade the shops as they step to the sound of gongs, drums, and firecrackers. *4151 Hazelbridge Way; 604-270-1234.*

The **Yaohan Centre,** one block north off No. 3 Road, is even larger and has more important shops, including an upscale supermarket with both Chinese and Japanese foods. This is a great place to buy fresh and unusual vegetables, seafood, and rare Asian dainties. There is a food court where diners indulge in such fast-food delicacies as durian milk shakes, suckling pig on a bun, Chinese oyster omelet, and the parent dish of San Francisco's "hangtown fry." *604-231-0601.*

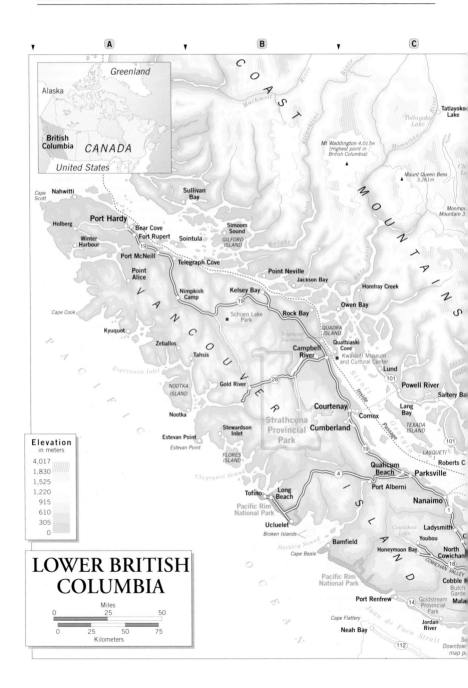

A **B** **C**

Greenland

Alaska

British
Columbia   CANADA

United States

COAST

MOUNTAINS

Machmell River

Klinaklini River

Homathko River

Mt Waddington 4,017m
(Highest point in
British Columbia) ▲

Tatlayoko
Lake

Tatlayoko
Lake

Mount Queen Bess
3,261m ▲

Monmou
Mountain 3

Cape
Scott

Nahwitti

Holberg

Port Hardy

Bear Cove
Fort Rupert
19

Winter
Harbour

Port McNeill

Point
Alice

Sointula

GILFORD
ISLAND

Simoom
Sound

Sullivan
Bay

Telegraph Cove

Nimpkish
Camp

Kelsey Bay
19

Knight Inlet

Point Neville

Jackson Bay

Homfray Creek

Owen Bay

Cape Cook

Kyuquot

Zeballos

Tahsis

Schoen Lake
Park ■

Rock Bay

Seymour
Narrows

Campbell
River

QUADRA
ISLAND

Quathiaski
Cove

Bute Inlet

Lund

101

Powell River

Saltery Ba

VANCOUVER

Esperanza Inlet

NOOTKA
ISLAND

Nootka

Gold River

28

Kwakiutl Museum
and Cultural Center

Courtenay

Comox

Lang
Bay

Strait of Georgia

Inside Passage

TEXADA
ISLAND

101

Stewardson
Inlet

Estevan Point

Estevan Point

FLORES
ISLAND

Strathcona
Provincial
Park

Cumberland

19

LASQUETI

Roberts C

Clayoquot Sound

Tofino

Long
Beach

Pacific Rim
National Park

Ucluelet

Broken Islands

Qualicum
Beach

Port Alberni

4

Parksville

Nanaimo

1

Barkley Sound

Cape Beale

Bamfield

Pacific Rim
National Park

Cowichan
Lake

Youbou

Honeymoon Bay

Ladysmith

North
Cowichan

COWICHAN VALLEY

18

Cobble I

Butch
Malat

PACIFIC OCEAN

Port Renfrew

14

Goldstream
Provincial
Park

Cape Flattery

Juan de Fuca Strait

Neah Bay

Jordan
River

112

Se
Downto
map p

Elevation
in meters

4,017
1,830
1,525
1,220
915
610
305
0

LOWER BRITISH
COLUMBIA

Miles
0   25   50

0   25   50   75
Kilometers

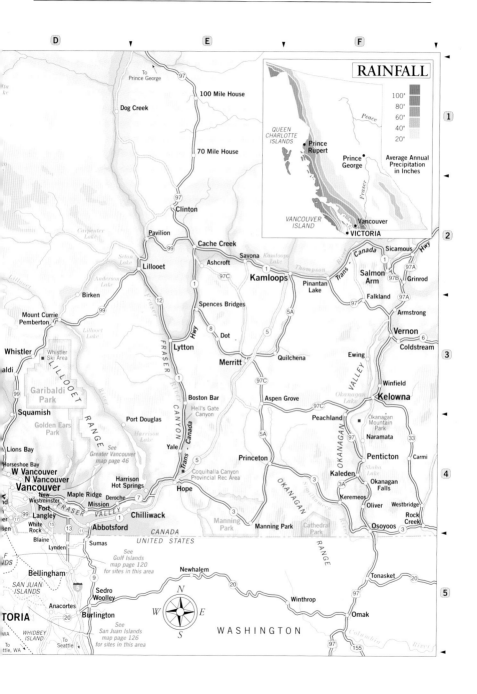

D   E   F

To Prince George 97

100 Mile House

Dog Creek

70 Mile House

RAINFALL

100"
80"
60"
40"
20"

QUEEN CHARLOTTE ISLANDS

Peace

Prince Rupert

Prince George

Average Annual Precipitation in Inches

VANCOUVER ISLAND

Fraser

Vancouver

VICTORIA

Clinton

Pavilion

Cache Creek

Savona Kamloops Lake

Canada Sicamous Hwy

Lillooet

Ashcroft

97C

Kamloops

Thompson

Trans

Salmon Arm 97B Grinrod

Birken

Spences Bridges

Pinantan Lake

Falkland 97A

Armstrong

Mount Currie
Pemberton

99

12

5A

97

Vernon 6

Whistler Whistler Ski Area

Lytton

Dot

8

5

Quilchena

Coldstream

aldi

Garibaldi Park

Merritt

Ewing

Winfield

VALLEY

Kelowna

Squamish

Golden Ears Park

Boston Bar

Hell's Gate Canyon

97C

Aspen Grove

Okanagan Lake

Peachland

97C

Okanagan Mountain Park

Lions Bay

Port Douglas

Harrison Lake

Yale

5A

Naramata

33

Horseshoe Bay

W Vancouver
N Vancouver
Vancouver

See Greater Vancouver map page 46

Princeton

Penticton Carmi

Skaha Lake

New Westminster

Fort Langley

Maple Ridge Deroche

Mission

Harrison Hot Springs

7

Hope

Coquihalla Canyon Provincial Rec Area

Kaleden

3A

Okanagan Falls

White Rock 15

Chilliwack

3

Keremeos

Oliver Westbridge

Blaine

13 11

Abbotsford

CANADA
UNITED STATES

Sumas

Manning Park

Manning Park

Cathedral Park

Osoyoos 3

Rock Creek

Lynden

See Gulf Islands map page 120 for sites in this area

RANGE

Bellingham

9

Newhalem

20

Tonasket 20

SAN JUAN ISLANDS

Sedro Woolley

N

97

Anacortes

W   E

Winthrop

TORIA

20

Burlington

S

WASHINGTON

Omak

WHIDBEY ISLAND

See San Juan Islands map page 126 for sites in this area

97

155

Columbia River

To Seattle

1

2

3

4

5

Parker Place, a few blocks south, has parking on the roof. Floata, one of the area's most popular restaurants, is in the center, and a superb tea shop, Arteas Chinese Tea, is at 1545-4380 No. 3 Road. Look for objects made from jade in the jewelry shops—the selection is good, because British Columbia is the world's top supplier of jade.

The **Richmond Public Market,** south of the Westminster Highway near No. 3 Road, has mostly Chinese vendors, with food booths, produce vendors, and fish mongers, knickknack merchants, and fast-food restaurants. It's open daily, but Tuesday is "optional open" day when most stalls are closed.

To reach the **Richmond Chinese District,** take Westminster Highway west from Route 99 to No. 3 Road.

■ RICHMOND NATURE RESERVES   *map pages 62–63, D-4*
You'll soon discover that there's more to this city than the long blocks of high-rise condominiums, palatial homes, and shopping malls lining the major roads. Richmond is also an agriculture and nature enclave, where some 39 percent of the urban lands has been set aside as reserves. Beyond the industrial parks, apartment blocks, and strip malls lie vast stretches of vegetable fields and gardens. Black-and-white dairy cattle graze in the pastures, and red-winged blackbirds sing and ducks dabble in reedy ponds and ditches. Beyond the levees, which shield this sea island from the fury of spring tides and winter tempests, stretch vast marshes—home of plovers, killdeer, and sandpipers, and a winter haven for golden plovers, yellowlegs, whimbrels, curlews, dunlins, dowitchers, snipes, phalaropes, loons, grebes, white-fronted geese, snow geese, and black brant. If you're lucky, you might even spot stints and spotted redshanks, uncommon visitors from Siberia who sometimes pause on these shores during migration.

Richmond Nature Park, surrounded by the city on all sides, is a boggy forest that provides a secure habitat for sparrows and goldfinches, owls and hawks, voles and lemmings. The boardwalks through the bogs and woods are much like the roads built by Northwest pioneers over the spongy ground of forest and meadows. The trees here are not stately coastal spruces, Douglas-firs, cedars, and hemlocks, but deciduous hardwoods—some of them stunted by the acid soils. This landscape is unique to the alluvial lands stretching from Washington's Nooksack Plain north through the Fraser Delta. This type of vegetation, more commonly found in eastern forests, is very rare on the West Coast. The bogs also contain wild cranberries, Labrador tea, and sundew (an insect-eating plant), as well as plants more commonly found in the muskegs and tundras of the far north. The **Nature House** has exhibits and interpretive programs. The park is just beyond No. 5 Road, which is one block west of Route 99, and its depths are accessed via boardwalks usable by wheelchairs and strollers. *11851 Westminster Highway; 604-273-7015.*

Reifel Migratory Bird Sanctuary, south of the Fraser River, is located 9.6 kilometers (6 miles) west of Ladner on Westham Island. Sandhill cranes, swans, bald eagles, and other birds can be seen here in season. Birdseed is for sale and there is an admission fee.

■ STEVESTON *map pages 62–63, D-4*

Steveston, a small fishing port on the south shore of Lulu Island, near the mouth of the Fraser River, looks as though it sprang straight from the pages of a John Steinbeck novel. It has kept its unique identity even though several chic shops and restaurants have opened in recent years. Once a separate community, Steveston is now part of Richmond but has, so far, kept urban sprawl limited to the fringes.

Until World War II, Steveston was home to many Japanese fishermen. During the war, the Japanese were interned and their boats sold to Anglo fishermen for a song. A few shops stocking Japanese goods, and a take-out sushi bar, are reminders of the town's Japanese period. An old cannery and shipyard along the refurbished waterfront have been turned into museums. At the public dock in the harbor, you can buy fish right off the boat. Look for boats with awnings draped across the boom—a sign they are selling that day.

You reach Steveston by taking No. 1 Road south from the Steveston Highway. If you continue to the end of the road, you can park your car in a small public lot and take a levee trail along the Strait of Georgia waterfront. The trail weaves through a virtual wilderness of reeds and other marsh plants, where you hear the sounds of the soughing of wind in the reeds, the trill of redwings and the chirping of sparrows, the screaming of seabirds, and the occasional putt-putt of a fishing-boat engine. Take No. 5 Road south for access to levee walks along the Fraser.

You can't miss a magnificent Chinese temple on the south side of Steveston Road. The red-and-gold structure has curved roofs decorated with dragons. Inside the great hall are golden images of Buddhas and bodhisattvas. Ancestor tablets are set up around the margins. Visitors are welcome, but remove your shoes before entering the building and take care not to disturb worshipers. A tearoom below the temple offers different Chinese teas. Tables in a courtyard garden have displays of miniature rock landscapes and pots of miniature trees.

The **Gulf of Georgia Cannery National Historic Site** (12138 Fourth Avenue; 604-664-9009) has exhibits about the British Columbia fishing industry from the days when salmon were plentiful and the industry boomed.

The **Britannia Heritage Shipyard** on the Steveston waterfront is a combination shipyard and park linked to the harbor by the Richmond trail system.

The **Steveston Hotel** (12111 Third Avenue; 604-277-9511), a renovated 1898 fishing port hotel, has quite a bit of history. The hotel served as headquarters for the Duke of Connaught's troops during the (sometimes violent) fishing strike of 1900, and it was one of the few buildings to survive the big Steveston fire of May 1918. It has served as a hangout and meeting place for local fishermen over the years.

■ THE COAST AND FRASER RIVER VALLEY

As you travel north or south on Route 99, you can spot the houses of the town of **Surrey** to the east among the trees on gravelly ridges left by continental glaciers. The flat lands in the foreground are farmland protected by an ordinance that allows urban expansion only on lands without value to agriculture.

Though workers in local vegetable fields often wear broad Chinese straw hats, Surrey's ethnic makeup is becoming largely East Indian, especially in its north end. Look for the gilded domes of two temples east of the freeway. Feel free to visit a temple, but maintain the respect due to a place of worship. During mealtimes, local Sikhs and Hindus may invite strangers to a free meal—after the food has first been offered to the local sage or deity, who "consumes its spiritual essence."

■ WHITE ROCK   *map pages 62–63, D-4*

This typical beach town north of Semiahmoo Bay (which is in the United States) has lots of sand, beachfront restaurants, and resort shops. In very warm summers, the coastline looks much like a California beach, and the houses, too, remind one so much of California that White Rock has been called Sausalito North. In cold or inclement weather, visitors bundle up and take long hikes along the tidal edge or enjoy a pint in a local pub.

■ NEW WESTMINSTER *map pages 62–63, D-4*

The once bustling capital and busy river port of British Columbia is today primarily a bedroom community of Vancouver. The grim, crenelated walls of the British Columbia penitentiary rose above the river here, until they were torn down in the mid-1980s to make room for condominiums.

New Westminster Public Market occupies a huge, modern building on the Fraser River quay. It is at the foot of Eighth Street west of downtown New Westminster and just a block from the SkyTrain terminal. Downstairs are a profusion of food shops: delis, produce vendors, fishmongers, and more. Upstairs are shops and restaurants ranging from fast-food joints to fancy eateries. All have window seats for river watching (tugs, barges, log rafts, and an occasional freighter). Tugboats tie up at the wharf outside, and an old stern-wheeler dredge, the *Samson V,* is permanently berthed at the quay (open weekends). The market is open daily and there's ample free parking. Take the SkyTrain from downtown Vancouver to New Westminster, or follow Marine Drive east until you see the market on your right. From Route 99, take the Annacis Highway north across the Alex Fraser Bridge to New Westminster. Follow this road until you see the market at Front Street near Marine Way.

Enjoy a meal or drink on a riverside terrace and watch the water flow by, or take a tour of the river. **Paddlewheeler River Adventures** will take you along the river from New Westminster to Fort Langley in a historic paddle-wheeler riverboat. *139-810 Quayside Drive; 604-525-4465.*

■ FORT LANGLEY *map pages 62–63, D-4*

This fort, a must-visit for history buffs, consists of a wooden palisade and half a dozen odd, reconstructed buildings. The fort was once the most important British stronghold in the Pacific Northwest. Founded in 1827, a dozen years after Hudson's Bay Company headquarters had been established at Fort Vancouver (now Vancouver, Washington), it is the oldest white settlement along the inland waters. Fort Langley predates Victoria, British Columbia's oldest city, which was founded as a fort in 1843. Founded as a trading post and supply house for the inland waters from Puget Sound to southeast Alaska, it was here that one of the Northwest's great industries got its start: salmon packing. Take the Trans-Canada Highway (TCH) Route 1 east from Vancouver toward Hope. Follow signs to Fort Langley National Historic Park. *23433 Mavis Avenue; 604-513-4777.*

A popular event at Harrison Hot Springs is the World Championship Sand Sculpture Contest.

■ **HARRISON LAKE**   *map pages 62–63, E-4*

Sixty-four-kilometer (40-mile)-long Harrison Lake is one of several long and narrow fjord-like lakes cutting through the spine of the mountains. Others are Stave Lake and Pitt Lake to the west, also accessible via Route 7. The westernmost of these lakes, Indian Arm, stretches north from Burrard Inlet. Tall mountains shield Harrison Lake's beaches from inclement weather. Harrison Hot Springs is a small resort community at the southern end of the lake, just north of Route 7, with a large resort hotel. A public pool fed by natural hot springs invites bathers at **Harrison Hot Springs Hotel** (100 Esplanade Street; 604-796-2244). The hot springs here have been popular for over a hundred years.

The historic Kilby Store and Farm in nearby Harrison Mills gives you a glimpse into British Columbia farm life during the 1920s, with a country store, farm kitchen, dairy house, and barn set among the orchards and fields. *215 Kilby Road, off Route 7.*

A road runs south from Harrison Lake to the TCH (Route 1). Take Exit 135 to visit the Minter Gardens, a 26-acre estate with several theme gardens, among them

Chinese, English, fern, fragrance, and rose gardens, and a giant evergreen maze in a style once popular on English estates. *52892 Bunker Road, Rosedale; 604-794-7191 (Apr.–mid-Oct.) and 604-792-3799 (mid-Oct.–Mar.) or 888-646-8377.*

■ FRASER RIVER CANYON

■ HOPE   *map pages 62–63, E-4*

The lower Fraser Valley extends east to Hope, where the river makes a big bend to the north. Hope is a pleasant small river town ringed by the dramatically serrated, snowcapped Cascade Mountains. A former fur trade and gold rush town, Hope sits at the junction of several major highways and provides services to travelers. If Hope looks vaguely familiar to you, this may be because the movie *Rambo: First Blood Part II* was filmed here.

The Fraser River and its canyon attract scores of bird-watchers. The unique blend of coastal and interior climates create a variety of different habitats for birds. **Greenwood Island,** across the river from Hope, is a blue heron sanctuary. In fall, the large snags along the river provide roosts for bald eagles that follow the spawning salmon upstream.

The Coquihalla Canyon Provincial Recreation Area, east of Hope, allows visitors to explore the **Othello Tunnels,** built from 1911 to 1918 to complete the Kettle Valley Railway. A suspension bridge over the 91-meter (300-foot)-deep Coquihalla Canyon links an impressive chain of solid granite tunnels. A leisurely walk (4 kilometers or 2.5 miles round trip) on the abandoned railway grade will take you though the tunnels and the spectacular Coquihalla Canyon gorge. (Plagued by washouts and rock slides, the railway line was closed in 1959.)

Just south of Yale, look for a sign directing you to the Spirit Cave Trail for a beautiful and panoramic view of the Cascade Mountains to the east.

■ YALE   *map pages 62–63, E-4*

Twenty miles north of Hope on the TCH, Route 1, Yale hugs the west bank of the Fraser River. Founded in 1848 as a Hudson's Bay Company fort, this small town played the important role of inland terminus for the stern-wheelers plying up the river during the Fraser River gold rush. Hill's Bar, just south of Yale, is the site of the first major gold find in British Columbia. From Yale, prospectors with their

(following pages) The resort town of Harrison Hot Springs.

supplies took the "Gold Rush Trail" through the canyon. Between 1858 and 1870, thousands of miners poured up the canyon, seeking fortunes on the Fraser River and, later, in the goldfields of the Cariboo. The trail was replaced by the Cariboo Wagon Road, built between 1862 and 1865 by the Royal Engineers. This treacherous cliffhanger of a track was so dangerous that freighters imported camels to see if these sure-footed beasts of burden would make the passage safer. They didn't and were set loose—"wild" camels roamed the sagelands of interior British Columbia for several decades.

Historic Yale, in the center of town, includes the 1863 **Church of St. John the Divine** and the **Historic Yale Museum** (604-863-2324). In 1871, the documents establishing the Confederation of Canada were signed in Yale.

■ **HELL's GATE** *map pages 62–63, E-3/4*

Between Yale and Boston Bar, the Fraser River squeezes through a narrow gorge. Here the Fraser River Canyon is several hundred meters deep and narrows to a mere 30.5-meter (100-foot) chute at Hell's Gate. In 1808, fur trader Simon Fraser was the first European to travel down the wild river that would one day bear his name. Even though Fraser was guided by native Salish Indians, he had harrowing experiences as his men paddled giant birch-bark canoes through the boiling rapids of the upper Fraser River. He did not attempt to run Hell's Gate, however, but portaged past its dangerous chute. The Swiss-engineered **Hell's Gate Airtram** (604-867-9277), which opened in 1971, will zip you down the cliff to an observation deck. You can also can hike down a dirt road to the river.

■ **BOSTON BAR** *map pages 62–63, E-3*

This village at the northern end of the Fraser River Canyon was founded by American prospectors during the Fraser River gold rush. The local Indians called the Americans "Boston men," hence the name Boston Bar. The village became a busy roadhouse stop during the gold rush, thanks to Boston Bar Alex, who ran one of the best inns with good food. The building of the Canadian Pacific and Canadian National Railways up the Fraser River Canyon sustained Boston Bar after the gold rush. Until the early 1980s, the Canadian Pacific Railway's divisional point, at North Bend, across the Fraser from Boston Bar, could only be reached by an aerial ferry. Today there's a bridge.

(opposite) A view down the Fraser River Canyon in the Hell's Gate area.

■ Travel and Climate

■ Getting There and Around

Most visitors to British Columbia arrive by car and drive into Canada at the Blaine, Washington, border crossing, one of the few that is open 24 hours. North of the border, I-5 changes to Route 99 but remains a freeway all the way to the Vancouver city limits. Because British Columbia has laws protecting its sparse farmlands, the road traverses a landscape of green pastures and fields, though you can spot suburban housing developments among the trees on gravelly ridges east of the freeway. About 10 miles north of the border, Route 10 turns west to the Vancouver Island ferry terminal at Tsawwassen.

The delta of the Fraser River has fallen victim to development, but east of New Westminster, the valley is still a pastoral idyll. To the north and east, the tall, craggy peaks of the Coast and Cascade Mountains rise straight from the valley floor. To the south, in northwest Washington, snowcapped Mount Baker towers over fir-clad foothills. The river winds placidly through green meadows and cottonwood and birch forests.

The **Trans-Canada Highway** (TCH) Route 1, a four-lane freeway, is the main route running east through level farmlands. Because of the proximity to the Vancouver metropolitan area—and because few travelers linger in this quietly beautiful landscape—there are few lodging facilities and restaurants of note. Scenic Route 7 skirts the rocky northern bank of the river, meeting the TCH west of Hope. Side roads lead to mountain lakes and to Harrison Hot Springs, the valley's major resort. Three two-lane highways—Routes 11, 13, and 15—run from the TCH south to the border crossings at Sumas, Lynden, and Blaine.

Note to travelers entering the region from the United States: Speed limits and distances in British Columbia are posted in kilometers, not miles!

■ Climate

The weather in the lower Fraser Valley tends to be a few degrees milder and less rainy than that in Vancouver; the upper valley is hotter in summer and colder in winter, with heavy snowfall near the mountains. Heavy rain melting the mountain snows can cause severe flooding of the lowlands in the fall and spring and force the closure of roads. Frigid northeasters can sweep down the valley in winter and freeze up creeks and ponds. Once or twice during the last century the weather turned so cold that the Fraser River froze to its mouth—most definitely an uncommon occurrence.

Okanagan Valley Winery Tour

■ East from the Fraser Valley

Among the high points of visiting British Columbia's Okanagan Valley are the approaches: no matter how you drive there, the road will be incredibly scenic. If you take Route 3, the Crow's Nest Highway, east from the Fraser Valley, you'll soon find yourself in an alpine landscape of tall peaks, deeply glaciated canyons, and colorful wildflower meadows alternating with dense forests. The scenery changes from forests to grasslands and bare rocks, as you cross the divide between the coast and the interior, but it remains beautiful.

The approaches from the south are equally beautiful—via Route 20, the North Cascades Highway, and U.S. 97 north to the border, or by taking U.S. 97 north from I-90. If you come from the south, you'll get a surprise as soon as you cross the border. The American Okanogan Valley is a sparsely populated region of orchards and range land; the Canadian Okanagan Valley is not. (Note that Americans and Canadians spell the name of the valley differently.) Just north of the line sprawls the city of Osoyoos, a retirement mecca. Don't be surprised when you see a profusion of whitewashed arches and red tile roofs rising above sandy beaches. The town decided on a Spanish theme for

The Okanagan Valley has only recently emerged as a producer of quality wine grapes.

its architecture (because it's so far south). On a sunny day, it makes you feel like you've been suddenly dropped into Southern California.

But as you head north, you're soon back in the farm country. Besides growing grapes, the Okanagan is British Columbia's fruit basket. In early summer, roadside stands sell cherries; in summer they're loaded to their canvas roofs with peaches; in fall, at grape harvest, it's apple time. The valley even has its own apple: the crisp, reddish-purple, tart-sweet Spartan, which was developed here in the 1920s. Its cultivation has spread to the United States, but it is nowhere better than here in the valley of its birth. Do yourself a favor. Stop at a roadside stand and buy some. This brings us to a curious customs law. While you cannot usually bring fruits from Canada into the United States, you are allowed to bring in British Columbia apples—by the box, if such is your desire. But you cannot bring Washington apples into British Columbia. It's against the law.

The Okanagan Valley is exceptionally scenic and gets prettier as you drive north. That's because it is a deep trough carved by a continental glacier. Places where the glacier encountered soft rock, and scoured deeper, are now filled with water. A chain of deep lakes, connected by the Okanagan River, stretches intermittently north from the U.S.

The bounty of a roadside fruit stand serves as a testimony to the abundant produce of British Columbia's interior valleys.

border to the head of the valley near Armstrong. Mountains rise steeply to heights of 1,800 to 2,000 meters (6,000 and 7,000 feet, respectively) from the waters of the largest of these lakes, appropriately called Okanagan, leaving little land for cultivation or settlements along its shores.

But without the mitigating influence of this lake, which has never been fathomed and is too deep to freeze over in winter, viticulture would be all but impossible in the valley. Even so, some growers have been known to bury their vines to protect them from killing freezes.

■ FIRST PLANTINGS

British Columbia's first grapes were planted in the 1860s, near Okanagan Mission on the lake's east shore, by Charles Pandosy, an oblate missionary, for religious use and personal consumption. The padre left no record about the quality of his wines.

Until the late 1980s, wine makers in British Columbia produced low-quality, high-alcohol wines. Though a few vintners planted quality grapes in the early 1980s, the tide did not turn until 1988, when a free trade agreement, plus a GATT ruling against Canada's protective tariffs, took effect. Until then, British Columbia vintners made wine from the cheapest fruit available: berries, apples, and hybrid grapes guaranteed by the Canadian government to withstand the severe winters.

With wineries free to set their own quality standards for grapes, they could now pay premium prices for high quality grapes. Almost overnight 2,400 acres (two-thirds of the British Columbia vineyards) were pulled up and replanted with European vinifera varieties—the vines that have made the wines of California, Oregon, and Washington famous. Less than a decade later, the results were spectacular. British Columbia wine promoter Jurgen Gothe declared, "We don't have to apologize anymore." He's right.

■ WINERIES

Gehringer Brothers Estate Winery

At the southern end of the valley between Osoyoos and Oliver on Route 97 is the turnoff road (326th Avenue) for Gehringer Brothers Estate Winery. This winery makes very good Rieslings and, if conditions are right in late fall, an ice wine, which is made from the intensified juice of grapes frozen on the vine. *RR No. 1, Site 23, Comp 4, Oliver; 250-498-3537.*

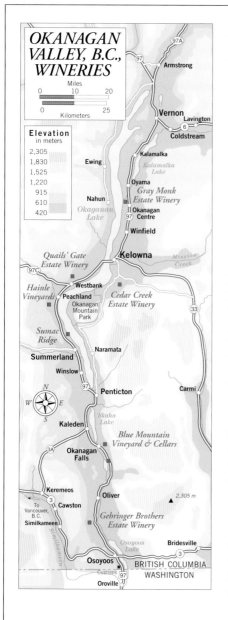

OKANAGAN VALLEY, B.C., WINERIES

Miles
0   10   20

0   25
Kilometers

Elevation
in meters
2,305
1,830
1,525
1,220
915
610
420

97A

97

Armstrong

Vernon

Lavington

6

Coldstream

Ewing

Kalamalka

Kalamalka
Lake

Oyama

Gray Monk
Estate Winery

Nahun

Okanagan
Lake

Okanagan
Centre

97

Winfield

Quails' Gate
Estate Winery

Kelowna

Mission
Creek

97C

Hainle
Vineyards

Westbank

Peachland

Okanagan
Mountain
Park

Cedar Creek
Estate Winery

33

Sumac
Ridge

Naramata

Summerland

Winslow

N
W   E
S

97

Penticton

Carmi

Kaleden

Skaha
Lake

Blue Mountain
Vineyard & Cellars

3A

Okanagan
Falls

Keremeos

Oliver

2,305 m

3

To
Vancouver,
B.C.

Cawston

Similkameen

Gehringer Brothers
Estate Winery

Osoyoos
Lake

Bridesville

3

Osoyoos

BRITISH COLUMBIA
WASHINGTON

Customs

97

Oroville

**Blue Mountain
Vineyard & Cellars**

A few miles to the north in Okanagan Falls, this winery makes very good sparkling wines, as well as pinot noirs, pinot blancs, and pinot gris. Most red wines made in this valley lack varietal character, but not the Blue Mountain pinot noirs. *Off Route 97 on Allendale Road; 250-497-8244.*

After Penticton, Route 97, the main north-south highway, runs along Lake Okanagan's western shore through a landscape alternating between steep cliffs and fertile alluvial fans.

Sumac Ridge Estate Winery

North of the small town of Summerland, you'll see a sign for this winery. Don't turn around when you see golf links. You haven't strayed. This pioneering winery was established in 1981 in the clubhouse of a golf course. Grapes were planted between the fairways. Sumac Ridge has gained a good reputation for its sparkling wines and gewürztraminers, and for a hybrid red called chancellor. It's quite good, though its taste will not remind you at all of, say, Sonoma merlot. *17403 Route 97, Summerland; 250-494-0451.*

The next town up the road is called Peachland, because peaches are what the area is famous for. There are also a few wineries high above the lake on benchlands.

Hainle Vineyards

Hainle, known for its pinot blancs, pinot noirs, and chardonnays, was British Columbia's first winery to make ice wines. The winery has a tasting room and a bistro and offers catering and cooking classes. *5355 Trepanier Bench Road, Peachland; 250-767-2525.*

At Westbank, Route 97C comes in from the west. This is the fast road to the coast, via Merritt and the Coquihalla toll road (Route 5).

Quails' Gate Estate Winery

This winery produces chardonnays, pinot noirs, and a late-harvest botrytis-affected wine from the German optima grape. To reach Quails' Gate, turn east on Gellatly Road, and north on Boucherie Road. *3303 Boucherie Road, Kelowna; 250-769-4451.*

Route 97 crosses the lake to the main part of Kelowna, the valley's largest city, on a floating bridge. Look for Ogopogo, purported to be a monster of the Loch Ness variety. Kelowna is the valley's cheapest place for food and lodging.

Cedar Creek Estate Winery

Off Route 97, Pandosy Street runs along the east side of the lake and takes you 14 kilometers (8.4 miles) south to this winery near the site of the mission where Father Pandosy planted British Columbia's first grapes. Cedar Creek makes good pinot blancs and gewürztraminers in addition to wines from pinot auxerrois, a somewhat obscure French white wine grape that has found a home in the Okanagan Valley. There's also a quaffable Proprietor's Reserve white. *5445 Lakeshore Road, Kelowna; 250-764-8866 or 800-730-9463.*

Gray Monk Estate Winery

A true pioneer of B.C. wines, this last winery on our tour occupies a splendid site in Okanagan Centre, high above the lake. For more than a decade, Gray Monk has made the valley's most exciting wines. The owners, George and Trudy Heiss, revolutionized grape-growing and wine-making techniques here in the early 1980s, succeeding with planting where government-paid experimenters had not and setting the stage for the production of high-quality vinifera wines. The winery takes its name from a pinot gris grape in the Heiss's native Austria. Pinot gris is among the best wines made by winemaker George Heiss, Jr. *1055 Camp Road, Okanagan; 250-766-3168.*

A tasting room in the Okanagan Valley.

V I C T O R I A

■ HIGHLIGHTS

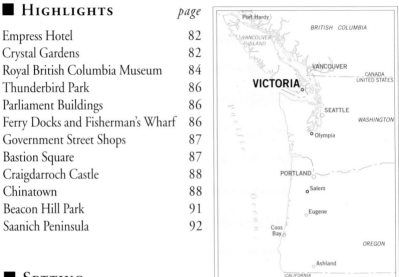

■ SETTING

VICTORIA SPRAWLS ACROSS A LOW, ROCKY HEADLAND at Vancouver Island's southeastern tip, at the base of the Saanich Peninsula. The city, the provincial capital of British Columbia, has an interesting, much indented waterfront, with a walled-in harbor downtown, a not-so-tidy fishing harbor farther out, and an even less tidy "Gorge," which is what locals call the long northwestern arm of the harbor that almost cuts Victoria off from the hinterland.

Some locals like to think of Victoria as the "southernmost" city in Canada, which it is not. Windsor, Ontario, is as far south as the Oregon-California border (about 42 degrees north). Even so, many retired civil servants have settled here because they like the mild "southern" clime with its low rainfall (Victoria is in the rain shadow of the Olympic Mountains and Insular Mountain Range).

In recent years, Victoria has raised a regional stink for insisting that it is safe for the city to dump its raw sewage into Juan de Fuca Strait. Though this stance has raised eyebrows in Seattle environmental circles, it has not hurt the tourist traffic.

■ HISTORY

Victoria was founded in 1843 as a fur-trading fort by the Hudson's Bay Company on Camosun Harbour, a natural port. By 1858, Victoria had made a transition from a sleepy outpost to bustling metropolis almost overnight, after gold was discovered on the Fraser River. The town's 500 residents were quickly outnumbered by the 25,000 miners who streamed into town to buy licenses and supplies. Their tents covered the waterfront and lined up along Front Street for a mile. During their short stay, many miners liked what they saw, and they settled in Victoria when they returned from the diggings—quadrupling the city's population by 1859 to some 2,000 people.

Since so many of these new settlers were Americans, the celebration of the Fourth of July soon took precedence over the Queen's Birthday, which, during Victoria's reign, was an almost sacred holiday. So how did the city get to look as "British" as it does now? Through what we now know as "psychological warfare."

Victoria in 1859 was growing rapidly due to the influx of thousands of would-be miners. (British Columbia Archives and Records Service)

The British government went all out to make the capital of British Columbia look as "British" as possible, mainly in the design of government buildings, to avoid secession to, or annexation by, the United States. It's exactly that "British" look that makes Victoria so appealing to American visitors today. But it didn't necessarily satisfy 19th-century Victorians.

In 1868, Victoria residents (those mostly of non-British origin) signed a petition to U.S. President Grant, asking him "to receive British Columbia into the American Union." While nothing happened, the petition may have paved the way for the favorable terms the British Columbians got in 1871, when they joined the Canadian Confederation.

Because the railroad from eastern Canada ran only to Burrard Inlet on the mainland, Vancouver became the province's dominant port. But because Victoria has remained out of the mainstream of industrial development, it has preserved its 19th-century character and charm.

■ **EXPLORING THE CITY** *map page 83*

Victoria has more sights than you can handle in a day—you should plan to spend at least a weekend in town. What makes Victoria unique, in the eyes of many visitors, is its Inner Harbour, compact and stone-walled, like no other port in western North America. What makes the city easy to explore is that most of the town's attractions are either on the Inner Harbour or within easy walking distance. Tubby little ferries connect several landings along the harbor; every morning at 10 A.M. they "dance" on the water—to music, of course. Flower baskets have brightened up lampposts at the harbor and around town since 1937. Every August, a huge barge, topped by a band shell, is towed into the Inner Harbour for the annual free concert by the Victoria Symphony, which attracts as many as 40,000 people.

■ **EMPRESS HOTEL AND CRYSTAL GARDENS** *map page 83, B-3*
The tall stone edifice of the Parliament Buildings to the south of the basin and the stone facade of the **Empress Hotel** to the east give focus to the harbor. The stately chateau-style hotel has dominated the Inner Harbour since 1908. But the solidity of the Empress is a bit deceiving. Before its construction, the "James Bay flats" occupied the site where the hotel stands. They were filled in, and the masonry is now supported by pilings driven through the mud. A large arch toward the north marks a spot where the pile drivers could find no ground to support the pilings—

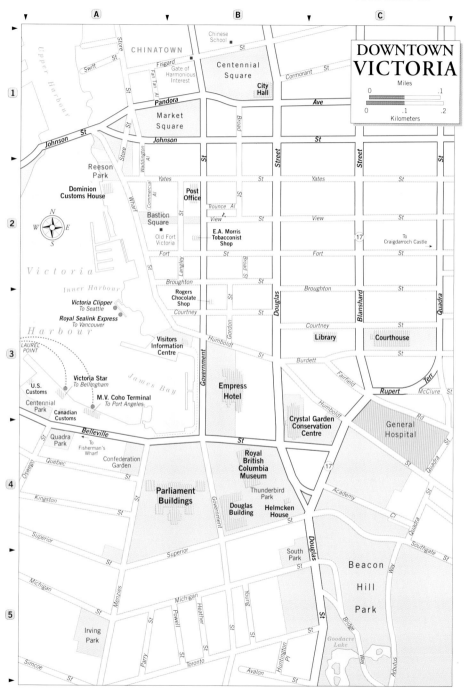

DOWNTOWN VICTORIA

Miles

0   .1

0   .1   .2
Kilometers

CHINATOWN

Chinese School

Swift St

Store St

Fan Tan Al

Fisgard St
Gate of Harmonious Interest

Centennial Square

City Hall

Cormorant St

Pandora Ave

Market Square

Broad St

Johnson St

Johnson St

Reeson Park

Waddington Al

Commercial Al

Yates St

Yates St

Dominion Customs House

Wharf St

Post Office

Trounce Al

Bastion Square

View

View St

Old Fort Victoria

E.A. Morris Tobacconist Shop

17

To Craigdarroch Castle

Victoria Inner Harbour

Langley St

Fort St

Fort St

Broad St

Broughton

Broughton St

Rogers Chocolate Shop

Gordon St

Douglas St

Blanshard St

Quadra St

Courtney

Courtney St

Harbour

LAUREL POINT

Visitors Information Centre

Humboldt St

Library

Courthouse

Victoria Clipper
To Seattle

Royal Sealink Express
To Vancouver

James Bay

Burdett

Fairfield

Terr

U.S. Customs

Victoria Star
To Bellingham

M.V. Coho Terminal
To Port Angeles

Rupert

McClure St

Centennial Park

Canadian Customs

Empress Hotel

Humboldt

Crystal Garden Conservation Centre

General Hospital

Rd

Quadra Park

Belleville

St

Quadra St

To Fisherman's Wharf

Confederation Garden

Royal British Columbia Museum

17

Oswego St

Quebec St

Parliament Buildings

Government St

Thunderbird Park

Douglas Building

Helmcken House

Academy

Cl

Quadra St

Kingston St

Superior

St

Superior St

South Park St

Douglas St

Beacon

Southgate St

Michigan St

Menzies St

Michigan St

Powell

Heather St

Young St

Hill

Way

Park

Irving Park

Parry

Toronto

Avalon St

Huntington Pl

Goodacre Lake

Bridge

Ker

Arbutus

Simcoe St

so they simply bridged it over. If the Empress and the Parliament Buildings seem to have similar stylistic features, that's because they were designed by the same architect, Francis Rattenbury. Unlike the Empress, however, the legislative house sits on solid rock. *721 Government Street; 250-384-8111 or 800-441-1414.*

For the "British" experience in Victoria, indulge in high tea at the venerable Empress or the huge **Crystal Garden Conservation Centre.** The Crystal Garden building was erected in 1925 above the former mudflats. But instead of driving piles, architect Percy James floated the glass-roof structure on a 0.75-meter (2.5-foot)-thick slab of concrete. The Crystal Gardens once had a giant saltwater swimming pool surrounded by palms; now it is a conservatory housing many exotic flowers and birds. *713 Douglas Street; 250-953-8800.*

■ ROYAL BRITISH COLUMBIA MUSEUM *map page 83, B-4*
This museum, still known to insiders by its old name, the British Columbia Provincial Museum, is the one place you absolutely don't want to miss. It has a superb collection of totem poles and Indian artifacts, historical exhibits (life in the

(above) The Empress Hotel graces Victoria's picturesque Inner Harbour.
(opposite) High tea at the Empress Hotel.

cold interior, a 19th-century street), and a series of superb natural habitat displays. A dramatic, life-size model of a Nootka whaling canoe, with the harpooner about to strike a whale, greets you as you enter the vast lobby, which is large enough to display several totem poles. The museum has an excellent bookstore with books on native tribes and British Columbia history, as well as a good selection of native jewelry, masks, and other art objects. *675 Belleville Street; 250-387-3014.*

■ **THUNDERBIRD PARK** *map page 83, B-4*
Just behind the museum, the tall totem poles of Thunderbird Park reach for the sky. They stand next to a scaled-down Kwakiutl longhouse built by chief Mungo Martin in the garden of the **Helmcken House,** the oldest house (1852) in Victoria still standing on its original site in its original condition. The building is named for Dr. J. S. Helmcken, a crusty pioneer medical doctor and politician.

■ **PARLIAMENT BUILDINGS** *map page 83, A/B-4*
These buildings on the south side of the Inner Harbour were completed in 1887, using local materials as much as possible. The exterior is made of stone quarried at tiny Haddington Island's neat Port McNeill in the northern inland passage. The gilded statue atop the main copper-covered dome is not of Queen Victoria, but of Capt. George Vancouver, the first navigator to circumnavigate Vancouver Island. Statues of Sir James Douglas, who chose the location of Victoria, and Sir Matthew Begbie, the "hanging judge," flank the entrance. Be sure to take a close-up look at the buildings' details. Figures from British Columbia's past and grotesque stone faces decorate the exterior walls. Inside, the ornate woodwork is trimmed with gold and silver leaf. Visitors are welcome inside and may take one of the free guided tours of the buildings. You may also watch the Assembly, when it is in session, from the galleries overlooking the Legislative Chamber. *501 Belleville Street; 250-387-3046.*

■ **FERRY DOCKS AND FISHERMAN'S WHARF** *map page 83, A-3/4*
Farther west on Belleville Street, beyond the Canadian Pacific Railway Steamship Terminal completed by Rattenbury in 1924 (and now housing a wax museum), is where the Port Angeles ferry and the passenger ferries from Bellingham and Seattle dock. A path from the Inner Harbour winds around **Laurel Point** to the west. Look for the tall poles of fishing trollers. A short stroll down side streets will bring you to **Fisherman's Wharf,** where purse seiners, gillnetters, trollers, and halibut

vessels now occupy the place where it is believed Sir James Douglas first landed. Farther down the harbor, freighters load lumber and visiting cruise ships dock—a fraction of the ship traffic that passed through after World War I, when Victoria was Canada's second busiest harbor (Montreal was the busiest).

■ VISITOR'S INFORMATION CENTRE *map page 83, B-3*
Back at the Inner Harbour, the Visitor's Information Centre sits on the waterfront. From here you get a good view across the harbor at Songhees Point of the **Welcome Totem,** the tallest totem pole in the world at 55.6 meters (182.5 feet). It was erected in 1994 for the Commonwealth Games. *812 Wharf Street; 800-663-3883 or 250-953-2033.*

■ GOVERNMENT STREET SHOPS *map page 83, B-2/3*
Government Street, between the Empress and the harbor, at one time ran over a wooden trestle, where the stone causeway rises now, when it connected the stockade of the fort to the residential areas to the south. Today, the section north of the Inner Harbour is downtown Victoria's prime shopping area. Here you'll find everything from top hats to heavy woolen sweaters knitted by Cowichan Indians, and from tartans to sweets.

    Rogers Chocolate Shop (913 Government Street) was established in 1885 by an American fruit dealer. It moved into its present (1903) building in 1918. Be sure to taste the famed Victoria creams.

    The **E. A. Morris Tobacconist Shop** (1116 Government Street) was established in 1892. Morris advertised in the Colonist newspaper that he "imported cigarettes for ladies"—a daring proposition back then. Its fine wood craftsmanship, beveled glass, and onyx columns remain virtually unchanged since a 1910 renovation. Cigars are kept moist in a walk-in humidor with a damp brick floor; they may be lit at a perpetual flame burning in an onyx column.

■ BASTION SQUARE *map page 83, A-2*
An alley leads to Bastion Square, which takes its name from one of the bastions of Fort Victoria. The first city jail stood here; condemned criminals were publicly hanged in the square until 1870. Built in 1889, the turreted old courthouse at 28 Bastion Square was the first concrete building in Victoria. Bastion Square was the city's original commercial hub.

■ CRAIGDARROCH CASTLE

A 15-minute walk east on Fort Street (you can also take Bus 11 or 14) will land you at lavish Craigdarroch Castle, built by Robert Dunsmuir, a coal magnate who was one of Victoria's wealthiest residents. Dunsmuir died in 1889, the year before his 39-room, four-and-a-half story structure was completed. Craigdarroch, which has splendid carved woodwork and beautiful stained glass, now serves as a museum of late-19th-century life. The house and its gardens are being restored to their original look in a multiyear project. On a clear day, you can see the Juan de Fuca Strait and the Olympic Mountains from the mansion's tower. *1050 Joan Crescent; 250-592-5323.*

■ CHINATOWN *map page 83, A/B-1*

North of Bastion Square on Fisgard Street is Canada's oldest Chinatown and, until Vancouver's surpassed it in 1910, the country's most populous one. Built in 1981, the red and gold **Gate of Harmonious Interest,** embellished with intricately carved dragons and other symbolic figures, is a monument to a period long past.

(above) The popular Butchart Gardens. (opposite) Victoria is a city for walkers. In the warm months, flowers bloom in flowerpots attached to lightpoles along downtown sidewalks.

These days the gate symbolizes the harmony that exists between Canada's eastern and western cultures. Two protective lions, sculpted in China, guard that concord. Local race relations were not always as congenial, however. In the 19th century, when the first Chinese arrived during the 1858 Fraser River gold rush, they were haunted by resentment, discrimination, and animosity. At the dawn of the 20th century, 3,500 Chinese lived in a six-block ghetto. Currently, Chinatown's population is in "decline" because Victoria's Chinese are now able to live throughout the city without facing discrimination, and no longer have to live tightly packed in a few downtown blocks.

Among Chinatown's noteworthy buildings is the **Chinese School,** which was completed in 1909. The combination of the pagoda-curled roof-tips and the Italianate details on the balconies, was the architect's riff on the chinoiserie style, which was popular in western Europe (particularly England and France) at the beginning of the 20th century. The playful design is unique in Victoria.

A few Chinese grocery shops, noodle shops, and restaurants still cater to the needs of the Chinese community with meals ranging in variety and price from simple dim sum luncheons to multicourse dinners. Chinatown's shops and restaurants are highly visitor friendly.

Fan Tan Alley, said to be the narrowest street in Canada—in places, it is only 1.2 meters, or 4 feet, wide—runs from Fisgard Street to Pandora Avenue, a distance of about 100 feet. (You'll find the alley on the south side of Fisgard between 545½ and 549½.) Taking its name from a Chinese gambling game, the alley once served as the main "entrance" to a maze of twisting passageways, camouflaged escape routes, hidden courtyards, opium dens, and gambling clubs.

Once known as the "The Forbidden City," this inner sanctum was off-limits to "round eyes." Only a few cemented-in doorways hint at the labyrinth that existed here a hundred years ago. Doors open into small stores selling knick-knacks, wicker ware, and artwork; there is even a barber shop. From here, it is a short walk to the Gorge waterfront of the Inner Harbour.

■ **DOMINION CUSTOMS HOUSE** *map page 83, A-2*
The Dominion Customs House on Wharf Street was built in 1876 in the Second Empire style. The nearby seawall still has iron rings where sailing vessels used to tie up. Many of the old buildings all along the waterfront once served as ship chandleries and warehouses.

■ **BEACON HILL PARK** *map page 83, C-4/5*

Walk south down Douglas Street, east of the Empress and the Royal British Columbia Museum, to Beacon Hill Park. Here some of southern Vancouver Island's native vegetation survives among plantings of shrubs and flowers, mostly because the city of Victoria didn't have enough money in the early days to "improve" the park. Horse races were once held here, and in 1878, guns were installed in Finlayson and Macauley Point to help defend Victoria, in case those pesky Americans to the south thought of attacking. Gunpowder stored in a shed became a source of civic disquiet. European skylarks released here in 1888 on the Saanich Peninsula adapted to the local climes and spread to the San Juan Islands.

Two blocks from Beacon Hill Park stands the handsome **Beaconsfield Inn,** completed in 1905. The mansion makes Anglophiles feel like they've come home. *998 Humboldt Street; 250-384-4044.*

Dallas Road and Douglas Street meet at the southwest corner of Beacon Hill Park, known as Mile Zero, where the Trans-Canada Highway officially begins. This drive passes the **Chinese Cemetery at Harling Point,** one of the major landmarks of Victoria's Chinese community. This cemetery was established in 1903 by the Chinese Consolidated Benevolent Association at a site selected because of its favorable feng shui. (Graves in an earlier cemetery, set on a beach, were repeatedly destroyed by the surf.) The graveyard was in use until 1950, and was designated a national historical site in 1996.

A recent refurbishing of the cemetery included the construction of new fencing and explanatory plaques. Although an open-air altar still stands, a "bone house" has been demolished. Until the 1930s, it was customary to exhume the bodies of Chinese who died in Canada after they had been interred for seven years. The bones were cleaned and shipped to their home villages to be buried with their ancestors in the family graves. Bones that were still in storage when the Chinese-Japanese war, World War II, and the Chinese revolution ended the practice are buried in mass graves marked by large new granite markers.

■ **TRIAL ISLAND**

Beacon Hill Park's southern slopes rise sufficiently to allow for great views across the water. The Trial Island Lighthouse, visible offshore, built in 1906, is one of the few B.C. lighthouses that still has keepers. The riptides here are quite powerful. In 1923, they pulled under the tug *Tyee,* and four crewmen were drowned.

■ **BUTCHART GARDENS** *map pages 62–63, C-5*

Butchart Gardens dates back to 1904, when estate owner Jennie Butchart decided to transform part of her limestone quarry into a sunken garden. The garden is popular during late spring, when a gaudy planting-out scheme with oodles of annuals create vulgar splashes of colors. The garden is the last in the world that adopts such Victorian landscaping schemes. *Route 17, 21 kilometers (13 miles) north of the city; 250-652-4422 or 866-652-4422.*

■ **SAANICH PENINSULA** *map pages 62–63*

This headland stretches north from Victoria to the ferry landing at Swartz Bay. Away from the main road, the Saanich Peninsula is a gentle place of low, rolling hills and rocky plains. Unlike other areas in this region, it does not have tall mountains and raging alpine creeks and wild rivers. It survives as a pastoral landscape at the edge of the metropolis, where quiet beaches invite beachcombers and upland ponds and lowland marshes make for perfect bird-watching. The peninsular roads wander this way or that, instead of following a land surveyor's grid, because they follow old Indian trails and stage routes. In an age that knew no automobiles, these routes followed the contours of the land.

The name Saanich comes from a Salish Indian word meaning "fertile soil," which seems like a bit of a misnomer when you look up at the great number of rocky outcroppings, topped by oaks and madrona trees. But in the draws and dells, the soil is indeed fertile. Even though this peninsula was settled by Canadian and European immigrants only a little more than 150 years ago, it has more than its share of quiet farmhouses, old barns, and weathered churches. Truck farms and orchards thrive here (look for roadside stands selling local produce from summer through fall).

But spring is perhaps the peninsula's most spectacular season. Japanese flowering cherries and plum trees bloom in the mild climate as early as February. Some 13 million daffodil blooms are shipped from here across the continent each March. The shoulders of back roads are bright with wildflowers in the spring, and roses, colorful annuals, and perennials spill from cottage gardens.

A short but steep hike to the top of the hill in **Bear Hill Regional Park** provides good views of the rustic landscape of the central Saanich Peninsula. Here, too, spring is the best time for a visit. Kayakers flock to the peninsula, because its inshore and nearshore waters are safe for small boats.

■ Travel and Climate

■ Getting There

Victoria's location at the southeastern tip of Vancouver Island makes the capital of British Columbia more challenging to reach than mainland cities. You'll have to take a plane, boat, or ferry, because no bridge crosses the Inland Passage to Vancouver Island from the mainland. Dress warmly if you plan to cross by ferry.

By Air

Victoria International Airport, about 18 kilometers (11 miles) north of town, has scheduled national and international flights. Charter planes will take you almost anywhere in the region. *VAA, 1640 Electra Boulevard, Sidney, 250-953-7500; www.cyyj.ca. For more information about British Columbia travel by air and rail see page 346.*

By Car Ferry

From Vancouver area, the B.C. Ferry leaves from Tsawwassen south of Vancouver and travels to Swartz Bay north of Victoria. Faster than the Washington State Ferry, this one makes more trips and costs half as much. The terminal is a half-hour drive from Victoria. *Information: 888-223-3779 or 250-386-3431 (in Victoria). Reservations: 888-724-5223 or 604-444-7890 (in U.S.); www.bcferries.bc.ca*

    From Anacortes, on Fidalgo Island, the Washington State Ferry heads to Vancouver Island. The Sidney B.C. terminal is about a half-hour drive from Victoria. *800-808-7977; www.wsdot.wa.gov/ferries*

    From Port Angeles (on the Olympic Peninsula), take the Black Ball car ferry *Coho.* The ferry unloads in the harbor. *360-457-4491 or 250-386-2202.*

By Passenger Ferry

From Bellingham, Washington: 360-738-8099.
From Seattle, Washington: 888-808-7977 or 206-464-6400; *www.wsdot.wa.gov/ferries*

■ Climate

The city of Victoria enjoys more sunshine than mainland places because it lies in the rain shadow of the Olympic Mountains and the Insular Range. This is a dry area, with an annual precipitation of less than 25 centimeters. Flowers bloom year-round. Spring comes early and autumn lingers. Winters here are generally mild.

VANCOUVER ISLAND

■ HIGHLIGHTS

■ LANDSCAPE

THE WEST COAST OF VANCOUVER ISLAND is one of the wildest and most beautiful places on the Pacific Coast: it is a rugged landscape of high mountains and deep fjords. Steep rock faces soar straight from the water to the clouds. Lowland woods and slopes tangle with the trees. The mosses and ferns of a temperate rain forest make the hinterland virtually impregnable. This is a world where the sea melts into the land and the land into the sky along fuzzy margins. Nothing seems real. Land and sea, mountains and clouds, men and animals, lose the defined edges of their being and blend into the landscape. In this misty world, it's difficult to distinguish the real from the supernatural. It is a silent world, the sounds muffled by the thick canopy of moss. Often the only sounds you hear are the dripping of water from the foliage, the chirping of forest birds, and the croak of a raven.

Roads touch the outer shore only at Port San Juan, Ucluelet, and Tofino. The eastern part of the island is a bit gentler and amenable to limited agriculture, but even here fertile fields are so rare that the island could most likely not survive on its own produce alone.

The island is dominated by the jagged, snow-covered peaks of the Insular Mountain Range, which runs along its spine; strips of lowland lie along the east and west coasts, and large regions of low rolling hills lie at the northern and southern tips.

■ HISTORY

The native population of Vancouver Island is divided into three major language groups: the Coast Salish of the southeastern coast and the Gulf Islands, the Kwakiutl (Kwakiulth) of the north-central and northeastern coast, and the Nootka, sometimes called West Coast People. These groups shared a similar culture, lived in cedar-planked longhouses, and traveled over salt water in canoes carved from giant cedar logs. The Kwakiutl carved totem poles, which the Salish and Nootka rarely did. The Nootka traveled far to sea in their canoes, hunting seals and whales. On one of these excursions, in 1788, they beheld massive objects, larger

The Kwakiutl village of Humdaspe on Hope Island off Vancouver Island's northern tip was photographed by Edward Dossetter in 1881. (American Museum of Natural History) (following pages) Sunset at Wickannish Bay.

TOTEM POLES OF THE NORTHWEST

Totem poles have been carved by the Indian tribes of the Pacific Northwest, from central Vancouver Island north, for many centuries. While the carving of them peaked during the 19th century—after traders introduced iron tools but before tribes began abandoning their villages—a few totem poles are still carved today, some by notable carvers. Made of cedar, totem poles usually succumbed to the region's steady rains within 60 to 70 years. During the last 100 years many poles have been moved to Vancouver, Victoria, and Seattle, where they have been preserved and may still be admired.

The animal and mythical beings displayed on the poles are family crests, acquired through inheritance, in war, or through purchase, much like European heraldic crests. More often than not, the figures, such as wolf or raven, represent the clan affiliation of the pole's owner. They may also tell a story or elucidate a myth owned by the family. While it is easy to tell which animals are represented in an abstract form—eagle, bear, raven, wolf, and others—the relationship of these figures to each other cannot be readily deduced, and needs a native interpreter. Fortunately, most poles displayed carry explanatory plaques.

Totem poles served different physical functions: they might be set up along a village waterfront like huge exclamation marks proclaiming the greatness of a particular chief and his family, or serve as house posts to hold up the huge roof beams of the single-room, barn-like native houses. Some rose in front of the house and had an entrance hole cut through the thick bottom section; others served as mortuary poles. A wealthy chief might set up a pole to ridicule a rival who had failed to meet an obligation, such as holding a potlatch. In that case, the person to be ridiculed was carved upside down.

than whales. Resembling floating houses, with strange wings spread to the wind, these odd-looking structures drifted from the ocean mists toward their shores. According to eyewitness reports preserved in Nootka oral history, the men reported after their hurried return that they had met fish looking like white men sailing across the sea in their houses.

> One white man had a real hooked nose, you know. And one of the men was saying to this other guy, "See, see…he must have been a dog salmon, that guy there, he's got a hooked nose."… "Yes! We're right. We're right. Those people must have been fish. They've come alive into people.…So they went ashore and they told the big Chief: "You know what we saw? They've got white skin. But we're pretty sure that those people on the floating thing there, that they must have been fish. But they've come here as people."

Nuxalt dancers from coastal British Columbia were photographed in 1886 in their elaborate masks and costumes. (Royal British Columbia Museum)

The exploring expedition of British seafarer Capt. James Cook had arrived on the Northwest Coast. While Cook had found a safe harbor for his ships, he missed many of prominent landmarks, including the mouth of the Columbia River and Juan de Fuca Strait.

Because of the roughness of the rocky coastline, the foggy, drizzly weather, and rough seas, the region gave up its secrets slowly. For a decade and a half, neither Cook nor the explorers and fur traders following in his wake learned that Vancouver Island was not part of the mainland.

In 1792, British navigator George Vancouver sailed around the island and proved that it was indeed separate from the mainland. After the Spanish withdrew, Nootka and the west coast of Vancouver Island once again became a backwater. But the inland passage Vancouver had discovered became a busy place for local shipping—a role it has not relinquished 200 years later.

■ JUAN DE FUCA STRAIT *map pages 62–63, C-5*

The coast west of Victoria has secluded beaches, some spectacular scenery, and, at times, a lot of rain. Route 14, the Sooke Road, was authorized by Gov. James Douglas in 1852 to open up the western lands along the coast of the Juan de Fuca Strait and to connect existing farms to the fort at Victoria.

Just west of Victoria is **Fort Rodd Hill,** built in 1895 to defend British Columbia against a feared U.S. naval attack. The guns are gone, but the batteries are still there. On a clear day they provide great views of the Olympic Mountains on the other shore of Juan de Fuca Strait. On the fort grounds is **Fisgard Lighthouse,** the oldest (1860) operational lighthouse on Canada's west coast. The military complex to the east is the **Canadian Forces base at Esquimalt,** the west coast headquarters of the Canadian navy. It was established as a naval station in the 1850s by the British during the Crimean War.

Farther down the road is **Royal Roads Military College,** the former Hatley Park estate of coal baron James Dunsmuir. The beautiful grounds with their elaborate gardens are open daily to the public.

A detour along **Metchosin Road** leads through pretty farm country, interspersed with beaches and great views of the strait. (Route 14 runs inland.) Metchosin Road also leads to **East Sooke Park,** a headland at the southernmost point of Vancouver Island. The park is a wilderness of twisted trees, hiking trails through the forest, swimming beaches, and the spectacular views so common on this coast. Trails also lead to secluded coves. (Don't leave valuables in your car: vandals and thieves can be active here.)

Sooke Region Museum, east of the town of Sooke, has an interesting collection of Indian and pioneer artifacts, plus a restored pioneer cottage. Sooke is a small town on Sooke Harbour, a quiet bay. The first independent settler on the island, Capt. Walter Colquhoun Grant, established a farm at Sooke in 1849. But the captain was no farmer. He soon followed the lure of gold to California and later returned to England and served in the Crimean and Indian military campaigns. *2070 Phillips Road; 250-642-6351.*

Whiffen Spit makes for a nice hike across the narrow mouth of the inlet. It ends at a narrow channel almost beneath the bluffs of East Sooke Park. Both sides of the spit are great for watching birds, with shrubbery and driftwood piles serving as natural blinds. Occasionally seals, sea lions, orcas, and dolphins drop by.

West of Sooke, the highway becomes rough and twisted, with many one-lane log bridges (watch out for logging trucks). Route 14 is not a fast highway even at the best of times, and it can get quite clogged up with traffic. But who's in a hurry? Sit back, relax, and take that lead foot off the accelerator. This road becomes

Entrance to the Juan de Fuca Strait *by John Meares, ca. 1790. (MSCUA, University of Washington Libraries)*

The Olympic Mountains rise above Juan de Fuca Strait.

rather lonely west of Sooke, but that doesn't mean you'll be stranded if your car breaks down. Several students once pulled me from a ditch after I had foolishly forgotten to set my hand brake. After they had lifted my car back on the road, they inquired what province I was from. I told them, "One of the American provinces," which they thought a good joke. In the meantime, I had asked a motorist to call the Canadian Automobile Association for assistance from Jordan River, the nearest community; instead, the proprietor of the Jordan River pub came out to help.

The coast west of Sooke has many parks and trails to the beach. There's the pleasant pub at **Jordan River,** halfway between Sooke and Port Renfrew, and not much else. Port Renfrew is an old British Columbia Forest Products company town that has livened up in recent years. The **West Coast Trail** of **Pacific Rim National Park** starts here. This is a trail for experienced hikers only. It started out as the West Coast Life Saving Trail, which was established after the American steamer *Valencia* ran aground on this treacherous rocky coast in January 1906. Of the 154 persons aboard, 117 lost their lives. A grisly finale was added the following summer when local Indians discovered one of the *Valencia's* lifeboats floating in a sea cave approximately 183 meters (600 feet) from the wreck. The boat held the bodies of eight survivors of the wreck, who died of exposure after the boat was swept into the cave over a huge boulder blocking the entrance.

While the trail has been somewhat improved in recent years, it is still very wet and slippery and demands exceptional backcountry skills, especially when it comes to fording swollen creeks and rivers. The grand scenery makes it all worthwhile. The trail ends in Bamfield on Barkley Sound.

Botanical Beach, at the mouth of Port San Juan has an exceptional aggregation of sculpted sandstone and marine life that is exposed during summer low tides.

■ FROM VICTORIA TO NANAIMO

Shortly after leaving Victoria, Route 1 crosses **Goldstream Provincial Park.** Gold was found here in 1885, but today's most valuable assets are the coho salmon that return to the Goldstream River each November to spawn. One of the largest concentrations of bald eagles anywhere in Canada come here to dine on the spawned-out chum salmon carcasses. Look for mink and river otter along lower Goldstream. A trail leads to Niagara Creek and to the top of Niagara Fall, a spectacular 30.5-meter (100-foot) cascade. The toughest part of the drive comes as the road winds its way up the sheer rock cliff of the Malahat to a 353-meter (1,156-foot) summit above the deep waters of Saanich Inlet.

Beaches in these protected waters can get warm enough for swimming, something almost unheard of in Puget Sound farther south. **Bamberton Provincial Park,** at the northern end of the Malahat Drive (just south of the Mill Bay ferry terminal, beside Route 1), is a quiet retreat with a sandy swimming beach. The warm and inviting waters of the Saanich Inlet are ideal for swimming, and fine sandy beaches stretch for miles. Picnic tables on terraces above the beach are shaded by fir and madrona trees. This is one of the more scenic parks on the inlet; from here the eye can roam far east to Mount Baker in Washington's North Cascades. **Mill Bay Nature Park** has easy oceanfront trails. In fall and spring, large flocks of shorebirds dabble in the shallow, muddy waters of the broad intertidal beach.

■ COBBLE HILL *map pages 62–63, C-5*

A bit farther up the road, the village of Cobble Hill leads the leisurely life of a retirement community and farm village. Many hobby ranches spread across the surrounding hills alongside well-established cow and goat dairies, horse farms, beef ranches, and fruit orchards. More recently, galleries have sprung up to show the works of local painters, sculptors, potters, and totem pole carvers. Cobble Hill's **Arbutus Ridge Golf & Country Club** (3515 Telegraph Road; 250-389-0070) is one of Canada's top public golf courses and regionally famous for its spectacular oceanfront links. Energetic visitors can rent kayaks at **Hatch Point Kayaks** (250-743-3505). The **Bakery Book Store** (3556 Garland Avenue; 250 743-8263), in the old bakery building downtown, specializes in out of print and old technical books. The **British Columbia Folklore Society** (250-743-3996) has a reference library of traditional and contemporary folklore of the people of British Columbia. It is open to anyone, but by appointment only. The **Asparagus/Apple Farm** (1550 Robson Lane; 250-743-5073) sells fresh white and green asparagus as well as apples in season.

■ COWICHAN BAY *map pages 62–63, C-5*
This seaside village, off Route 1, is well worth a stop for its attractions. Salish villages stood on the beach near the mouths of the Cowichan and Koksilah Rivers before European settlers arrived in the mid-1800s. The natural harbor played a major role in the opening up of the Cowichan Valley for these early settlers, particularly for exporting farm produce and lumber from the region.

A substantial fishing fleet took advantage of rich local fish stocks and the protected moorage, but the arrival of the railways in the late 1880s supplanted the harbor's role as a prime mover of people and goods. Today, the harbor remains as a base for a small fishing fleet, though diminishing fish stocks have reduced the importance of the local fishing industry.

A walk along **Cowichan Bay Road** gives visitors an overview of this working coastal village. Cottages rest on stilts above the water, and piers, pilings, fish boats, and freighters loaded with lumber abound.

Along the pier, the **Maritime Centre** has some fine exhibits that interpret the history of Cowichan Bay and a collection of restored marine engines and boats. The **Marine Ecology Station,** a part of the Maritime Centre, provides a fully equipped teaching lab, with aquariums and seawater systems, for local schools and colleges. The local tide flats and marshes attract more than 200 species of birds during fall and spring migration.

■ COWICHAN VALLEY WINERIES
The Cowichan Valley just north of Malahat and south of Duncan has emerged in recent years as British Columbia's newest wine region. Cool climate grapes like pinot noir thrive here.

Cherry Point Vineyards is the southernmost of these vineyards and wineries. The 24 acres here are planted with five main varieties: gewürztraminer, ortega, pinot blanc, pinot gris, and pinot noir. Cherry Point has British Columbia's only winery–B&B, inside a balconied chalet. The breakfasts are legendary. Each evening at cocktail hour, the wine-maker conducts a private wine tasting for guests. Visitors can stroll through the vineyard and pastures or walk to a public beach. *840 Cherrypoint Road, Cobble Hill; 250-743-1272.*

You'll need to make an appointment to visit nearby **Venturi-Schulze Vineyards,** which makes pinot gris, kerner, and pinot noir, grown in its 15 acres of vineyards. Venturi-Schulze also makes a traditional-method balsamic vinegar, aged in small barrels of cherry, chestnut, acacia, ash, and oak. *4235 Trans-Canada Highway, RR1 Cobble Hill; 250-743-5630.*

Blue Grouse Vineyards & Winery is a family-run winery. The wines include pinot gris, pinot noir, ortega, bacchus, müller-thurgau, dry muscat, and an ortega late-harvest dessert wine. *4365 Blue Grouse Road, Duncan; 250-743-3834.*

Vigneti Zanatta occupies a 1903 farmhouse with a wraparound porch. Plantings include cayuga, muscat, merlot, ortega, pinto auxerrois, pinot grigio, pinot nero, and Madeleine X sylvaner. The 120-acre farm produces much of the food served in Vinoteca, the food and wine bar here. *5039 Marshall Road, Duncan; 250-748-2338.*

Alderlea Vineyards has 10 acres of vineyards planted on rocky soils above Quamichan Lake. Some of British Columbia's best pinot gris and pinot noir come from here. *1751 Stamps Road, Duncan; 250-746-7122.*

Much farther north, near Nanaimo, is **Chateau Wolff,** which makes only a few varieties of handcrafted (as well as hand-bottled) wines from organically grown grapes. *2534 Maxey Road, Nanaimo; 250-753-4613.*

■ DUNCAN *map pages 62–63, C-5*
Local hills and Salt Spring Island to the east protect this northern Cowichan Valley community from north and northeast winds. It has been called "The most English village in Canada," though it is actually a city. Once a mere whistle-stop at William Duncan's farm in the 1880s, Duncan is now the commercial hub of the

Cowichan Valley. In 1985, Duncan began to transform itself into a "City of Totems," a unique urban forest with distinctive hand-carved cedar poles from local native artisans. Many of the totems on display were removed from original sites and private collections and re-erected here. Beside City Hall stands an unusual totem carved by a Maori craftsman. A self-guided walking tour (follow the yellow footprints), which starts at the **Cowichan Valley Museum** (130 Canada Avenue; 250-746-6612), winds past 41 totem poles; others have been erected elsewhere in town and along the Trans-Canada Highway (TCH), making for a total of more than 80 different poles.

At the **Quw'utsun' Cultural and Conference Center** in Duncan you can watch women knit the famous Cowichan sweaters. The sweaters are hand-knit in one piece from dyed wool that still has its lanolin. There's also an open-air carving shed where native carvers create totem poles. The poles are now an integral part of the town's identity—even though totem-pole carving is not one of the traditional crafts of the local Cowichan tribe of Salish Indians, but was practiced by the Kwakiutl and other tribes to the north. *200 Cowichan Way; 250-746-8119.*

Seaplanes in the harbor of Nanaimo (above) may be rented for flight-seeing trips to view Vancouver Island's scenery, such as this coastal area near Tofino (right).

Duncan's prosperous entry into the 20th century can be attributed to the flow of capital funds for the development of copper and mineral deposits within the region. Duncan became the main distribution center until the mines closed in 1908. As the mines died, agriculture and sawmilling took the place of minerals. The boom years of 1909–1913 gave the settlement around Duncan's Station a solid footing.

People with money retired from the Imperial Army or Navy and flocked into the district. So many new settlers went into the egg and poultry business that the Cowichan District became known as the "Egg Basket of the World."

The **Fairburn Farm Country Manor** (2310 Jackson Road; 250-746-4637) is in a restored 1884 manor house on an organic sheep farm. The farm's made-from-scratch breakfasts are renowned.

Just north of Duncan, on 100 acres of forest and meadows at Somenos Lake and Marsh, the **B.C. Forest Discovery Centre** offers a "hands-on" historical tour of the forest industry with a logging camp, logging machinery, sawmill equipment, and a blacksmith's shop. Visitors can ride a restored narrow-gauge steam train, the Cowichan Valley Railway, through the grounds and across a wooden trestle over the lake. *2892 Drinkwater Road; 250-715-1113.*

■ CHEMAINUS *map pages 62–63, C-5*
The small town of **Chemainus** lost its major employer, a lumbermill, in 1981. The townsfolk hired artists to paint murals that told this story, and the murals—about three dozen of them—are now a major attraction in their own right, as are the many restored Victorian-era homes.

■ LADYSMITH *map pages 62–63, C-4/5*
The 49th parallel passes near Ladysmith, where the U.S.–Canadian border would be, had the treaty of 1846 not curved around the southern portion of Vancouver Island. The **Crow & Gate Neighbourhood Pub,** north of Ladysmith on Yellow Point Road, adds the perfect British touch to the region. With its rose-arbor entrance, lawns, and duck pond, it could have been lifted straight from the English countryside. Inside, there's a blazing fire, a dartboard, and a collection of English magazines. The pub fare is excellent. *2313 Yellow Point Road; 250-722-3731.*

■ NANAIMO *map pages 62–63, C-4*

The town has preserved a bastion (1853) from the old Hudson's Bay Company fort. Nanaimo's value to the company was not in furs, but in the coal that was found here and fueled Hudson's steamers. Robert Dunsmuir (the father of James Dunsmuir) became the island's richest man when he took over the mines. The **Nanaimo District Museum** tells the fascinating story of the Snunymuxm people and of the coal-mining industry of this region. It even has a replica of a coal mine entrance. *100 Cameron Road; 250-753-1821.*

■ TRAVELING TO THE OUTER COAST

The Trans-Canada Highway (TCH) turns east at Nanaimo and from here you must travel via ferry to the mainland. Route 19 continues up the east side of the island. Route 4 branches off north of Parksville and takes you first to Port Alberni at the head of the Alberni Channel and eventually, after many twists and turns, to the outer coast at Long Beach and north to Tofino. A branch road goes south to Ucluelet. The road is some 150 kilometers (94 miles) long; plan on at least two-and-a-half to three hours of driving time.

Thanks to the **Alberni Channel,** a long, steep-walled fjord that cuts into the island from Barkley Sound for some 64 kilometers (40 miles), the timber town of **Port Alberni** has a deepwater port. Roger Creek Park, in the center of town, has a popular swimming hole right in the creek.

On Tuesdays, Thursdays, and Saturdays (and Fridays and Sundays in July and August), the *Lady Rose,* a 30.5-meter (100-foot) vessel built in Scotland in 1937, departs from Harbour Quay at the foot of Argyle Street in Port Alberni and travels down the inlet to **Bamfield,** on the southern shore of Barkley Sound. This just has to be the most romantic boat ride in the Northwest—traveling down the steep fjord on a boat that once plied the stormy coasts of Scotland. En route, the boat makes side trips to the Broken Islands, where kayakers and canoeists can have themselves dropped off and picked up. From early June to mid-September, the *Lady Rose* and the *Frances Barkley* make trips to Ucluelet via the Broken Islands. *250-723-8313.*

You must travel a logging road to reach Bamfield, a village with wooden walkways and a fjord. Only the *Lady Rose* docks at both sides, which as one resident learned, can lead to complications. In the mid-1980s, after the road first opened,

his new lawn tractor was carried across the inlet on the *Lady Rose* with what he called an "outrageous" fare. "We charged him the full freight rate," said the mate.

If you decide to drive to the Pacific coast, the road becomes rather scenic after Port Alberni; cliffs along the road have polished faces and lateral striations left by glaciers. The road follows the short but pretty Kennedy River to Kennedy Lake, the island's largest. The lake is almost at tidewater level, and shortly after you reach it, you arrive at Long Beach, the largest unit of Pacific Rim National Park. Here dense, often boggy forests grow right up to an 11-kilometer-long (7-mile) flat beach of hard-packed sand, where the only sounds you may hear are the roar of the breakers and the croaking of ravens. Watch for gray whales playing in the surf.

The road turns south to Ucluelet and north to Tofino. Ucluelet is a fishing village on a protected bay where Native Americans lived for thousands of years. It is close to the Broken Islands and to banks where migrating salmon feed. Until 1959, when the road from Port Alberni was completed, it could be reached only by boat or floatplane.

If you're not interested in fishing or kayaking, you might want to take a nature cruise to the coast and the Broken Islands. Few things are more dramatic than having the boat nose up to a sea lion on a rock right where the ocean swells run into the calm waters of the bay. The rise and fall of the waves is tremendous: at one moment, you're staring an annoyed sea lion right in the eye, and the next instant you're looking at huge sea anemones clinging to the rock.

It's easy to understand why the Broken Islands in Barkley Sound, the central unit of Pacific Rim National Park, are so popular with kayakers and divers. Not only are they beautiful, all 98 of them, but they possess a rare mystic quality. Native villages once lined the beaches of quiet sandy coves, where canoes were drawn up onto the sand. Today, the villages are gone, but some of the land still belongs to the natives. Tread with respect wherever you go.

As you drive north to **Tofino,** you may notice sea kayakers tumbling about in the surf. Don't try to emulate them in a rental kayak. It takes a lot of experience to kayak in these waters. Tofino, a hamlet on the southern edge of **Clayoquot Sound,** has a huge airport, left over from World War II, when Tofino was a major air base. Today, it is the only commercial airport of the region. The town has beachfront resorts, motels, and bed-and-breakfasts. To get away from the crowds, you can take a water taxi to hot springs north of town.

(opposite) Floating homes in Tofino Harbour.

Clayoquot Sound was a favorite place of American and British fur traders, who dealt with the clever local chief, Wickaninnish. Some Americans came to grief in their dealings with native people. John Kendrick's *Lady Washington* was unsuccessfully attacked in 1791, but in 1811, the Astorian's *Tonquin* was captured. After the British government was established on the coast, Indian attacks were dealt with harshly: when the trading vessel *Kingfisher* was captured and its crew murdered by Clayoquot Sound Indians, the naval vessels *Sutlej* and *Devastation* destroyed nine Indian villages and 64 canoes by shelling. Permanent European settlers arrived in 1875 to build the first trading post on Stubbs Island just offshore. Today, many countercultural squatters live on the sound's remote islands.

As you stand by the shore and look out across the waters of the sound, you can understand why some people would want to move into these quiet recesses. If you are truly searching for peace, you may well find it here. This shore in many ways is much more remote than it was in prehistoric times. The rains that seem to fall incessantly onto this shore purify it; the scars made by man, storms, and landslides heal much more quickly here than they would on drier shores.

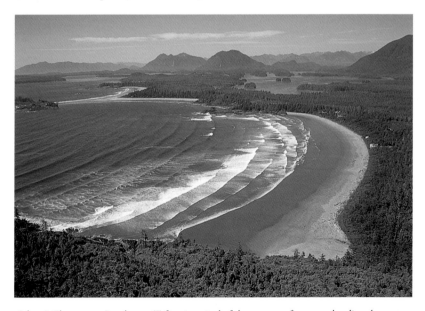

(above) Chesterman Beach near Tofino is typical of the many perfect coves that line the west coast of Vancouver Island.

■ QUALICUM BEACH TO CAMPBELL RIVER

Qualicum Beach, north of Parksville, is by far the most popular bathing beach on the island. The water here and all around the islands gets quite warm in the summer. This has the benefit of causing Pacific oysters—which need warm water to spawn—to reproduce in such great numbers that Puget Sound oyster growers have come up here to collect oyster "seed"—that is, spat, the young oysters—so they can restock their farms. Many tidal rocks are covered with oysters. Unfortunately, these are barely edible during the summer spawning season but are at their best in late fall and winter, when hardly anyone likes to poke about the beach to collect them. Perhaps that's why they're still plentiful.

Courtenay and its twin sister **Comox** attracted the first white settlers in 1862—New Zealanders who had been lured to British Columbia by the Fraser River gold rush but decided to farm instead. In 1876, the first wharf was built and the navy established a training base on the spit. Since then the area has depended largely on the military for its support.

The **Forbidden Plateau,** to the east, got its name from a story told by the local Indians. Fearing an attack by the Kwakiutl, the Chowichans hid their families here. After the attackers were beaten off, the Chowichans searched for their families, but could not find them. They surmised that "skookums," evil spirits, had thrown them off a cliff, so the plateau became taboo. Today, the Forbidden Plateau is an all-season recreation area, with subalpine wildflowers gracing the higher elevations in summer. A car ferry runs between Courtenay and Powell River on the mainland.

Campbell River, halfway up the island from Victoria, is famous for its giant trees and huge king salmon—both of which are history. Offshore is **Quadra Island,** separated from Vancouver Island by **Discovery Passage,** so named by George Vancouver in 1792. This narrow defile, which is plagued by treacherous winds, tides, and whirlpools, is the main passage north. It was made even more dangerous by Ripple Rock and the Euclataw band of Kwakiutl, who had driven the Salish Indians from the their Cape Mudge village early in the 19th century. The Euclataws raided and exacted tolls from Indian and white trading parties using the passage to and from Victoria. They stopped only when the British, using the gunboat *Forward,* subdued the tribe.

Ripple Rock stood right in the middle of the narrowest part of the passage. Its two summits were just below the water, in easy reach of ships' hulls, but also, potentially, of bridge piers. The rock had to be removed to make shipping safe, but the idea incensed islanders, who feared that with Ripple Rock removed they'd never get the government to build the bridge to the mainland promised them in the 1871 federation agreement. To remove the rock, a shaft was drilled on nearby Maude Island, followed by a tunnel under the seabed, and a "raise" to within a few feet of the rock's tips. After two-and-a-half years of boring, 34 boxcars full of explosives were packed into the cavity. In April 1958, the rock was blown up.

■ THE ROAD TO NOOTKA SOUND

Route 28 runs from north of Campbell River to Muchalat Inlet, an arm of Nootka Sound. Seventy-two kilometers (45 miles) west of Campbell River, you'll pass Strathcona Park Lodge and Outdoor Education Centre on Upper Campbell Lake at **Strathcona Provincial Park.** Strathcona Park has Vancouver Island's highest mountain, the Golden Hinde at 2,200 meters (7,218 feet), and Canada's highest waterfall, Della Falls at 440 meters (1,143 feet).

From **Gold River,** the ferry *Uchuck III* takes passengers north of Nootka, where Cook landed, along the rugged west coast of Vancouver Island, to the remote old village of **Kyuquot.** Passengers spend the night at a bed-and-breakfast and return the next day. *250-283-2325 or 250-283-2515.*

■ CAMPBELL RIVER TO PORT HARDY

The road north from Campbell River to Kelsey Bay was built during World War II to facilitate troop shipment in case an invasion threatened from the north (Yorke Island in Johnstone Strait was fortified at that time). The road north from Kelsey Bay to Port Hardy was not completed until 1979. Until then, ferries connected Kelsey Bay to Beaver Cove in the north; from here a road continued to Port Hardy. As you drive north, keep a lookout for the resident pod of orcas living in Johnstone Strait.

Port McNeill was named after an American skipper in the employ of the Hudson's Bay Company who was famous for the subterfuges he used to avoid becoming a British citizen. The Kwakiutl village of Alert Bay is a short ferry ride from Port McNeill. It is well worth visiting for the **U'mista Cultural Centre** (Front Street; 250-974-5403), an excellent museum. In *Guests Never Leave Hungry,* Kwakiutl chief James Sewid talks about the problems the builders faced in 1965, when they erected a large ceremonial house. After a giant forklift was unable to lift the huge beams, Sewid successfully used the traditional Indian method of rocking up the logs on a tower of eight-by-eight timbers. "....that big log just rolled into the grooves that we had made for it. It was really quite easy and we did both of those logs inside of a day."

Fort Rupert, on Beaver Harbour, was established by the Hudson's Bay Company in 1849 to protect coal miners working the local seams. After the fort was built, a part of the Nahwitti tribe of Kwakiutl Indians moved here. The Edward Curtis film *In the Land of the War Canoes* was filmed here. The village is one of the best places to buy native art.

Port Hardy is the terminal for the ferry to **Prince Rupert** on the northern mainland, just below the Alaskan border. (Ferry reservations should be made well in advance.) Port Hardy was named after the commander of the British ship-of-the-line *Victory*, on whose deck Horatio Nelson died during the Battle of Trafalgar. Nelson's last words were, "Kiss me, Hardy."

■ TRAVEL AND CLIMATE

■ GETTING THERE AND AROUND
Beyond the main highways, most backcountry roads are not paved, and some that are paved don't stay that way for long, due to heavy logging-truck traffic. If you're planning to take a logging road into the backcountry, check the signs posted at the road entrance for the hours during which it is open to the general public.

By Car Ferry. Ferries run between Victoria and Port Angeles, between Sidney and Anacortes, and between Swartz Bay and Tsawwassen on the lower British Columbia mainland. *(See page 347 for details.)* Ferries also connect Nanaimo to Horseshoe Bay north of Vancouver and to Tsawwassen on the lower mainland and they connect Courtenay to Powell River on the Sunshine Coast. Car ferries travel to the Gulf Islands and from the islands to the mainland.

■ CLIMATE
The climate is generally wet and cool all year long on the island's west coast. Inland shores are sheltered by the Insular Range from Pacific storms and by the Coast Mountains from the cold weather of the interior. For the most part, the area is pleasantly warm in summer.

I S L A N D S

■ HIGHLIGHTS

■ LANDSCAPE

ISLANDS ARE SPECIAL PLACES, miniature continents with moods uniquely their own. In the Pacific Northwest, with its misty days and foggy nights, you sometimes wonder if they are terra firma at all, or whether they float this way or that at the whim of the tide.

The inland waters of the Pacific Northwest, between the southern end of Puget Sound and the Canadian Inside Passage, have hundreds of islands of various sizes, shapes, and elevations. Some are little more than reedy sandbars in river mouths; others have peaks that rise straight from the water for almost 915 meters (3,000 feet). Some are so close to shore they have been tied to the mainland by bridges. Others are separated by deep, swift-running tidal channels or saltwater straits. Those can be reached only by boat, ferry, airplane, or floatplane.

What really sets these islands apart is their exceptional beauty, which expresses itself with dramatic cliffs where eagles soar, lush seaside meadows, gnarled trees, and multicolored wildflowers that cling to seemingly infertile rocks. The islands have valleys and mountains, forests filled with birdsong, and leafy glens where the tiny island deer browse. Even a species of prickly pear cactus *(Opuntia fragilis)*

Sunset over Canada's Gulf Islands as seen from Ruckles Park on Salt Spring Island.

grows here. Beaches can be pebbly or sandy, but all are scenic. Offshore, seals haul out on sandbanks, and orcas patrol the deep channels.

The islands are visited by ducks and swans, herons and hawks, humans and whales. Many islands are settled; some have picturesque villages—more often than not near a ferry landing—and a few have resorts for visitors. Many have campgrounds and ample beaches or meadows where boaters (or hikers) can haul out and pitch a tent.

■ ISLAND HISTORY

The most beautiful of the Pacific Northwest's islands lie north of Juan de Fuca Strait, between the northwest Washington mainland and Vancouver Island. These islands were once part of Vancouver Island, from which they were separated by the grinding action of continental glaciers during the last ice age. Because the ice—some 915 meters (3,000 feet) thick—pressed the land down into the earth's crust, the islands have been rising slowly ever since the ice melted. Humans moved in as soon as the islands were free of ice.

Excavation of ancient shell middens proves that the islands have been inhabited for at least 5,000 years. But in Indian days, these were summer settlements only. According to Ken Pattison, writing in *Milestones on Vancouver Island,* "None of these native visitors established permanent settlements in the Islands, and the first recorded settlers were a group of American Negroes who had purchased their freedom in the U.S. and applied to Sir James Douglas for permission to settle on Salt Spring Island [in 1859]."

The islands were stopping-off points for Nanaimo and Cowichan Indians from Vancouver Island; for Salish, Musqueam, and Tsawwassen from the mainland of present-day British Columbia; and for Lummi and Samish from present-day Washington State. The visitors used them as summer homes, camping in shelters of woven mats, and as a sort of natural supermarket, taking salmon and halibut from the reefs and harvesting camas root and berries on the land.

Perhaps the islands were not inhabited continuously because they were regularly raided by Haida, Tlinkit, and Kwakiutl warriors from the north out to capture booty and slaves. (The Tlinkit name for Puget Sound was the same as their term for slave.) In 1858, northern Indians—reportedly Stikine Tlinkit from southeast Alaska—raided a Lummi summer village on the east shore of West Sound on

Orcas Island. According to contemporary reports, the beach was soon littered with "over a hundred bodies." The site of that ill-fated village has ever since been known as "Massacre Bay." These raids continued long after Americans and British had settled along the inland waters and did not cease until the latter half of the 19th century. The Canadian Gulf Islands and the American San Juans belong to two different political jurisdictions. Back in 1846, when the Oregon Territory was divided between Britain and the United States, it was decided that, south of the 49th parallel, the border should run down the middle of the main channel between Vancouver Island and the mainland.

The vagueness of that diplomatic language caused a bit of grief back in the late 1850s, when the British decided that Rosario Strait, not Haro Strait as previously agreed upon, was the "main channel" separating the British from the American domain. War almost erupted between the two nations when an American settler shot a Hudson's Bay Company pig that had been raiding his San Juan Island potato patch. This so-called "pig war" remained an *opera buffa* episode because cooler heads prevailed, leading to a joint occupation of San Juan Island by British and American troops until 1872. In that year, the German emperor, who was asked to settle the dispute, awarded the San Juans to the United States.

■ **GULF ISLANDS** *map pages 62–63, C/D-4/5, and page 120*

The best way to explore this archipelago, which lies north of the San Juan Islands just off the eastern shore of Vancouver Island, is to travel there by car ferry, boat, or kayak, and explore by bicycle or on foot. Island roads are limited and most parks and campsites are accessible by sea. Bald eagles, murres, pigeon guillemots, harlequin ducks, and an occasional puffin can be seen over or in island waters. Gnarled madronas (called arbutus trees by British Columbians), Garry oaks, and Douglas firs make dramatic statements atop cliffs and hills. Writers, artists, craftspeople, weekend cottagers, and retirees make up much of the resident population, which is augmented by a heavy influx of weekend and summer visitors.

Both Vancouver Island and the Gulf Islands have seasonal farmers markets and farm stands where visitors can stock up on local fruits. Look for strawberries, blueberries, raspberries, and loganberries from June to September, blackberries in July and August, cherries in June and July, and local kiwi fruit from October to December.

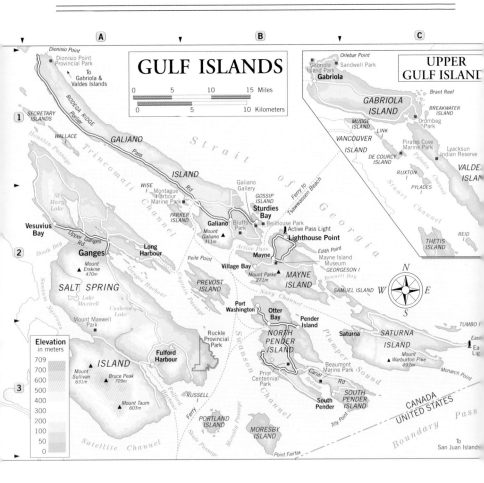

GULF ISLANDS

0   5   10   15 Miles

0   5   10 Kilometers

UPPER GULF ISLAND

Dionisio Point
Dionisio Point Provincial Park
To Gabriola & Valdes Islands
SECRETARY ISLANDS
WALLACE I.
Houston Passage
BODEGA RIDGE
Porlier
GALIANO
Trincomali Channel
Strait
Pass

Orlebar Point
Gabriola Island Park
Sandwell Park
Gabriola
GABRIOLA ISLAND
MUDGE ISLAND
LINK
VANCOUVER ISLAND
DE COURCY ISLAND
RUXTON I.
Brant Reef
BREAKWATER ISLAND
Dromberg Park
Pirates Cove Marine Park
Lyacksun Indian Reserve
PYLADES I.
VALDE ISLAN

ISLAND
WISE I.
Montague Harbour Marine Park
PARKER ISLAND
Galiano
Mount Galiano 311m
Bluffs Park
Galiano Gallery
GOSSIP ISLAND
Sturdies Bay
Bellhouse Park
Active Pass Light
Lighthouse Point

Ferry to Tsawwassen Beach
of
Georgia
Stuart Channel
THETIS ISLAND
REID I.

St Mary Lake
Vesuvius Bay
Booth Bay
Upper Ganges Rd
Ganges
Mount Erskine 470m
SALT SPRING
Long Harbour
Peile Point
Ganges Harbour
Captain Passage
PREVOST ISLAND
Village Bay
Mount Parke 271m
MAYNE ISLAND
Mayne
Active Pass
Edith Point
Mayne Island Museum
GEORGESON I.
Bennett Bay
SAMUEL ISLAND
TUMBO I.
East Ea Lig

Samson Narrows
Lake Maxwell
Cusheon Lake
Mount Maxwell Park
Navy Channel
Port Washington
Otter Bay
Pender Island
Saturna
Plumper Sound
SATURNA ISLAND
Mount Warburton Pike 497m
Monarch Point

Elevation in meters

709	
700	
600	
500	
400	
300	
200	
100	
50	
0	

ISLAND
Mount Sullivan 631m
Bruce Peak 709m
Mount Taum 603m
Fulford Harbour
Ruckle Provincial Park
Swanson Channel
NORTH PENDER ISLAND
Prior Centennial Park
Beaumont Marine Park
Canal
Bedwell
Rd
SOUTH PENDER ISLAND
South Pender
CANADA
UNITED STATES
Boundary
Pass

Fulford Harbour
Ferry
RUSSELL I.
PORTLAND ISLAND
Shute Passage
Moresby Passage
MORESBY ISLAND
Tilly Point
To San Juan Islands

Satellite Channel
Point Fairfax

N W E S

■ GABRIOLA ISLAND *map page 120, inset*

Eleven kilometers (7 miles) long, Gabriola Island is the northernmost of the Gulf Islands and a 20-minute ferry ride southeast of Nanaimo. This residential island has few facilities for visitors. Yet there is one attraction well worth seeing: the **Galiano Gallery** on Descanso Bay, a 300-foot-long, 12-foot-high, spectacular sandstone formation near Malaspina Point that looks like petrified surf and sea foam. It shows what power the sea has when it exerts its full force to hollow out rock. The Galiano Gallery is also sometimes confusingly called Malaspina Gallery, after the Italian-born explorer and sea captain Alexandro Malaspina, who explored the Northwest for the Spanish in the 18th century.

■ GALIANO ISLAND   *map page 120, A/B-1/2*

Galiano Island is the first stop after the Tsawwassen ferry crosses the Strait of Georgia, and it retains much of the rustic character of its densely forested hillsides, towering bluffs, wildflower meadows, and sheltered harbors (only in these bucolic islands would anyone think of describing a harbor as "rustic"). Trails along **Bodega Ridge** wind through old-growth forest, past wildflower meadows, and open up to great views of the Olympic Mountains to the southwest. From **Bluffs Park** and **Mount Galiano** you can watch riptides swirl through Active Pass and observe bald eagles as they scan the channel for fish or carrion.

This long, skinny sliver of rock is considered by many to be the most scenic of the Gulf Islands—perhaps because residents have fought to keep it unspoiled. It lies between two famous salmon fishing areas: Porlier Pass on the north, separating Galiano from Valdes Island, and Active Pass on the south, separating Galiano from Mayne. Active Pass is also an incredibly scenic as well as busy shipping and ferry lane.

Cormorants nest on the rocks and small islands separating Montague Harbour from Trincomali Channel. **Montague Harbour Marine Park** has campsites, a picnic area, floats, a boat launch, and sheltered swimming beaches. Bellhouse Provincial Park at Sturdies Bay overlooks Active Pass, the saltwater passage that separates Galiano and Mayne Islands.

Galiano Island has resorts, a nine-hole golf course, and about 1,200 residents, but no bank, one gas station, and only a few stores, all clustered at the southern end. Restaurants are scarce. **La Berengerie** (Montague Harbour Road; 250-539-5392) is about as gourmet as things get around here. The pub fare at the **Hummingbird Inn** (47 Sturdies Bay Road) at the junction of Sturdies Bay and Georgeson Bay Roads is a less expensive alternative. **Dionisio Point Provincial Park,** at the north end of the island, has challenging trails and primitive camping.

■ MAYNE ISLAND   *map page 120, B/C-2*

Mayne Island is pastoral in a woodsy way. Middens of clam and oyster shells have been dated back 5,000 years, which shows that the island has been visited seasonally for a long time. Mayne was a stopover point for miners headed to the Fraser River and Cariboo gold fields. By the mid-1800s it was the commercial center of the inhabited Gulf Islands. Japanese established farms and orchards in the 1930s and worked until their owners were interned during World War II. Farms and orchards still prosper, but there's no longer anything Japanese about the island. A farmers market is open on Saturdays during harvest season. There's a ferry dock at **Village Bay** and a trail to the top of **Mount Parke** (look for the carved wooden archway marking the entrance). It's a short 15-minute hike to the highest point on the island. From here you are rewarded with great views of Active Pass, Vancouver Island, and the Strait of Georgia. Miner's Bay has a tiny museum of local history in the small former jail, the 1896 Plumper Pass Lockup. The **Mayne Island Museum** (Miners Bay, at Fernhill and Minty Roads in Miner's Bay Village; 250-539-2283) has a collection of island artifacts, including a number from an old shipwreck. According to one local source the jail "was built to cool off those whose tempers were not soothed by either the church or the saloon." Nearby St. Mary Magdalene Chapel was built in 1898.

Active Pass Lighthouse, at the end of Georgia Point Road, was built in 1855 and is still operating. The grassy grounds are open to the public on afternoons and are great for picnicking.

A perfect vacation home rests on the shores of Mayne Island.

■ NORTH AND SOUTH PENDER ISLANDS   *map page 120, B/C-2/3*
These two islands are normally treated as one because they are connected by a picturesque 91-meter (297-foot) bridge. **Port Washington,** on North Pender, is the largest settlement and has the ferry terminal. **Bedwell Harbour** is the customs port of entry for air and seacraft entering Canadian waters from the south.

The numerous coves and harbors on South Pender now attract pleasure boaters. During the Prohibition era they were used by rumrunners, despite their proximity to the Canadian Customs office.

The Pender Islands have few facilities but many beaches. **Prior Centennial Park,** 3.2 kilometers (2 miles) south of Port Washington, has campsites. **Beaumont Marine Park,** on South Pender, has a fine swimming beach near Bedwell Harbour Village with its commercial marine facilities. Travelers who have left their car at home can rent bicycles. **The Stand** has the islands' best hamburgers.

■ SALT SPRING ISLAND   *map page 120, A-2/3*
This island got its name from 14 salt springs discovered on its north end by officers of the Hudson's Bay Company, who thought the briny emissions of 3,446 grains of salt per imperial gallon were a bit too salty. Salt Spring is the most popular and commercialized of the Gulf Islands. But don't let that scare you off. "Commercial" here means a gas station or two and a few stores, art galleries, and shops selling handmade candles and tie-dyed T-shirts.

With 135 kilometers (83 miles) of shoreline, Salt Spring is also the largest and most populous of Gulf Islands. It has 160 kilometers (100 miles) of road and several hamlets, including Fulford Harbour, Ganges, and Vesuvius Bay, each with a ferry terminal. The first thing you note when you land are the steep hills. The highest is 709-meter (2,325-foot) Bruce Peak. From the top you can enjoy panoramic views of islands and mountains without end.

Ganges, the island's cultural and commercial center, is a pedestrian-oriented seaside village where you should drop in at the rather ramshackle Mouat's Mall, built in 1912 and still serving as a community store. Many studios of local artists are open to the public. Pick up a tour map at the chamber of commerce on Lower Ganges Road. Two miles south of Ganges, **Mount Maxwell Park** has views as well as picnic sites. The permanent population of a few thousand souls is more than doubled in summer months, but sheep ranching remains the island's most important industry. If you've ever tasted Salt Spring Island lamb, you know why. Seaside

Ganges Harbour on Salt Spring Island.

meadows, with their abundant sprinkling of wild herbs, put special flavors into that tender meat. If you don't eat red meat, you'll be glad to know that the island has 11 freshwater lakes stocked with bass and trout.

Salt Spring Island has two **Saturday markets.** They're held between April and October—one on top of the hill next to the Harbour House, the other in the center of town on Fulford-Ganges Road near Centennial Park. Look for locally grown produce, seafood, crafts, clothing, herbs, candles, toys, home-canned foods, and more. If you're not equipped to cook while traveling, go for the berries, apples, and other fruits, and for smoked salmon and other smoked or pickled seafood.

Ruckle Provincial Park is an 1872 heritage homestead with extensive fields still farmed by the Ruckle family. This working farm/park has camping and picnic spots as well as trails leading to rocky headlands.

■ SATURNA ISLAND   *map page 120, C-3*
Tucked away at the southern end of the Gulf Island chain, and difficult to reach, Saturna Island may well be the least spoiled of the Gulf Islands. Regardless, it is popular with visitors for its excellent hiking, cycling, kayaking, swimming and

fishing. Saturna's big social occasion, and the Gulf Islands' most celebrated event, is the annual **Lamb Barbeque**, held on Canada Day (July 1) at the ball field in Winter Cove Marine Park.

The 497-meter (1,630-foot) summit of **Mount Warburton Pike** offers a panoramic view of the surrounding Gulf and San Juan Islands, to be shared with feral goats, soaring eagles, falcons, and turkey vultures.

Saturna Island Vineyards, a family-owned winery, occupies a rustic barnlike structure just off Quarry Trail. Sixty acres of vines are under cultivation in four vineyards, which makes Saturna one of the province's largest estate vineyard and winery operations. *Quarry Road; 250-539-5139.*

■ **OTHER ISLANDS OF THE STRAIT OF GEORGIA**

Denman and Hornby Islands, north of Nanaimo, are sometimes included among the Gulf Islands though they are quite separate, as are Quadra, Sonora, and Cortes Island, of the Discovery Group at the northern end of the Strait of Georgia. Denman has old-growth forests and long sandy beaches; Hornby, too, has spectacular beaches. Both islands have thriving communities of potters, sculptors, and wood carvers. Ferries leave from Buckley Bay near Comox/Courtenay.

■ **QUADRA ISLAND** *map pages 62–63, B/C-3*

Quadra is separated from Campbell River by Discovery Passage, crossed in a 10-minute ferry ride. When the first fur trappers arrived in the region, the island was part of the traditional territory of the Coast Salish. But these people were driven out by Kwakiutl moving south.

The invaders built a fortified village at Cape Mudge. From here they raided Indian canoes traveling north and south through Discovery Passage. They exacted toll from white ships as well, until the provincial gunboat *Forward* shelled the village and stockade in 1860.

The **Kwakiutl Museum and Cultural Centre** (34 Weway Road, Cape Mudge Village; 250-285-3111), 4.8 kilometers (3 miles) south of the ferry terminal, has an outstanding collection of native masks, blankets, and carvings.

The **Tsa-Kwa-Luten Lodge** (1 Lighthouse Road; 250-285-2042 or 800-665-7745) of the Cape Mudge band of Kwakiutl is a contemporary lodge overlooking Discovery Passage. It serves a weekly buffet of regional foods in the summer, followed by tribal dancing.

■ SAN JUAN ISLANDS *map pages 62–63, D-5, and page 126*

The San Juan Islands are a cluster of large and small tree-clad rocks scattered across the lower end of the Strait of Georgia in northwest Washington, just below the Canadian border. They are pleasurably reached by ferry, and blessed with a temperate climate, lovely countryside, quiet beaches, and fine vistas.

Many of the smaller San Juan Islands are off-limits to visitors because they are either bird sanctuaries or privately owned. But a few are marine state parks. These are accessible by private or chartered boat, and by the **San Juan Island Commuter Ferry** (360-734-8180 or 888-734-8180) from Bellingham; the ferry also carries camping equipment and kayaks. Visiting these islands means roughing it.

Fresh water is limited (bring your own); camping and toilet facilities are primitive at best (carry your garbage out with you).

Why visit? Because these islands are truly off the beaten path and have a rugged beauty that is unique even in the midst of the natural beauty of the Gulf and San Juan Islands. You will be surrounded by wildlife—harbor seals or sea lions hauled on tidal rocks or sandbanks, river otters frolicking in a secluded cove, auklets, pigeon guillemots, and puffins hanging out on steep cliff sides, great blue herons stalking prey along the shore, and bald eagles soaring overhead or resting on high snags. With luck, you may spot a passing gray or humpback whale, or see a pod of orcas cruise by.

State parks worth visiting include Blind Island, Clark Island, Doe Island, Jones Island, Matia Island, Patos Island, Posey Island, and Stuart Island.

■ **LOPEZ ISLAND** *map page 126, B/C-3*
The first stop on the ferry run from Anacortes, Washington, is Lopez, the flattest of the big islands. Its gentle topography has fostered agriculture since white settlers first arrived on the island in the 1850s. Farmers raise everything from sheep to llamas, and from kiwi fruit to wine grapes.

In summer, the island's 1,800 year-round residents are joined by throngs of vacationers who descend on Lopez every sunny weekend. Like the rest of the San Juans, Lopez struggles to hold on to its identity as a vital community.

Lopez Village, on the island's western shore, has a few good restaurants, a winery, a supermarket, and a great local history museum. To reach Lopez Village from the ferry terminal, follow Ferry Road south about 8 kilometers (5 miles). Along the way you will pass two splendid parks. Both **Odin County Park** and **Spencer Spit Park** are ideal spots to while away an afternoon hiking, beachcombing, picnicking, and even clamming.

The **Lopez Island Vineyard** (Fisherman Bay Road; 360-468-3644), the only vineyard in the San Juans, has a tasting room that is open between Memorial Day and Labor Day. **Edenwild** (Eades Lane at Lopez Village Road; 360-468-3238) is a large, gray 1890 Victorian-style farmhouse and inn, which is surrounded by gardens and framed by Fisherman's Bay. The two-story **Mackaye Harbor Inn** (949 Mackaye Harbor Road; 360-468-2253 or 888-314-6140) is a 1920s sea captain's frame house with half a mile of beach that rises above the rocks at the southern end of Lopez Island.

■ ORCAS ISLAND *map pages 126, B/C-1/2*

On the map, Orcas Island—the largest of the San Juan Islands—looks like a pair of well-worn saddlebags divided by the long, narrow body of East Sound. Up close, Orcas is lush and steep, and its roads are narrow and contorted. Luxury homes occupy much of the coastline, but along the island's one main road, the landscape remains mostly rural or thickly forested with tall, old second-growth fir and alder.

At the end of the 19th century, fruit orchards and hop fields flourished in the fertile soil of Crow Valley, on the island's western side. All the crops went to market by boat, and as water transportation lost ground to railroads and then trucks, the island became commercially stranded. After irrigation projects converted the arid Wenatchee and Yakima valleys of eastern Washington into fruit-growing centers, most of Orcas Island's orchards were abandoned.

A handful of resorts, from posh Rosario to low-budget Doe Bay, as well as beautiful Moran State Park, draw hordes of visitors in the summer. The massive hump of **Mount Constitution**, the highest point in the San Juans, rises 2,409 feet above sea level on the eastern side of Orcas Island. A steep, narrow road climbs to the

The Olga Store on Orcas Island.

mountain's summit. At road's end stands a watchtower built of hand-cut stone by the Civilian Conservation Corps (CCC) from 1934 to 1936. An open deck on top of the tower affords a spectacular 360-degree view.

To the east, Mount Baker's snowy cone rises over the North Cascades. (In the San Juans, Baker is the peak of reference, as Rainier is from Seattle to Olympia.) The jagged ice-and-granite Cascade Range and the Canadian Coast Range close out the eastern horizon. The Olympics are etched onto the western sky.

Mount Constitution is surrounded by **Moran State Park,** a forested 3,325-acre tract of land that covers most of Orcas Island's eastern lobe. The park includes isolated lakes, sandy beaches, and campsites. A few ancient spruce and fir, 4 to 5 feet in diameter, grow near the cool, mossy gorge of Cascade Falls, a short walk from the Cold Springs trailhead.

The park was the gift of shipyard tycoon Robert Moran, who served as Seattle's mayor during the fire of 1889, made a fortune building steamships for the Klondike gold rush, then retreated to the San Juans. Moran bought thousands of acres on Orcas and built a 19-bedroom mansion with two bowling alleys and an indoor pool in 1906. In 1921, he donated most of his land to the state. Today, Moran's mansion is the centerpiece of the **Rosario Spa & Resort** (Horseshoe Highway; 360-376-2222 or 800-562-8820).

During the Great Depression, the CCC cleared the park's campsites and trails and built its stone gazebos. The CCC also built the Mount Constitution Observation Tower and the stone guardrails along the mountain's treacherous, winding road.

The island has a regional reputation for the high quality of work produced by local artists, especially pottery and metal sculpture. One of the oldest and best loved galleries is **Crow Valley Pottery**, at 2274 Orcas Road. The **Orcas Island Artworks** in Olga on the waterfront in the shadow of Mount Constitution, sells a variety of works created by local artists and also has a small, locally popular cafe. **Howe Art**, on the road from the Orcas ferry landing to Eastsound, is well-known for its kinetic sculptures that sparkle in the sun and flutter, twist, and gyrate in the slightest breeze. They range from small patio pieces to large garden installations. **Darvill's Rare Book Shop**, on Eastsound's Main Street, has a national reputation for the quality of its hard-to-find books and prints.

If you want to get a feel for what island living was like in the old days, when the local economy was based on fruit and lamb, not tourism, check out the

Turtleback Farm Inn (Route 1; 360-376-4914 or 800-376-4914), which dates from the late 1800s. Eighty acres of meadows, woods, and farmland surround the Crow Valley forest-green farmhouse in the shadow of Turtleback Mountain. Sheep and black cattle graze below an ancient apple orchard; chickens cluck near the barn; and ducks lounge by the pond. To meet the locals and get involved in deep conversations on a long winter night, dine at **Christina's** (North Beach Road and Horseshoe Highway; 360-376-4904). More than a homey waterfront restaurant serving superb food, it's an area institution and popular hangout.

■ SAN JUAN ISLAND   *map page 126, A-2/3*

The most developed and second largest of the islands, San Juan is the last stop in U.S. waters on the ferry run from Anacortes. The seat of San Juan County government, San Juan National Historic Park, vantage points for whale-watching, restaurants, hotels, and campgrounds attract droves of fair-weather visitors.

A few ribbons of two-lane blacktop cross the island from coast to coast, winding past the small farms of the San Juan Valley. The roads are confusing and poorly marked, but eventually they all lead back to Friday Harbor. Traffic, both cars and bicycles, fills them every summer. Many cyclists will tell you that the best way to enjoy the islands is to leave your car in Anacortes, take ferries between the islands, then bike and camp at your leisure.

Friday Harbor, with a population of 1,900, is the largest community in San Juan County. It was named for Joe Friday—not the "Dragnet" detective, but a Hawaiian shepherd who once lived here. Friday Harbor climbs the hill above the ferry landing and a neighboring marina. The town's brightly painted, remodeled, turn-of-the-19th-century homes have been converted into an assortment of chi-chi bistros, health food stores, and gift shops. A jumble of houses old and new, fashionable and funky, surrounds the business district.

Friday Harbor's **Whale Museum,** a yellow two-story building kitty-corner from the old brick courthouse on First Street, about three blocks north of the ferry dock, houses whale skeletons, models, and informational displays. Speakers in the stairwell broadcast what first seem to be the sounds of creaking docks and keening seagulls, but in fact are the recorded voices of local whale pods, often observed at

(opposite) A spectacular view from the summit of Mount Constitution out across Rosario Strait to the islands and mainland. The towering volcanic cone of Mount Baker is visible in the background.

Lime Kiln State Park, on the island's west side. *62 First Street; 360-678-4710.*

One place you should check out while visiting Friday Harbor (even if you're not staying there) is the 1873 **San Juan Inn** (50 Spring Street; 360-378-2070 or 800-742-8210), which has been accommodating travelers since the days when steamers instead of ferries called at the islands. Another place to visit is the **Roche Harbor Resort** (4950 Tarte Memorial Drive; 360-378-2155 or 800-451-8910), 10 miles northwest of Friday Harbor off Roche Harbor Road at the island's north end. The main lodge, the 1886 Hotel de Haro, was built as a company guesthouse to accommodate visitors to the island's once thriving limestone quarries.

Westcott Bay Sea Farm is a rustic oyster farm, tucked into a small bay 2 miles south of Roche Harbor, on the west side of the island. The farm has some of the tastiest oysters in the season from November through April. *4071 Westcott Drive; 360-378-2489.*

The collection of outdoor sculpture at the **Westcott Bay Reserve** is set into a former horse pasture overlooking a freshwater pond at the northern end of Westcott Bay, to the immediate west of the Roche Harbor airstrip. The sculptures look

The seaside perch of the restaurant at San Juan Island's most famous hotel, the Roche Harbor Resort.

like they have stood here from time immemorial. As befits an outdoor sculpture collection, most of the pieces are quite large and are done in a wide variety of styles, from abstract rusty metal pieces to an almost naturalistic great blue heron, owls, and a horse's head. A small duck pond serves as the reserve's reflecting pool. Unlike museum art, these sculptures are touchable—feel the smoothness of polished granite and marble, the roughness of unfinished basalt. A surprisingly comfortable, free-form basalt loveseat makes a great bench for contemplating the pond and its dabbling ducks. A kingfisher has staked out a bronze dragonfly (the only sculpture in the pond) as a fishing perch. There is no admission fee, but a contribution is recommended. *Roche Harbor Village; 360-370-5050.*

American and British troops occupied San Juan Island jointly for 12 years in the mid-19th century. American Camp, where the U.S. forces lived, and English Camp, the British stronghold on the island's north end, are now both administered as **San Juan Island National Historical Park** (360-378-2240 or 360-378-3902). To reach the visitors center from Friday Harbor, take Spring Street west to Mullis Road. Turn left on Argyle, which turns into Cattle Point Road.

American Camp occupies most of San Juan's southern tail, 6 miles south of Friday Harbor, and includes an information center, interpretive trails, two restored military buildings, and a few miles of public beach. The open plain around American Camp is honeycombed with rabbit warrens over which eagles, hawks, and owls glide, looking for dinner.

British Camp overlooks Garrison Bay, a sheltered inlet on the island's northeast corner. The camp is a 10-mile drive from Friday Harbor. A couple of neat whitewashed buildings, including a two-room barracks with brick fireplaces, are scattered across the manicured lawn that slopes down to the bay. A blockhouse built of unpeeled, whitewashed logs stands at the water's edge.

The joint occupation was a peaceful affair, and relations between the occupation troops were friendly. The soldiers often attended holiday parties at each other's encampments and spent most of their time gardening, hunting, and maintaining their tidy settlements. The structures remain here thanks to the preservation efforts of a local named Jim Crook, who homesteaded the land following the departure of British troops.

A trail leads uphill from the parking lot, across the road and up to the British cemetery on the slope of Mount Young. Here lie the oak-shaded gravestones of eight Englishmen who died during the joint occupation. These men were

ISLAND DREAMTIME

Imagine yourself on a sandy beach of a quiet little cove. On the far shore, almost cutting off the bay from the strait, rise sandstone cliffs carved by the action of wind and water into weird shapes. Some resemble dragons, others look like petrified sponges, mushrooms, or giant fish heads.

Below the cliffs, the waves have cut deep tide pools. Their sides are encrusted with colorful lichen that all but match the mottled colors of sculpins, making them difficult to see. Limpets and snails crawl on tidal rocks, tiny crabs scurry among piles of seaweed, a large purple starfish clings to the side of a boulder.

Hidden in a dark crevice, you spot a tiny octopus, its tentacles barely hidden from the light. Octopuses are secretive and usually emerge only at night, when they stalk crabs and other prey. The inland waters of the Pacific Northwest are home to the largest octopus in the world—with an arm spread of more than 3 meters (9 feet) and a weight of about 100 pounds. But this harmless monster is rarely encountered near the beach.

Ducks chatter as they dabble among the eelgrass in the shade of a large cedar whose flexible boughs hang out far over the water. Behind you tower tall firs, all but cutting off the view of the snowcapped Cascades to the east, where the glaciers atop the volcanic cone of Mount Baker glow pink in the setting sun. A robin trills its nightly song from a blackberry thicket as the booming hoot of a great horned owl echoes from the cliffs.

You've been fishing all day, and your boat is now safely anchored just offshore. Several kayaks are pulled up on the beach near you; an aluminum skiff rests in the sand farther on. You've tidied up your campsite and spread out your sleeping bag. Now you're ready for dinner.

Fishing was good, today. You've caught a lingcod, a couple of rockfish, and three Dungeness crabs. A pot of salt water you've set on the hot rocks of the campfire is beginning to boil. You drop in the crabs one by one. You spread the lingcod, Indian fashion, between sticks, brush it with butter, sprinkle it with salt and pepper, and set it up by the fire. You invite your neighbors for dinner. They contribute some pink scallops they gathered while diving and a pail of wild blackberries. As you open a bottle of wine, the sun sets behind Vancouver Island. You're in paradise.

A paradise like this can be found in many of the small coves of the Gulf and San Juan Islands. And you don't even need a boat to reach it. On many of the larger islands served by ferries, trails lead to hidden coves like this.

casualties not of war, but of accidents. Above the graveyard are the steep, arid slopes of Mount Young, with meadows of tall, golden grasses, mossy slabs of exposed granite, and ancient, twisted oak trees.

■ **SHAW ISLAND** *map page 126, B-2*
Shaw Island and the four islands that it serves, is home to a few hundred permanent residents. Among them are a community of Franciscan nuns who run the ferry dock and the grocery store. Shaw's residents value their seclusion and have thus far resisted the tourist trade that thrives on the neighboring islands. Shaw offers neither restaurants nor overnight accommodations—the island's community plan forbids both.

■ **SUCIA ISLAND** *map page 126, B-2*
Once accessible only by private boat or floatplane, remote Sucia Island can now also be reached from Bellingham by the San Juan Island Commuter Ferry. Sucia has the most wildly sculpted of the San Juan Island sandstone formations. Surrounding several quiet coves, the formations are topped by red-and-beige-barked, gnarled madrona trees. It's hard to believe they actually grew that way—they're all natural. These rocks and trees alone are worth a visit. The eccentric beauty of the sandstone formations did not stop 19th-century entrepreneurs from quarrying them. Many of the stones have paved downtown Seattle sidewalks.

Some interesting remnants of the region's past have been found in **Fossil Bay**. The island is composed of sandstone, siltstone, and conglomerate that have been eroded by waves and glaciers. Ridges in the harder layers of sandstone and conglomerate have formed, and fossils of clams, snails, and ammonites can be found. (The island is a state park and removing fossils is illegal.)

■ **WALDRON ISLAND** *map page 126, B-1*
Waldron Island has no public access, but it has numerous small rocky coves off its dramatically steep eastern shore where boats may anchor, as well as tiny beaches, unreachable by land, where kayakers may haul out and camp. Here the locals may see you, but they can't reach you. The steep sandstone cliffs near Point Disney were once quarried for the building stone that changed Seattle from a wooden city into a stone one.

■ **Travel and Climate**

■ **Getting There and Around**

By Air and Floatplane

Tiny air services using single-engine planes fly between the San Juan Islands and Bellingham and Anacortes.

Floatplane companies, among them West Isle Air and Harbour Air, offer scheduled and charter flights from Vancouver to the Gulf Islands. Seattle-based Kenmore Air offers floatplane trips to Sucia Island.

Harbour Air. *800-665-0212*
Kenmore Air. *206-364-6990*
West Isle Air. *800-874-4434*

By Ferry

Car and passenger ferries travel among the Canadian Gulf Islands and among the U.S. San Juan Islands but not between the two island groups themselves.

If you travel by car and ferry, you might want to plan a loop trip, boarding the Washington State Ferry in Anacortes, Washington, and exploring the San Juan Islands; continuing by Washington State Ferry to Vancouver Island and Victoria; and from there taking a British Columbia ferry to the Gulf Islands. Close the loop by taking a ferry from the Gulf Islands to the British Columbia mainland and the city of Vancouver. Be sure to bring your passport.

Gulf Island Ferries

Active Pass between Galiano and Mayne Islands is the most scenic route in these islands, with the riptides of the pass swirling around the ship, and the more than 2,000-foot-high peaks of southern Salt Spring Island looming above the channel's northwest shores.

All British Columbia ferries from Tsawwassen on the mainland and from Vancouver Island (Swartz Bay, Nanaimo, and other docks) have regularly scheduled services. Since departure and arrival times are a bit confusing and since not all of the ferries go to or stop at the same islands, you should call in advance, especially if you're planning to bring your car.

For information and reservations in British Columbia phone 888-223-3779. From Victoria phone 250-386-3431. For route reservations in British Columbia, phone 888-724-5223.

San Juan Island Ferries

In the San Juan Islands, the four largest—Lopez, Shaw, Orcas, and San Juan—are served by the Washington State Ferry from Anacortes or Vancouver Island. Many of the others can be reached only by private boat or plane.

The San Juan Island Commuter Ferry takes hikers, bikers, kayakers, nature lovers, and residents to some of the smaller San Juan Islands not reached by Washington State Ferry, and to state parks only accessible by boat or floatplane. For information call 360-734-8180 or 888-734-8180.

Washington State voters passed two restrictive tax initiatives that have left the ferries short of money. Schedules are being cut and rates raised. The specifics change almost monthly. Check schedules and rates before you set out, and allot extra travel time, especially during the busy season.

■ CLIMATE

The San Juan and Gulf Islands lie in the rain shadow of the Olympic Mountains and the Insular Range and receive about 29 inches of rain annually. Winters are generally mild, with temperatures above freezing level. Winter brings much of the annual rainfall, though. The temperature during summer usually doesn't get higher than 80 degrees Fahrenheit.

Ganges Harbor Salt Springs Island boats at docks.

NORTHWEST INTERIOR

■ HIGHLIGHTS

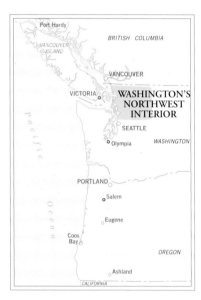

■ LANDSCAPE

THE CITIES OF THIS REGION of Washington State, on a clear day, are always in sight of salt water and mountains. The relatively flat land on which they have been built was gouged out by rivers of ice that left deep valleys, which were then filled by gravels and clays left behind by the glaciers or by silt carried by rivers from the rugged Cascade Mountains, which form the eastern boundary of the region. The lower parts of these valleys—Puget Sound and its channels and inlets—are filled with water from the sea. The Cascades, from Snoqualmie Pass north to Canada, have been set aside as national park, wilderness, or national recreation areas. Hundreds of miles of hiking trails wind through wilderness areas, Ross Lake National Recreation Area, and North Cascades National Park. To the west, killer whales, ferries, kayaks, and sailboats travel through the channels of the inland sea.

■ NORTH CASCADES *map page 139, C-1/2*

The granite peaks of the North Cascades are far more rugged and ancient than the eroded hills south of Snoqualmie Pass. Drive into these mountains on a cloudy day, and the evergreens on the steep slopes look almost black. The rock walls reach

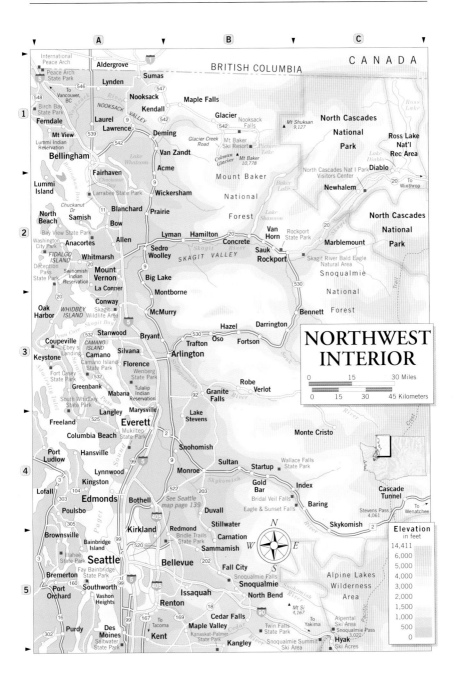

NORTHWEST INTERIOR

0   15   30 Miles

0   15   30   45 Kilometers

Elevation
in feet

14,411
6,000
5,000
4,000
3,000
2,000
1,500
1,000
500
0

for the clouds, like mountains in a Chinese landscape painting, and seem to rise from earth to heaven. On the lower slopes in the heat of summer, the soil of the rocky trail may be dry as dust, while farther up patches of snow linger among wildflower meadows in full bloom with white or golden lilies, bright red-orange Indian paintbrush, and intensely purple lupines. As you climb higher, ridge succeeds ridge, their misty outlines towered over by the great, snowcapped volcanoes.

In the solitude of the mountains, hikers may not encounter any other humans, but they will always be in the company of wild animals—whiskeyjacks, juncos, buntings, pikas, chipmunks, ptarmigans, mountain goats, and, in rare instances, cougars. The heavy snows of winter, and the rock and ice of the high country, have not made the mountains inhospitable to wildlife. Wolves, once hunted nearly to extinction in the North Cascades, are making a comeback. Threatened northern spotted owls and marbled murrelets nest here. Salmon spawn in many of the rivers. Though rarely seen, grizzly bears are not uncommon in this region.

North of Snoqualmie Pass, the half-million-acre **Alpine Lakes Wilderness,** a haven for hikers, fishermen, and backpackers, comes nearly to the road's shoulder.

■ SNOQUALMIE PASS *map page 139, C-5*

Despite its modest elevation, Snoqualmie Pass (3,022 feet) can easily receive 35 feet of snow a year making this a perfect destination for skiers, who head for the groomed slopes, nordic trails, and warm firesides of ski areas like Alpental, Ski Acres, and Snoqualmie Summit.

In the foothills west of the pass, popular trails lead through the so-called **Issaquah Alps** or climb the steep southern slope of 4,167-foot **Mount Si,** the crag that looms over the upper Snoqualmie Valley. Nearby, the Snoqualmie River plunges 268 feet over a stone ledge at Snoqualmie Falls. The spot has always been sacred to the Snoqualmie Indians, who believe that the mists rising from the catch basin below ascend like prayers to heaven.

A hydroelectric powerhouse carved out of the solid rock below the falls has been producing electricity here since 1899. The steam train **Puget Sound & Snoqualmie Valley Railroad** runs along a scenic route between North Bend, at the base of Mount Si, and Snoqualmie, near the falls. Purchase tickets for the ride at the Snoqualmie Depot Museum on Railroad Avenue. *425-888-3030.*

■ EVERETT *map page 139, A-4*

Everett, a port 30 miles north of Seattle, lies on the shore of Port Gardner Bay, an inlet of northeast Puget Sound. Just south of town, **Boeing** manufactures 747s in the largest space under one roof in the world. The weekday tour of the plant, which allows visitors to view the huge aircraft in various stages of assembly, is arguably the premier industrial tour of the state. From I-5, take Exit 189 to Route 526 West. Drive for about 3.5 miles and then follow the signs to the Tour Center. It is near the west end of the assembly building. *800-464-1476 or 206-544-1264.*

A former mill town, Everett was plotted in 1890. Frederick Weyerhaeuser subsequently built what became the world's biggest sawmill on its shore. Beautiful examples of building styles popular in the early decades of the 20th century decorate downtown. Within a few blocks you see the grand old wing of the Spanish mission–style courthouse with its clock and bell tower, the ornate art-deco brick of City Hall, and the massive, Romanesque Federal Building. Many of the mansions built by lumber barons still stand on Grand and Rucker Avenues at the north end of town. Several blocks farther north on 18th Street are the marina and **Marina Village**, a string of waterfront restaurants and shops. It's here that you catch the ferry to **Jetty Island** for a day of picnicking, hiking, and bird-watching. Other sites in Everett include the **Everett Museum** (2915 Hewitt Avenue; 425-259-8849), housed in a century-old brick building, and the **Everett Publick Market** (284 Grand Street), a two-story structure consisting of shops, galleries, cafes, and an antique mall.

Northeast of Everett off Route 530 in the Cascade foothills lies the town of **Darrington,** originally settled by loggers from North Carolina. A **Bluegrass Festival** (360-436-1006) held here on the third weekend in July celebrates the town's Tarheel roots. In this scenic valley, dairy cattle graze in wet meadows with the crags and spires of the North Cascades rising behind them.

■ SKAGIT RIVER VALLEY *map page 139, A/B-2*

The jade green Skagit River rises in Canada and flows down through the North Cascades, entering Puget Sound in a wide delta southwest of the town of Mount Vernon. Much of it is protected as the Skagit National Wild and Scenic River. At the river's mouth, the Skagit Wildlife Area provides habitat for whistling swans, snow geese, and other birds. For a look at the Skagit River delta farmlands, turn off the freeway south of Mount Vernon and head west to **Conway,** a quiet hamlet with a white-steepled church built in 1916 and a tavern popular with visitors.

Between Conway and La Conner, the delta spreads out in a patchwork of fallow and green fields. Farmhouses with their huge old barns sit by the side of the road at regular intervals; drainage ditches wind through the green fields. On a clear day, white-topped Mount Baker dominates the landscape.

■ LA CONNER *map page 139, A-2*

La Conner lies along the eastern bank of the Swinomish Channel, a narrow inland waterway used as a sheltered marine passage from Bellingham Bay to Puget Sound. Quaint "olde tyme" boutiques, craft stores, and antique marts occupy the early-20th-century storefront buildings along La Conner's First Street. Visitors browse the trinket shops and dine al fresco in restaurants overlooking the channel.

La Conner's reputation as an artists' colony dates back to the late 1930s, when Northwest School painters Guy Anderson and Morris Graves took up residence in a dilapidated cabin here. It got a boost in the 1970s when novelist and pop philosopher Tom Robbins became the town's most famous resident. Fine old Victorian homes and churches stand on the cliff above the commercial district. The **Skagit County Historical Museum** (501 South Fourth Street; 360-466-3365) sits atop the hill. The two-story brick wedge of City Hall, built in 1886, rises above Second Street at the south end of town. Between City Hall and the high, orange arch of the painted steel bridge that spans the channel, fish-processing plants stand near the water in a jumble of green nylon nets and crab pots. On the west side of the channel you might want to visit the studio of **Swinomish carver Kevin Paul** (open by appointment; 360-466-3906).

■ SKAGIT WILDLIFE AREA *map page 139, A-2/3*

To reach this bird-watcher's paradise, take the Conway–La Conner Road off I-5 heading west. After winding past fields and farms, the road crosses a bridge to the top of the Skagit River levee. Look for signs directing you to the wildlife area. In spring, summer, and fall, this place is truly idyllic.

Ducks and geese are most common in spring and fall, when huge flocks stop here on their way to and from wintering marshes in California's Sacramento Valley. But many waterfowl, especially swans, stay here all winter. It is quite stirring to watch a skein of trumpeter swans flying overhead, their melodic bugling drifting across the marsh. In summer, watch for goldfinches collecting thistledown for their nests. Swallows twitter in the air, the boom "oonk-ka-ch'oonk" of a bittern may resound from the reeds, a great blue heron may wade in the shallow water, carefully measuring each step, as it searches for frogs, fish, and muskrats. You may be startled by the rattling call of a kingfisher while listening to the melodious gurgling of a meadowlark.

If your meditations are interrupted by a loud splash, hold still. The beaver that slapped its tail on the water to scare you off may slap again and again before deciding you may be harmless after all. If you're lucky you can see a beaver carry sticks and twigs to a lodge. And if you're really fortunate, a beaver may climb from the water, lumber up a bank, and begin cutting down a willow or cottonwood (often you can hear a beaver's gnawing long before you spot the animal itself). Or you might see a family of otters cruising a slough in search of crayfish. This is truly a magical place.

The **Padilla Bay Interpretive Center,** just north of Bayview State Park, has a trail through woods and past meadows, a trail to an overlook platform and muddy beach, and (south of Bayview) a trail along the shores of Padilla Bay. All make for great bird-watching. *1043 Bayview-Edison Road; 360-428-1558.*

The Skagit Valley has the largest concentrations of trumpeter swans in the lower 48 states. In an average winter, about 3,100 swans winter in Skagit County. The swans arrive from their summer breeding grounds in Alaska around October, and leave by March. The best place for getting up close to the swans is the **Johnson DeBay Swan Reserve,** northeast of Mount Vernon, which is visited by hundreds of migrating trumpeter swans, tundra swans, and Canada geese and tens of thousands of mallards, pintails, and other ducks, as well as bald eagles, northern harriers, and Cooper's hawks. At the reserve, the swans and ducks feed on corn specifically grown for them. The corn is knocked down in late January—making this the best time to view these often elusive birds.

To reach the reserve, take I-5 to College Way in Mount Vernon; turn east, then turn left at LaVenture Road and follow it to DeBay Isle Road, which is located at the beginning of a major right bend in the main road. If you miss the left turn, go straight into a gravel parking lot and turn around—DeBay Isle Road adjoins this intersection. Continue along the dike road until you see a gate. The reserve is open to the public every day. If the gates are closed, you can still park in the outer lot and walk around the gate.

Bald eagles are the second most common raptors you are likely to encounter in this region (after red-tailed hawks). At times they seem to be everywhere—soaring overhead, patrolling beaches, or sitting on snags and roadside utility wires. Long stretches of the Northwest Interior mainland shores are bordered by extensive stretches of tideflats where the water recedes far offshore during low tide (especially in Port Susan, Padilla Bay, and Samish Bay). You don't see many different species of shorebirds on these flats, but the ones you see are plentiful in numbers. Look for flocks of dunlin in shallow water, as well as western sandpipers. Killdeer tend to hang out on gravelly beaches and in shoreside meadows. Black oystercatchers prefer rocky outcroppings, where they dine on mussels and other shellfish. These are fascinating birds to watch; almost anything they do is interesting.

■ **Mount Vernon** *map page 139, A-2*
Mount Vernon, on I-5, straddles the Skagit River. From Mount Vernon west to the Swinomish Channel, a saltwater slough separates Fidalgo Island from the mainland. To the north, the area is bordered by Route 20; to the east and south by

Mount Shuksan (above) is one of the many Northern Cascades peaks that rise above the Skagit River Valley. (opposite) The valley is one of the world's foremost tulip-growing regions.

the Skagit River and its delta. Downtown Mount Vernon has a successful food co-op, a winery, a Mexican grocery, two bike shops, a good bakery, and a small bookstore with an entire shelf devoted to UFO abductions.

The beautiful valley of the Skagit River runs east into the Cascade Mountains, but the daffodil, tulip, and Dutch iris fields that make the valley famous occupy only a small portion. Flowers are in bloom from March (daffodils) and April (tulips) to May and June (Dutch irises).

The **Skagit Valley Tulip Festival** celebrates the spring blooms and also includes exhibits, salmon barbecues, picnics, a parade, and fireworks. *From I-5, take Exits 221-231. Exit 226 takes you to the tulip festival office and Visitors Information Center; 360-428-5959.*

Among garden-related highlights are the **Museum of Tulip History** (15379 Route 536; 360-424-6234), at the Lefeber Bulb Farm, the 3-acre display garden at **Roozengaarde** (15867 Beaver Marsh Road; 360-424-8531), and the tulip displays at **Skagit Valley Gardens** (I-5 near Exit 221; 360-424-6760).

■ UPPER SKAGIT AND NORTH CASCADES NATIONAL PARK *map page 139, C-1/2*

The Skagit tumbles out of some of the state's most wild and beautiful country. Upstream from the vacation town of Rockport, the **Skagit River Bald Eagle Natural Area** attracts some 500 bald eagles every winter, when they come to feed on spawned-out chum and other salmon. Beyond the eagle refuge, Route 20, the North Cascades Scenic Highway, follows the river through **Ross Lake National Recreation Area,** a buffer zone between the northern and southern units of North Cascades National Park. Campgrounds, trailheads, lodges, resorts, and boat launches are found here as well as in adjacent national forest lands. The drive along the highway is invigoratingly scenic. Stop for the views from Goodall Creek Viewpoint and the Diablo Lake, Ross Lake, and Washington Pass overlooks.

North Cascades National Park is home to 1,700 species of plants, more than botanists have found in any other national park. The highway's climax is Washington Pass (5,477 feet), from which short hikes lead to spectacular views of Snagtooth Ridge, Cooper Basin, and the jagged peak of Liberty Bell.

The national park itself is a roadless wilderness accessible only by foot. Trails connect the national park and recreation area with the Pasayten Wilderness to the east, and to the Glacier Peak Wilderness and the Lake Chelan National Recreation

Area to the south. Water taxis take hikers up 24-mile-long Ross Lake to trailheads far north of the road. One trail leads to the nation's largest stand of old-growth western red cedar. There are also short trails that start at campgrounds or the side of the highway and can easily be covered in less than a day. Fishermen can rent boats and motors at the **Ross Lake Resort** or the **Diablo Lake Resort.**

Both Ross and Diablo Lakes were created early in the 20th century by Seattle City Light power dams. The scenic trip up Diablo Lake ends at the foot of Ross Dam. A 4-mile hike takes you to Cascade Pass and back, through acres of lupines and white-tufted beargrass. Water seeps out under glaciers, tumbles over boulders in gray streambeds, and drops down sheer vertical walls. In a nearby cirque filled with fireweed, dozens of nameless waterfalls cascade over granite cliffs.

■ FIDALGO ISLAND *map page 139, A-2*

Wooded and rural, with outcroppings rising straight from the sea on one side and tideflats stretching across Padilla Bay on the other, Fidalgo Island is an appealing place. Its only town, Anacortes, has the ferry landing for the San Juan Islands ferry. But Fidalgo is more than just a ferry stop. It's worth exploring itself. The island is connected to the mainland by a bridge (Route 20) across Swinomish Channel, a winding saltwater slough. South of the highway lies the Swinomish Indian Reservation, a woodsy place with a village across the channel from La Conner.

Anacortes, at the island's northwestern shore, has attractive parks and maritime views, the ornate 19th-century residential neighborhood of Causland Park, and an attractive old downtown area. A refurbished steam engine of the **Anacortes Railway** (360-293-2634) pulls cars and tourists through the town from the old Burlington Northern Depot. South of town, accessible by paved road, Mount Erie (1,270 feet) offers views of Campbell Lake, of Deception Pass (a churning saltwater channel, to the south) and, on clear days, of Mount Rainier and Mount Baker. Exhibitions at the **Anacortes Historical Museum** (135 Eighth Street; 360-293-1927) focus on the cultural heritage of Fidalgo and nearby Guemes Islands.

From the air, the rocky hill of **Washington City Park** looks like a sounding whale, half risen from the water. Mostly covered with a dense tangle of Douglas fir, cedar, madrona, and alder, broken now and then by clearings and meadows, the park rises from the waters of Rosario Strait to the rocky crest of Fidalgo Head. You can navigate it by car on a narrow, 2.4-mile loop road, or you can explore it on one of the many trails winding through the woods.

Grass-covered cliffs on **Fidalgo Head** rise from the churning currents of Burrows Channel in a series of rocky steps to forested ridges. Bedecked with wildflowers in spring, the cliffs appear like well-tended rock gardens, though the artifice of man played no role in their creation. Fidalgo Head is composed of serpentine and ultrabasic rocks, which also make up the southern part of Cypress Island, to the immediate north. These rocks are akin to the dunite rock of the Twin Sisters at the edge of the North Cascades, but are totally unrelated to any other rocks found in the vicinity. Twisted junipers crouch on the exposed rocks of Fidalgo Head. Their tangled roots grip the convoluted rocks; their gnarled branches reach defiantly into the sky with wind-burned tips. Hawks and bald eagles ceaselessly patrol the shore, riding the updrafts caused by the cliff face.

■ WHIDBEY ISLAND   *map page 139, A-3*

Across Deception Pass Bridge from Fidalgo Island is Whidbey Island, the second-longest island in the country at almost 50 miles. (Long Island, New York is the longest.) Lying in the Olympic Mountains rain shadow, Whidbey receives little

(above) Deception Pass between Fidalgo and Whidbey Islands. (opposite) Whidbey Island Bridge at Deception Pass State Park.

rain even in the wet season. Sunny summer days attract many visitors. Farms, woods, and native prairies cover most of this peaceful island; the towns are small.

Deception Pass State Park borders both shores of the channel that British navigator Capt. George Vancouver sighted in 1792. Hoping the rock-bound passage would lead to a secure harbor, Vancouver found otherwise and named it Deception Pass. Visitors to the park can hike, swim, fish, or go boating.

When you see strands of seaweed swirling in the tidal eddies of Deception Pass, consider yourself fortunate, for you are beholding the hair of a beautiful maiden of the Samish people who married the spirit of Deception Pass. Seeing the maiden brings good luck: you shall have wealth and ample food for the rest of your life.

Whidbey Island changes with the seasons, from the wildflower-covered meadows of spring to the wind-ruffled days of winter, when new colonies of lichen spread across the decaying concrete walls of the abandoned forts like so many colorful ice flowers. Not that you'd ever see many real ice flowers here. The climate is dry, with some of the lowest rainfall averages west of the Washington Cascades,

Kayaks for rent on Coupeville Pier, Whidbey Island.

and mild throughout the year. An occasional wild rose may bloom on New Year's Day; rain and snow never stay for long. Turquoise cabbage fields, van Gogh–yellow wheat patches, lush meadows, and scattered copses of conifers cover the low, undulating landscape of the island's center. Plowed fields, black with the fertile loam of prairies, terminate in tall sand bluffs crowned by sculpted trees and by weathered snags turned to bronze and pewter by sea breezes and salt air. One of the prairies has been preserved as **Ebey's Landing National Historic Park.** No recreational development will take place, since the arable land has been leased back to farmers to ensure the preservation of the prairie as farmland, in homage to the early settlers whose back-breaking toil first cleared the land for cultivation. The park is on the western shore of the island on Admiralty Inlet, about 2 miles southwest of Coupeville at the junction of South Ebey and West Hill Roads.

At the north end of this park, a small turnout marks the beginning of the bluff trail and beach walk to **Perego's Lagoon.** (The land just off the trail is private property, so respect the rights of the owners by treading carefully here.) The trail climbs along the leading edge of the prairie until it reaches a point of about 240 feet above the waters of Admiralty Inlet. The hilltop affords a sweeping view of the water and the Olympic Mountains to the west.

The lagoon and bluff take their name from George Perego, a Civil War veteran who homesteaded here in 1876. Perego never attempted to farm the land, and today it remains a wilderness—a windswept bluff, a lagoon, a low spit of sand, rocks, and driftwood. Many of the rocks are not native to the island. Carried here as ballast in sailing vessels, they were dumped onto the beaches before the ships loaded Puget Sound lumber. Ravens and bald eagles may fly past, and don't be surprised if you see a rare peregrine falcon zip by.

Much of Whidbey Island is a wildflower-lover's paradise in the spring, but the steep meadow at the head of Penn Cove is especially noteworthy. This is one of the few places west of the mountains where the wild blue flag grows in profusion.

From the head of Penn Cove you can drive along winding, scenic Madrona Drive to the **Captain Whidbey Inn,** a long two-story madrona lodge on a wooded promontory. It is bordered on one side by Penn Cove and on the other by a secluded saltwater lagoon. The Captain Whidbey has a special kind of hospitality and charm now rarely found. Gracefully aged, surrounded by native shrubs and trees, it is the perfect hideout for those who wish to escape from the worry and stress of the world. The bar at the Captain Whidbey is a favorite hangout of local characters. Here you may think and talk, and, after a relaxing day, doze off by the fire over a cup of mulled wine. *2072 West Captain Whidbey Inn Road; 360-678-4097 or 800-366-4097.*

Continuing down Madrona Drive brings you to **Coupeville,** a village founded in 1852 and little changed since the late 19th century. The town is well known for its art galleries, restaurants, and antique shops. The main street is lined by old buildings with false storefronts. A pier and a few historic houses perch above the tidelands on mussel-encrusted wooden stilts. The oldest dates from the early 1850s. Whidbey Island pioneers built blockhouses in the 1850s to protect themselves from raids by marauding Indians (in 1857, a band of Tlinkit Indians from Alaska raided the homestead of Col. Isaac Ebey and took his head to avenge the killing of a chief by U.S. marines). Some of the log structures still stand in Coupeville. On a clear day, Mount Baker looms to the northeast, its white glaciers reflected in the waters of the cove. The best view is from the back room at **Toby's Tavern** on the waterfront.

The **Island County Historical Museum,** next to the Alexander Blockhouse near the waterfront just off Front Street, offers a self-guided walking tour describing many houses surviving from the mid- to late 1800s. Most of the old homes are still occupied, and all are carefully maintained by their present owners. *908 NW Alexander Street; 360-678-3310.*

The 53-acre **Meerkerk Rhododendron Gardens** in **Greenbank** contain 1,500 native and hybrid species of rhododendrons, numerous walking trails, and ponds. The flowers are in full bloom in April and May. *Resort Road; 360-678-1912.*

Another attractive walking village is **Langley,** to the south, with galleries, restaurants, an excellent bakery, and small, well-stocked shops. For four days in late August, its **Island County Fair** brings together local agricultural exhibits, a parade, and logger competitions. *819 Camano Avenue; 360-221-4677.*

Fort Casey State Park, on the western shore, preserves army fortifications built in the 1890s. Also here is the 19th-century Admiralty Point Lighthouse. You can explore the grounds and casemates, check out the period cannon, or hike on the bluff, through the woods, or on the long sand-and-cobble beach. Divers flock to the underwater park, on the south side of the Keystone/Port Townsend ferry landing, but because the park's attractions are subtidal, there's not much for the casual visitor to see. The spit separating Crockett Lagoon from Puget Sound offers great hiking and bird-watching. *About 3 miles south of Coupeville; 360-678-4519.*

The **Inn at Langley** (400 First Street; 360-221-3033) is Langley's most elegant and comfortable inn. A concrete-and-wood Frank Lloyd Wright–inspired structure perches on the side of a bluff. If you want to know what Northwest food is all about, the **Country Kitchen**, the Inn at Langley's restaurant, is the place to go. The **Dog House Backdoor Restaurant** (230 First Street; 360-221-9996) is a friendly and relaxed waterfront tavern and family restaurant. Listed on the National Register of Historic Places, the tavern is filled with collectibles including a 1923 nickelodeon.

■ CAMANO ISLAND   *map page 139, A-3*

Camano Island is one of western Washington's best-kept secrets. Even though this island is just a few miles off I-5, and is connected to the mainland by a bridge, it receives far fewer visitors than Whidbey Island to the west. The proximity to the freeway and the Seattle-Everett metropolitan area has brought an influx of suburbanites to Camano in recent years.

Luckily, most of the new construction is near the shore and atop the bluffs above Saratoga Passage (which separates Camano from Whidbey Island), leaving the center of the island relatively undisturbed. While there is a supermarket now (in the north end, near the county offices), islanders shop mostly at a handful of small neighborhood groceries and dine at the island's cafes.

Camano's landscape is rustic, with fields that alternate between pastures and Douglas-fir woods. Farmhouses and weathered barns dot the low, rolling slopes of the island's hills. Island farms raise chickens and dairy cattle as well as more exotic animals like alpacas and llamas.

Unlike its sister island, Camano has no towns—but this was not always the case. Before American loggers arrived on the shores of the Salish Sea, Camano was densely covered with giant Douglas firs. Old-growth logging started in the 1850s near Utsalady ("place of berries") at the northern end of the island. The logging soon involved all of the island's old-growth forests, and was at its most active from about 1895 to 1910.

Island towns like Utsalady, Camano City, and Mabana began as logging camps. They grew into flourishing communities supplied by the steamers that ran up and down the inland waters between Bellingham and Seattle. But the automobile began to make its impact felt: after a swing bridge was built in 1909 to connect Camano to the mainland, "auto resorts" sprung up on the island shore.

APPLE AND CHEESE TOUR

Owing to differences in climate throughout Washington, different types of apples grow east and west of the Cascade Mountains. Most people know about eastern Washington apples but are unaware that western Washington also grows great apples.

Apples and cheese make a great duo, and it's likely that you'll find just the right cheese to enhance the flavor of the locally grown fruit. Start the tour in Whatcom County, north of Ferndale, by taking Grandview from I-5 west to Kickerville and turning left. Pleasant Valley Dairy is on your left.

Pleasant Valley Dairy *map page 155, A-1*
The gouda and farmstead cheeses here are made from raw cow's milk and go well with Whatcom and Skagit County apples. The dairy is open on Saturdays from January through June. *6804 Kickerville Road; 360-366-5398.*

Appel Farms *map page 155, A/B-1*
The Appels make four cheeses: gouda (aged or smoked), quark (German-style sour cream cheese), *paneer* (East Indian fresh cheese), and squeaky cheese (unpressed, unaged cheddar), named for the sound produced when you bite into it. *6605 Northwest Road, off I-5, Ferndale; 360-384-4996.*

Samish Bay Cheese *map page 155, B-4*
Excellent aged gouda made from unpasteurized milk, a montasio, and a delightful Mont Blanchard are made here. A sign on the east side of Chuckanut Drive (south of where the road enters the flats) directs you to the cheese works. Call for hours. *15115 Bow Hill Road, Bow; 360-766-6706.*

Merrit's Apples *map page 155, B-4*
On a clear day, with snowcapped Mount Baker looming in the eastern sky, you are likely to think you've rediscovered the Garden of Eden here. When you bite into one of the Gravenstein or Jonagold apples, you'll know you have. *896 Bayview-Edison Road, Bow; 360-766-6224.*

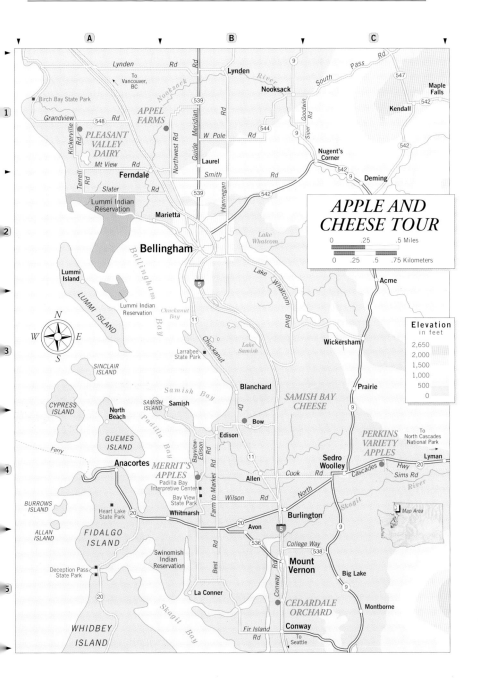

APPLE AND CHEESE TOUR

0   .25   .5 Miles

0   .25   .5   .75 Kilometers

Elevation
in feet
2,650
2,000
1,500
1,000
500
0

Cedardale Orchard *map page 155, B-5*

If you're in a hurry, skip the northern leg of this tour and stock up on westside apples at Cedardale Orchard, where you'll find the diverse flavors of Akane, Gala, Jonagold, Jonamac, Melrose, and Summered. *South Mount Vernon Exit, off I-5 on Conrad Road; 360-445-5483.*

Continue the tour by taking Route 20, the North Cascades Highway, east from Burlington across the mountains.

Perkins Variety Apples *map page 155, C-4*

Your next chance to stock up on apples comes on Route 20, the North Cascades Highway, 3 miles east of Sedro Woolley, at Perkins Variety Apples. More than 100 varieties of apples are grown here, including Akane, Jonamac, and Melrose. Lay in a good supply. There are no more orchards until you reach the valleys on the far side of the mountains. *816 Sims Road; 360-856-6986.*

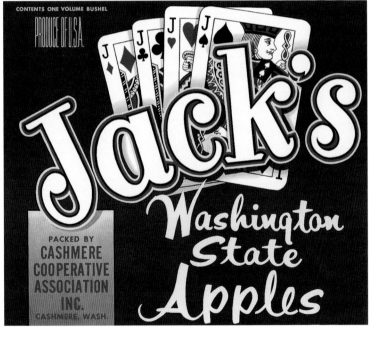

Apple crate art.

Golden delicious apples are the ideal storage apple and the perfect accompaniment to cheese and dessert wines.

The logging towns declined in the 1920s and all but vanished after the trees ran out, but the resort towns flourished until World War II. For a while it seemed that every low-bank waterfront had its resort, with cabins and boats to rent. Tourists hired row boats or boats with outboard engines to fish for salmon, cod, or rockfish in the protected waters of Saratoga Passage. After World War II, when trailer boats became popular, boaters ventured farther and farther afield, and the Camano Island resorts declined. One of these resorts, **Cama Beach**, was acquired by the state in 1998, with its surviving cabins and boats, and will be opened as a state park "sometime after 2002."

Cama Beach is just north of **Camano Island State Park**, a 134-acre camping park with 6,700 feet of rocky shoreline and beach. The park provides sweeping views of the surrounding mountains and has a limited clam-digging season (usually in spring), plus breathtaking views of Puget Sound and the Olympic Mountains across Saratoga Passage. The park is located 14 miles southwest of Stanwood. Take Exit 212 from I-5 and travel west on Route 532 for 7 miles. Cross the Mark Clark Bridge and you've arrived. *2269 Lowell Point Road; 360-387-3031.*

In 1949, with the property in hand, the Camano Island Grange requested that the Parks Commission develop the area as a state park. Finally, the Commission was able to allot $5,000 to the development project. The dollars were granted to create the park, if the local community would furnish a workforce of about 500 volunteers. A "Camano Island Park Day" was scheduled and some 900 Camano Islanders responded with excitement.

The Parks Commission surveyed the area and provided some skilled workers. By the end of the day, the park was finished. Picnic areas were set up, complete with picnic tables; a natural spring was cleaned and then tiled; roads and a parking area were built; and a scenic trail was cleared. The park had become usable and it has been popular ever since.

Be sure to stop at the island information center, **Camano Gateway**, as you first come onto the island for updates on Camano's parks and recreation sites, local businesses, and other interesting facts about the island. The center also serves as a showcase for island artists, and the staff will gladly direct you to local studios and galleries. The park has two boat ramps and watercraft launch permits are available for $4. For information about locations where permits may be purchased, call the boating office of the state park at 360-902-8608. This is a first-come, first-served park. No picnic area or campsite reservations are taken.

There are other sites worth visiting on Camano Island. **Utsalady Bay** was once the busiest port in Puget Sound, and still shows traces of its lumber and sawmill past. Today, it is a peaceful retreat, with views of Whidbey Island, the Skagit River delta and its flocks of migratory birds, and snowcapped Mount Baker and the North Cascade Mountain range. A small county park has picnic tables and a free boat launch.

Triangle Cove is a remarkably peaceful, secluded lagoon with a variety of bird and marine life. **Cavelero Beach** is a small county park in an east shore cove beneath tall bluffs, with beach access, a boat launch, and views of the sheltered waters of Port Susan and the North Cascades beyond. The **Stillaguamish Delta** and **Livingston Bay** have extensive tide flats that attract flocks of snow geese, as well as blue herons, marsh hawks, and shorebirds.

■ BELLINGHAM   *map page 139, A-1*

The last big town south of the Canadian border is Bellingham, whose commercial core has fallen on hard times since a mall opened north of town. Cobbled together from four pioneer communities in 1903, Bellingham is mostly a fishing port, but it's also home to **Western Washington University,** whose campus rests high on Sehome Hill. From the freeway, all you see of Bellingham is a strip mall, but downtown you'll find the elegant **Mount Baker Theater** (104 North Commercial Street) and the **Whatcom Museum of History and Art** (121 Prospect Street; 360-676-6981), a late-19th-century brick affair north of Champion Street. The collection here includes Native American artifacts, exhibits on pioneering and logging, and Northwest contemporary art. The museum faces Bellingham Bay from its perch atop a steep bluff.

Fairhaven

Fairhaven's downtown is filled with coffee shops, bookstores, and restaurants. Farther afield of downtown, you'll find cottages and gardens, green woods bordering a purling creek, wildflower meadows, and, along the bayfront, sandstone cliffs, tide flats, and fishing boats. The ferry to Alaska docks here, at the former site of one of the world's largest salmon canneries. In summer, passenger ferries carry visitors to the San Juan Islands and Victoria on Vancouver Island.

Ancient shell middens and stone tools, many of them thousands of years old, are proof that the mouth of Fairhaven's Padden Creek has long been occupied by humans. The Lummi Nation once had a fishing village here, and there are legends of a fierce battle between the local tribes and Spanish pirates in Padden Marsh in the 1600s. There is no historic proof of the battle, but pioneers recorded their discovery of a Spanish chalice, dated 1640, embedded in a muddy bank.

Few historic remains of the 19th-century waterfront survive, but a local historical society has put down plaques throughout the village, marking such sites as the city's drowning pool (for dogs only, it says, where the local constable killed stray pets); the shore where Fairhaven moored its prison (a barge); the site of the town pillory (Fairhaven had one as late as the 1890s); and the place where a saloon owner died in a gun battle.

Fairhaven residents are a motley lot of fishermen, college professors, poets, ship-fitters, painters, and the sons and daughters of hippies who settled here in the 1960s. They're a friendly bunch, meeting at the **Colophon Cafe** (1208 11th Street) for breakfast or a bowl of African peanut soup; sipping coffee at **Tony's Coffee House** (Harris Avenue and 11th Street); or browsing the shelves of **Village Books** (1210 11th Street). Come evening, folks crowd into **Stanello's** (1514 12th Street) for the best pizza in town, or congregate at Post Point to watch the red sun sink behind the San Juan Islands.

To reach Fairhaven, take Old Fairhaven Parkway off I-5 and head west toward the water. Turn right on 12th Street and then left on Harris Street.

■ CHUCKANUT DRIVE   *map pages 139, A-1/2, and 155, A/B-3*

Route 11, also known as Chuckanut Drive, got its start early in the 20th century as the first highway heading south from Bellingham, Fairhaven, and Skagit County (before the road was built, people moved by steamer or railroad). For a dozen miles, this narrow, 23-mile road, winds above Chuckanut Bay and Samish Bay. The steep and heavily wooded Chuckanut and Blanchard Mountains limit the roadway to a narrow passage that moves along sandstone cliffs and turnouts in the road, framing magical views across the water to the San Juan Islands.

The drive begins in Fairhaven, and after skirting the mountains and traversing the flat farmlands of the Samish Valley near Bow, joins up with I-5 at Burlington. Along the way, you'll pass **Larrabee State Park** at the foot of Chuckanut Mountain. The mountain has been logged assiduously, but there are still areas of virtual wilderness. At Larrabee are miles of trails leading through fir and maple forests to lakes and cliff-top lookouts offering dramatic views. There are sandy beaches

Live music on a summer's weekend in Bellingham's Fairhaven district.

warm enough for summer sunning, a rocky shore with tide pools, and headlands occasionally graced by passing gray whales and orcas. Picnic and campgrounds are available, and there is a small boat ramp perfect for kayaks. Crabbing and bird-watching opportunities abound. *245 Chuckanut Drive; 360-676-2093.*

At the southern end of Chuckanut Drive lies **Bow**, just east of Samish Bay, where oysters and clams are farmed on the tidelands. Bow is not a "town" in the traditional sense, not even a hamlet, but consists of a post office, a couple of shops at a crossroads, and a few widely spaced houses and barns.

Lower Chuckanut Drive has two classic regional restaurants. The **Chuckanut Manor** (302 Chuckanut Drive; 360-766-6191) is a former residence with an old-fashioned, glassed-in dining room and bar overlooking Samish Bay and several San Juan Islands. The restaurant serves traditional American-Continental fare with an emphasis on steak and fried seafood. Diners can not only watch shorebirds and seabirds out on Samish Bay, but there are bird feeders right outside the windows. The **Oyster Bar** (240 Chuckanut Drive; 360-766-6185), to the north, is poised above the shore on a steep, wooded bluff with perhaps the best marine view of any Washington restaurant.

■ NOOKSACK VALLEY AND MOUNT BAKER *map page 139, B-1*

From Bellingham, Route 542 takes you east to 10,778-foot Mount Baker and the trails of the northernmost and wildest parts of North Cascades National Park.

As you get beyond Glacier, the steep cliffs rise higher and higher, the trees become taller, and the boulders in the north fork of the Nooksack River become bigger. A few miles south on twisting Glacier Creek Road, you will encounter the trailhead for **Coleman Glacier.**

A short path leads to the glacier's snout, where ice pushes into the alders; a longer, steeper hike brings you to the glacier's side, where you can peer down into the crevasses and listen to the ice as it grinds downhill. The scenery looks like it was snatched from an Alaska tourism brochure. Take a close look at the edges, where the ice meets the land. In midsummer, pink and white wildflowers cover this fertile verge.

The next stop is Nooksack Falls, reached by a short gravel road. Notice the nearly impenetrable tangle of trees, shrubs, ferns, and deep mosses as you head down the slope. This is a typical western Washington forest. Water from this tree-girded falls plunges over a rocky ledge 170 feet into a narrow canyon, and a nearby grove of cedars is thousands of years old. If you're driving to Mount Baker in August or September, you'll see high-bush huckleberries by the road. The shrubs are chest-high and have light-green leaves and blue-black berries. (Check with someone knowledgeable before you eat berries you pick.)

Picture Lake, one of the most photographed spots in the entire state of Washington, is near the end of the road, high up on the eastern slope of Mount Baker. The lake has some great picnic areas along its shores. Dramatic 9,038-foot **Mount Shuksan** looms across the valley. The blueberries here grow on low bushes, but they're worth every stoop you make to pick them. They ripen from August until late fall.

If the snow has melted, you can drive to the end of the road, past the ski lodge, and hike along alpine ridges for good views of both Mount Baker and the glacier-cut valley of Baker Creek.

Mount Baker itself attracts rock climbers in spring and summer and downhill and cross-country skiers in winter, and many hiking trails lace the 117,528-acre Mount Baker Wilderness Area. The mountain, which is volcanic, spouted smoke as recently as 1975. The precipitation on the upper elevations can be as much as 150 inches per year; snow accumulation has been known to top 18 feet.

■ TRAVEL AND CLIMATE

■ GETTING THERE AND AROUND

By Ferry

A car ferry crossing from Mukilteo, just south of Everett, takes you to the southern end of Whidbey Island. This crossing affords some spectacular views of the snow-covered Cascade and Olympic Mountains. A two-lane highway running north along the island's spine takes you to the Keystone ferry landing. The landing can also be reached from Mount Vernon via Route 20. From here you can catch a ferry to Port Townsend, Anacortes, or the San Juan Islands, and eventually back to the interstate highway (I-5).

North of Bellingham, narrow, two-lane Route 542 winds its way through the Cascade foothills into the chasm of the Nooksack River's north fork and up the slopes of Mount Baker.

By Car

The traffic artery of this region, I-5, has its scenic spots north of the Seattle suburbs and Everett. Green fields, pastures, and woods stretch from the freeway to the foothills of the snow-covered Cascade Mountains to the east and the waters of Puget Sound to the west. The blue peaks rising above the water are the mountainous San Juan Islands. On clear days, the massive snow cone of Mount Baker rises above the lesser mountains at its base.

From the Skagit Valley, you can look upriver into the heart of the northern Cascades. North of the valley, the freeway runs through rugged mountains and passes Lake Samish before it descends to Bellingham and the Nooksack River lowlands.

An even more scenic freeway, I-90, crosses the Cascades on Snoqualmie Pass. Narrow, winding U.S. 2 takes travelers east via 4,061-foot Stevens Pass. Route 20, the slowest but most scenic of the highways (closed every winter because of deep snow and avalanche danger), crosses 5,477-foot Washington Pass.

■ CLIMATE

Weather here is usually wet in spring and fall, and sunny and warm in summer, though on the average about 10 degrees F cooler than Seattle. Winters are generally mild, but on the uncommon occasions when the northeasters blowing down the Fraser River canyon turn south, the air can chill down in a hurry (while Lake Washington rarely freezes over, Lake Whatcom occasionally does).

S E A T T L E

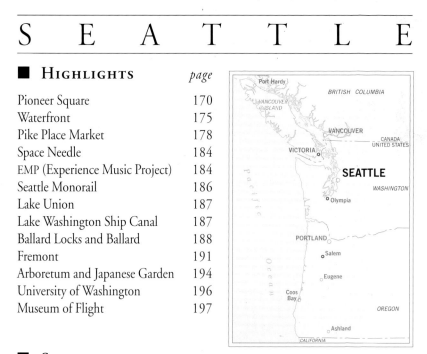

■ Setting

SEATTLE SITS AMONG saltwater bays, lakes, and forested mountains. To the west, the waters of Puget Sound lap up against piers and beaches, and to the east, Lake Washington delineates the city. On most days, you can see craggy, snow-covered peaks across the Sound from downtown, as well as the snow cone of 14,411-foot Mount Rainier to the south; on a clear day you can see 10,750-foot Mount Baker to the north. The high-rise office and apartment buildings of the downtown business district rival the city's hills in height and on most days can be seen far up and down Puget Sound.

The pioneer founders of Seattle envisioned a city to rival the world's greatest (they originally named it New York), but locals think of their metropolis as a collection of urban villages, each with a unique personality. Much of this has to do with the way Seattle is spread out over several hills and valleys, and split into sections by the Lake Washington Ship Canal, Lake Union, Green Lake, the Duwamish River, and I-5.

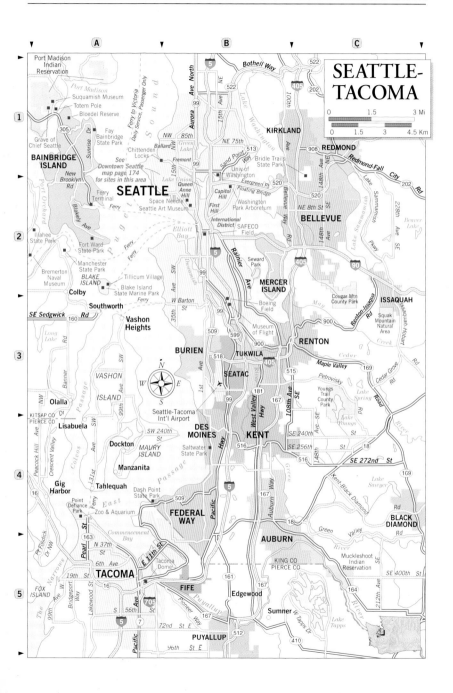

SEATTLE-TACOMA

0   1.5   3 Mi
0   1.5   3   4.5 Km

On many days, the city is shrouded in mist. Its glass-and-steel monoliths are swathed in fog, and seagulls drift like ghosts between the downtown office towers. The lugubrious "wail-honk" of a ferry horn sounds somewhere beyond the shrouded waterfront as clean-cut citizens in Eddie Bauer raincoats clutch briefcases and lattes and wait for traffic lights to change.

When the sun comes out, though, sidewalk cafes on the piers and picnic tables on the decks of Waterfront Park fill up with Seattleites who abandon their workday schedules with the speed of a sunburst. Sunlight brings out uncommon levity in the residents of the gray city by the Sound. On one sunny afternoon, I watched a staid-looking businessman in a three-piece suit, briefcase in hand, raincoat draped over his left arm, stride into the Waterfall Fountain downtown and emerge on the far side slightly moistened, with a smile.

Once you get to know Seattle, you'll learn that it hardly ever rains in summer, never mind how much residents moan and groan about the constant overcast. But perhaps Seattleites need the specter of rain to justify the energy they radiate. They never sit still for long and are always up to something, whether it's walking, running, sailing the Sound, or hiking in the mountains.

Maybe it's the Scandinavian work ethic that Norwegian, Swedish, Finnish, and Icelandic immigrants brought to this area early in the 20th century. Along with that energy and industry came a lighthearted, self-mocking humor. A favorite old folk song, "The Old Settler," goes:

> No longer a slave of ambition,
> I laugh at the world and its shams,
> As I think of my happy condition
> Surrounded by acres of clams.

■ AMBITIOUS BEGINNINGS

The first settlers to establish themselves in Seattle, in 1851, were a party of Americans from the Midwest under the leadership of Arthur Denny. Though Denny never said in his autobiography what made him pull up stakes, he did admit that he wanted to find a place where he would be the first to put down roots and make a killing in real estate. When his party reached Portland, Oregon, Denny was dismayed to find a booming town of 2,000 people. He had come too late. That's when he heard about an unsettled place called Puget Sound.

The Dennys joined forces with another pioneer family, the Terrys, who hailed from New York, and together they established their new town on a sandy spit just south of Elliott Bay. They called it New York. It soon gained the epithet *Alki,* a Chinook jargon word meaning "by and by," a name the site has kept to this day. The Dennys and Terrys soon discovered that in bad weather, or at low tide, the exposed sloping beach of their site was a poor place from which to load ships. But load they did, as the town's emerging income came from lumber sold to ship captains who sailed north from another enterprising place on the coast, San Francisco.

■ SEATTLE RELOCATED

Reluctantly, the settlers picked up their belongings and moved across Elliott Bay, a less desirable place, but one where ships could sail right up to the shore. They built houses here, on steep, overgrown hillsides. It was a wet place, cut by deep ravines. Springs flowed down from the bluffs and water, seemingly everywhere, dripped from the moss-covered trees. But the trees were soon cut down. Early pictures of Seattle show mostly stumps, not trees, between the cabins. The tree cutting accelerated when Henry Yesler built a sawmill, making timber-cutting the

Yesler Way, the original "Skid Road," so called because of the log skids placed in the street to enable timber to be moved easily to the docks. Pioneer Square now exists where the flagpole appears in this photo. (Museum of History and Industry)

new city's main industry. Yesler used rocks carried as ballast on inbound ships to build a wharf hundreds of feet out into the bay, so the largest ships could unload on any tide. A handsome plaque near Colman Dock marks the site of that first wharf.

Yesler's dock was also the landing place for the early steamboats that plied the waters of Puget Sound. One amusing anecdote tells of a group of legislators bound for Olympia on the *Eliza Anderson*. Wakened one morning by what they thought was the steamer's whistle, they stumbled down to the wharf on a dark, rainy morning and headed straight for the open door of a boiler room that promised warmth. But the "ship" didn't appear to move from the dock. Checking his watch and noting that it was well past sailing time, one of the legislators tapped the fireman on the back and asked, "May I ask when we are going to pull out for Olympia?"

"Olympia?" replied the fireman. "This sawmill don't run to Olympia." The legislators had mistaken the mill's boiler room for that of the steamer. By now, the *Eliza Anderson* had left, and the lawmakers had to return to the provincial capital by canoe.

The regrading of James Street allowed for the construction of the cable car system. (Museum of History and Industry)

■ ON TO THE KLONDIKE

A little over a century ago, Seattle became the point of departure for prospectors heading to Alaska and the Yukon during the Klondike gold rush. The excitement started one day in 1897 with the arrival of the ship *Portland,* which happily unloaded its "ton of gold" near Colman Dock. Seattle's mayor at the time, W. D. Wood, as enthusiastic as everyone else at the thought of getting rich, immediately deserted his post to join a shipload of eager-beavers going north.

Colman and other area docks served as the headquarters of the Mosquito Fleet, the flotilla of boats that ferried passengers and freight around Puget Sound from the mid-19th century through World War II, making Seattle the hub of local trade. Vestiges of these docks—double rows of gray pilings—still march two by two into deep water at spots where steamboats used to call.

■ COLORFUL CHARACTERS

Early Seattle was a bit rough around the edges, a place of unlimited optimism, despite streets that sometimes became so muddy that horses and wagons might get stuck in them. When the Northern Pacific Railway snubbed Seattle in favor of Tacoma, denizens decided to build a railroad of their own. They didn't get far, but they did scare the railroad moguls into connecting Seattle to the main line.

The town's early population was lively, to say the least. Native American women sold butter clams on the sidewalks of the business district, and saloons boomed, especially in the Lava Bed—the bustling red-light district south of Yesler's mill. One of early Seattle's more colorful characters was David "Doc" Maynard, who moved to Seattle after he was kicked out of more sedate Olympia. Maynard had married a widow he met on the Oregon Trail, without first getting a divorce from the wife he had left behind in Ohio. Things became tense when his first wife sailed into port, but the two supposedly settled matters amicably, and Maynard continued to live with wife number two.

Maynard was known as a man who always helped folks in need. He had filed a homestead claim on what is now downtown Seattle but died a poor man because he sold most of his land below its value, and in some cases even gave it away, to help the budding city grow. Nard Jones reported in his book on Seattle that Maynard was given the largest funeral in the city's history when he died in 1873, and adds, "An unidentified citizen, whether friend or enemy is not known, stood up to say, 'Without Doc Maynard...Seattle would never have reached its present size.

Perhaps, had it not been for Doctor Maynard, Seattle might not be here now.'"

One reason Maynard did not get along with civic-minded teetotalers like Henry Yesler and Arthur Denny is that he drank too much. In *Totem Tales of Old Seattle,* Gordon Newell and Don Sherwood record an argument Maynard had with Denny when the latter asked him to attend a temperance lecture at Yesler's hall. "'Temperance!" Doc roared. "That's the only thing I believe in taking in moderation. In fact I'm a total abstainer."

Early Seattle may have had more citizens of the Maynard ilk than of the Denny and Yesler kind, because vice prospered well into the early decades of the 20th century, despite repeated civic campaigns to stamp it out.

By the late 1800s, most of Seattle's 40,000 inhabitants lived and worked in the 50-plus blocks of one- and two-story clapboard buildings that comprised downtown. The big fire of 1889 had burned most of Seattle's waterfront business district but spared residents on the hill. The gutsy citizenry didn't sit around Yesler's cookhouse complaining, however. Instead, they erected a new downtown, of brick, and elevated the streets a full story above their previous level to solve the city's chronic sewage problem. Elevating the streets meant that many ground-floor storefronts were now belowground, thus creating Underground Seattle.

■ PIONEER SQUARE   *map page 174, C-4*

The city's original 19th-century center was Pioneer Square. This name applies both to the triangular cobblestone park on First Avenue, where James Street meets Yesler Way, and to the ornate brick and stone buildings at the south end of downtown. The triangular square itself marks the site where Henry Yesler built the first steam-driven sawmill on the shore of Elliott Bay. First Avenue, then called Front Street, was the waterfront in those days, and logs cut on the forested ridge above town were skidded down what is now Yesler Way to the mill, where they were sawed into boards that built the embryonic city of Seattle.

Yesler Way was the original Skid Road, a label that most of the country has since corrupted to "skid row." The street got its name because logs were skidded down it but also because it marked the boundary between the city's business district and the Lava Bed red-light district to the south (called the Tenderloin after the fire, and now known as the Pioneer Square district).

The well-preserved facades of the buildings in Pioneer Square lend historical continuity to an area packed with art galleries, bookstores, and missions serving

Victorian-era buildings behind the Pioneer Square totem pole, a replica of one stolen by early Seattleites from the Tlingit Indians.

the needy. For a taste of local color, sign up for the **Underground Seattle tour,** which starts at Doc Maynard's Public House at First Avenue and James Street, across from Pioneer Square. This restored pub with its carved back bar gives you a feel for what Seattle was like in the early days; the rock bands that perform here on Friday and Saturday nights put you in touch with what's happening in Seattle now. On sunny days, you can sit at one of the tables outside and watch Pioneer Square's highlife and lowlife flow by (expect to be panhandled; it's a time-honored Seattle custom). *Underground tour, 608 First Avenue; pub, 610 First Avenue; 206-682-4646 for tour and pub.*

The **totem pole** in Pioneer Square is a replica of one that was spirited away from a "deserted" Tlingit village by a "goodwill committee" of prominent Seattle citizens in 1899. When the Tlingits learned where their missing pole had gone, they demanded and received payment for their purloined property. The pole's figures relate several Tlingit tales, including one about a raven and a mink that go to sea in the belly of a killer whale.

Microbrewery pub in Pioneer Square.

For a peek at Seattle's role in the gold rush of 1897, see the exhibits at the city's outpost of the **Klondike Gold Rush National Historic Park**. *Union Trust Annex, 117 South Main Street; 206-553-7220.*

At the **Waterfall Garden** (South Main Street and Second Avenue South), an enclosed courtyard, the soothing sound of a tall waterfall shuts out the noise of the city. Tables and chairs placed near the water are usually packed at lunchtime with workers from nearby offices. A few blocks to the south are two stadiums, the high-tech home of the Seattle Seahawks pro football team, and Safeco Field, where major league baseball's Seattle Mariners play.

■ **INTERNATIONAL DISTRICT**   *map page 174, C/D-4*

Inland from the stadiums, the International District holds the city's largest concentration of Asian restaurants, food stores, and social services. Many of the area's first residents were Chinese, and their descendants have largely moved on, though some older Chinese have remained to run shops and other concerns that have been in Seattle for generations. In recent decades, people from many Asian lands, most notably Vietnam, have settled here.

The exhibits at the **Wing Luke Museum** document the lives of Asian immigrants to the Pacific Northwest. The collection includes costumes, crafts, photographs, and Chinese medicines. *407 Seventh Avenue South; 206-623-5124.*

The pan-Asian **Uwajimaya** department store sells groceries and sake, kitchenwares, garden tools, and Japanese fabrics, papers, and objets d'art. Also here are a food court and a branch of the Kinokuniya Bookstore, which specializes in Asian-language texts and periodicals. *600 Fifth Avenue South; 206-624-6248.*

■ **DOWNTOWN AND THE WATERFRONT** *map page 174, C/D-4*

From downtown hotels, it is only a short walk into the central business district. The 42-story **Smith Tower** (506 Second Avenue) was the tallest building west of the Mississippi River when completed in 1914, and it remained the tallest building in Seattle for 55 years.

High-rises dwarf the Smith Tower these days, the result of an office-building boom in the 1980s that transformed the look and feel of downtown Seattle. The

Smith Tower under construction behind the Grand Trunk Pier, where Puget Sound ferries, known as the Mosquito Fleet, docked. (Puget Sound Maritime Historical Society)

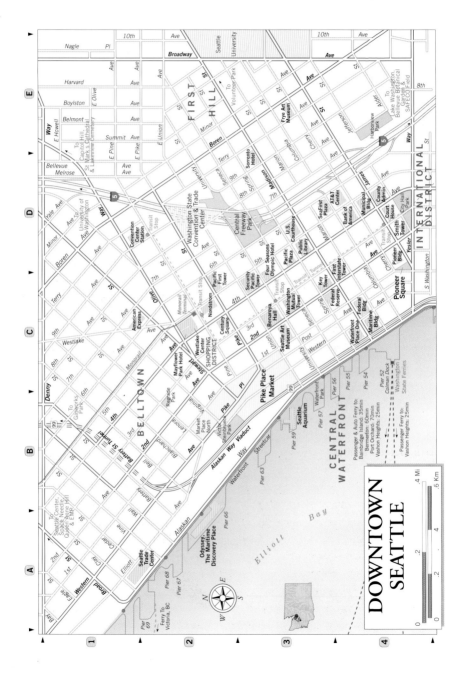

DOWNTOWN SEATTLE

city's skyline stretches north and northwest from the Smith Tower and includes another noteworthy high-rise, the 76-story **Bank of America Tower** (701 Fifth Avenue). At 997 feet, it is Seattle's tallest skyscraper. The skyline's most distinctive element, north of downtown, is the **Space Needle** (400 Broad Street).

The Waterfront *page 174, B-3/4*

Although it is no longer Seattle's economic focal point, the downtown waterfront area remains vital to the city's character. Many old piers have been transformed into shops, museums, restaurants, and amusements. **Harbor tours** depart from **Pier 55** weekdays and **Pier 57** on weekends, providing passengers with great views of the city skyline, the docks of Harbor Island, and the Ship Canal, a narrow waterway cutting a gorge from Shilshole Bay to Lake Union and Lake Washington. Some tour boats traverse the Ballard Locks, the world's second largest after those of the Panama Canal.

Many visitors stroll the mile and a half north to **Pier 70,** now a commercial complex, detouring over the harbor on the boardwalks and fishing piers of Waterfront Park, and returning on a 1927 streetcar.

On Pier 59, children can get a sense of life beneath Puget Sound in the underwater dome of the **Seattle Aquarium** (206-386-4320), or see a film at the **IMAX Theater** (206-622-1868). A short walk south of Pier 59 along First Avenue to the corner of University Street takes you to the **Seattle Art Museum,** designed in a flashy postmodern style by Robert Venturi. The grand entrance hall to the five-story structure is connected to state-of-the-art galleries by an approach that makes you think you've wandered through the service entrance. The museum's extensive collection surveys Asian, Native American, African, Oceanic, and pre-Columbian art. Highlights include the anonymous 14th-century Buddhist masterwork *Monk at the Moment of Enlightenment* and Jackson Pollock's *Sea Change.*

Outside the museum you'll see the tall perpetual-motion sculpture *Hammering Man,* by Connecticut sculptor Jonathan Borofsky. The piece has had its share of adventures. When first installed, the huge steel form toppled over—fortunately not flattening any workers or pedestrians, but doing enough damage so that the sculpture had to be shipped back to Connecticut for repairs. After it was installed a second time, a group of local artists, working under cover of darkness, fastened a huge ball and chain to one leg. Some people liked the idea, but the museum promptly removed the fetters. *100 University Street; 206-654-3100.*

DAY TRIPS BY FERRY

Puget Sound ferries are Washington State's number-one tourist attraction. On several, you can travel as a passenger or bring your car; other ferries are passenger-only. Avoid rush-hour traffic: eastbound in the morning, westbound in the afternoon and evening. A high-speed passenger-only catamaran also runs from Seattle to the San Juan Islands and to Victoria, on Vancouver Island. *Washington State Ferries, 206-464-6400, outside Washington and British Columbia; 888-808-7977 in Washington and British Columbia; www.wsdot.wa.gov/ferries*

Seattle to Bainbridge Island. The Puget Sound crossing to Bainbridge Island is popular. The big boat drops you off in Eagle Harbor, in the heart of **Winslow,** a former logging town turned suburb. The Winslow waterfront is made for walking. Pick up the fixings for a picnic at Seattle's Pike Place Market and picnic right off the ferry at **Waterfront Park.**

After lunch, walk to **Bainbridge Island Vineyards and Winery**, where Gerard Bentryn sells wines made from local grapes and strawberries. *682 State Highway; 206-842-9463.*

You can also sample the food at one of the waterfront cafes, among them **Pegasus Coffee,** at the foot of Madison Avenue, and **Bainbridge Bakers,** at Winslow Green. For trips into the interior of Bainbridge Island, or to do a loop trip and return to Seattle via Bremerton (or via the Kingston/Edmonds ferry), you'll need a car.

Seattle to Bremerton. You'll enjoy this trip if you're a navy buff, as Bremerton has one of the country's largest naval bases and shipyards. The **Bremerton Naval Museum,** near the ferry terminal, has displays going back to the days of the sailing navy. The USS *Turner Joy,* docked nearby, saw action off Vietnam and played a role in the Gulf of Tonkin affair; it's open for self-guided tours. *130 Washington Avenue; 360-479-7447.*

You can take a boat tour of the **Navy Shipyard** and a mothballed fleet through Kitsap Harbor Tours. Boats depart hourly from the boardwalk on the waterfront. *360-377-8924.*

Bremerton's waterfront has several restaurants and bars, the most notable being the **Boat Shed** on Shore Drive. You'll need a car to take a loop trip back to Seattle via the Bainbridge Island ferry. The **Naval Undersea Museum,** in nearby Keyport, has the country's largest collection of undersea artifacts, mines, and torpedoes; displays on the ocean environment; and an antique submarine. *Highway 3, Keyport; 360-396-4148.*

The **Marine Science Center,** in Poulsbo, has touch tanks for kids and a giant octopus. *18743 Front Street; 360-779-5549.*

Other Puget Sound Ferries. Additional ferries travel from Fauntleroy Cove in West Seattle to Vashon Island, from Edmonds (north of Seattle) to Kingston on the northern Kitsap Peninsula, and from Mukilteo in Snohomish County (south of Everett) to Whidbey Island. The passenger-only *Flyer* makes daily runs from Everett to Friday Harbor on San Juan Island. *800-325-6722.*

Seattle to Victoria, B.C. (Canada). The *Victoria Clipper* runs from the Seattle waterfront to Victoria, British Columbia, and to Friday Harbor and Rosario on San Juan Island. *206-448-5000.*

A ferry crosses Puget Sound as the sun sets over the Olympic Mountains.

Benaroya Hall is the concert facility Seattle Symphony Music Director Gerard Schwarz built, or, rather, the one he got as a reward for staying in Seattle after gaining international fame (he cofounded the New York Chamber Symphony and recently became music director of the Royal Liverpool Philharmonic Orchestra). The hall, completed in 1998, takes up the entire block across Second Avenue from the Seattle Art Museum. *200 University Street; 206-215-4747.*

■ PIKE PLACE MARKET *page 174, B/C-3*

Pike Place Market, which perches above the waterfront, is a riot of color. Fish stalls gleam with silver-scaled salmon and red rockfish, pearly squid, and orange Dungeness crab, bright red shrimp, and blue-black mussels. Produce stalls are piled high with red and green apples, golden pears, crimson cherries, purple plums, orange chanterelles, cream-colored oyster mushrooms, and brown morels and shiitakes. It's a hectic scene, but fun. Fishmongers hurl huge salmon back and forth, joking

Pike Place Market in 1915.
(Museum of History and
Industry)

Pike Place Market remains the best place to buy fresh fruit, vegetables, and seafood in the city.

with each other and their customers, who jostle with tourists. The market is one place where you'll see few people without a smile. The mood here is invigorating, but it can also be exhausting. Relax and take it easy. Treat yourself to a cup of coffee or a glass of wine, grab a window seat at a cafe or restaurant, and watch the freighter and shipping boats far below in Elliott Bay. Or buy picnic fixings, head down to Waterfront Park, snag a table, and enjoy an alfresco meal.

In season, you'll find fresh strawberries, raspberries, blueberries, melons, apricots, peaches, nectarines, and quinces. Cheese shops stock a sophisticated hodgepodge of cheeses, and butchers sell some of the city's best racks of lamb, steaks, and sausages. Bakeries specialize in tantalizing French, Greek, and Chinese pastries, and restaurants serve everything from plain sandwiches, spaghetti and meatballs, and dim sum to fresh fish cooked and sauced to perfection.

The market began back in 1907, when Seattle's civic leaders and businessmen, influenced by socialist ideas, started to think up ways to eliminate the middleman. In 1970, the city caught the nationwide redevelopment virus that replaced beat-up but picturesque old downtowns with Brutalist concrete structures. It looked as if

(following pages) Downtown Seattle skyline and Elliott Bay.

HOMES AWAY FROM HOME

Seattle has its share of fine homes, cute cottages, and elegant apartment buildings, stylish architectural testaments to the rainy city's endearing way with hearth and home. But the city also has many fine hotels that carefully balance coziness and cosmopolitan panache.

The **Four Seasons Olympic Hotel** (411 University Street; 206-621-1700 or 800-223-8772) has been the classiest place in town since it opened in 1929. The elaborate lobby is worth a special visit (and perhaps a drink).

The **Mayflower Park Hotel** (405 Olive Way; 206-623-8700 or 800-426-5100) isn't much to look at from the outside, but it has a handsomely appointed lobby and Seattle's most urbane bar, Oliver's, whose tall windows overlook one of the city's busiest intersections. Oliver's is a perfect place to wait out Seattle's notoriously bad rush hour over one of the best martinis in town.

The boutique **Sorrento Hotel** (900 Madison Street; 206-622-6400 or 800-426-1265) occupies a 1908 Italianate building on First Hill. The ornate lobby is a fine setting for a warming drink on a rainy day. The hotel uses the top floor dining room for private functions, but the antique elevator to it is worth a look.

the market's days were numbered. Demolition plans were derailed, however, by a local architecture professor, Victor Steinbrueck (he is memorialized by a grassy park at the market's north end), who spearheaded a grassroots campaign.

A series of ramps leads to the Hillclimb, a broad stairway flanked by shops and restaurants that extends from the cliff on which the market rests down to the waterfront. Beneath the arcade, the "down under" section of the market descends several stories to Western Avenue, where shops selling inexpensive imported olive oil, exotic spices, folk art—even parrots—can be found. The Main Arcade and the open-air vendors' stalls on the east side of Pike Place are the central arteries of the market. At the Main Arcade's north end, you'll find silver bracelets, pottery, carved wooden bowls, and other handmade objects.

Many shops have been here almost from the beginning. **Three Girls Bakery,** founded in 1912, sells wonderful breads and pastries. **De Laurenti Specialty Foods Market,** which opened in 1928, is a classic Italian deli with a great selection of olive oils, wines, and cheeses.

■ REGRADE AND BELLTOWN   *page 174, B/C-1/2*

The streets north of Pike Place Market run almost level to Seattle Center and steep Queen Anne Hill. The Regrade hasn't always been so flat. At the dawn of the 20th century, the rounded cone of Denny Hill rose 140 feet above what is today the more level neighborhood of Belltown. The missing hill is a non-monument to city engineer Reginald Thomson, who wanted Seattle's downtown to stretch to the base of Queen Anne Hill, the result being one continuous business district. And, darn it, Denny Hill was in the way. Determined to flatten things, Thomson and his workmen, between 1902 and 1930, sluiced Denny Hill into Elliott Bay.

Today's Belltown, bounded by Queen Anne Hill, Pike Place Market, and First and Third Avenues, is worth checking out for its mix of neo-grunge attitude and bohemian chic. To get a feel for the neighborhood, check out Second Avenue near Bell Street, where you'll find clothing stores, furniture shops, florists, antiques dealers, art galleries, bookstores, and several impressively stocked music stores.

A few property owners fought against the Regrade, with the result that their properties were left atop sluiced-away pinnacles. (Washington State Historical Society)

Towering over Seattle Center is the **Space Needle,** the trademark structure built for the 1962 World's Fair, an event that drew John F. Kennedy and Elvis Presley. According to the "Official 1962 World's Fair Guide," the Space Needle is 606 feet tall. Its legs are 500 feet high, which puts the restaurant on its top at just above 500 feet and the observation deck a bit higher. There is an admission charge for the observation deck, but you ride free if you have a reservation for the restaurant. The top rests on a turntable mounted on a pair of twin rails and revolves 360 degrees once every hour. There are two high-speed elevators, but in case the power goes off, you'll be glad to know you can escape down two stairways—each with 832 steps. The restaurant's food does not match the view. *400 Broad Street, at Fourth Avenue; 206-905-2100.*

Seattle Center, a 74-acre cluster of buildings and gardens, has something for everyone, from plays, operas, and concerts at the **Bagley Wright Theater** (155 Mercer Street; 206-443-2222) to big traveling shows at the exciting **Pacific Science Center** (200 Second Avenue North; 206-443-2001).

The **Seattle Children's Museum** (305 Harrison Street; 206-441-1768) is in the basement of the Center House, and the Fun Forest amusement park has carnival rides. Pro basketball's Seattle SuperSonics play in **Key Arena.** Crowds jam the **Northwest Folklife Festival** (206-684-7300) on Memorial Day weekend and the **Bumbershoot** (206-684-7337) musical extravaganza on Labor Day weekend.

All the buildings within Seattle Center looked pretty much the same until Microsoft billionaire Paul Allen commissioned architect Frank Gehry to design the ultramodern **EMP (Experience Music Project).** A museum of rock 'n' roll and blues, the unusual complex includes a Sky Church concert hall for live performances, a sound lab, exhibition galleries, and a cinema. EMP's permanent collection has more than 80,000 artifacts, including Quincy Jones's trumpet from his Seattle days, a 12-string guitar once owned by Roger McGuinn of the Byrds, and the original Stratocaster guitar used on the Kingsmen's recording of "Louie, Louie." There's also a Jimi Hendrix Gallery showcasing, among other things, the Stratocaster Hendrix played at Woodstock in 1969 and the kimono he wore at the Newport Pop Festival. You don't have to pay museum admission to enjoy the Turntable restaurant, Liquid Lounge bar, or EMP Store. *325 Fifth Avenue North; 206-367-5483.*

The Space Needle, originally built for the 1962 World's Fair,
has become a popular symbol of the city.

■ **SEATTLE MONORAIL** *page 174, B/C-1/2*

The Seattle Monorail whisks two million passengers each year between Seattle Center and the **Westlake Center** (1601 Fifth Avenue; 206-467-1600), a mall with several dozen stores and many restaurants. The 0.9-mile ride takes about 90 seconds. The monorail was built as a demonstration project for the 1962 Seattle World's Fair by Alweg, a German company that had designed systems for Disneyland and cities in Europe and Japan. Construction took 10 months and the cost, $3.5 million, was underwritten by Alweg.

The monorail was never meant to be permanent, but it proved such a success with residents that the city purchased the system in 1965 from the fair's sponsor. The price tag: a mere $600,000. Over the years, the monorail has become a touchstone for environmentalists and urban planners around the world who consider it a reasonably priced, eco-friendly solution to the problems of mass transit and urban pollution. With Seattle's burgeoning population causing increased car traffic, there is talk of expanding the system. Seattle voters went to the polls in late 2002 to decide whether or not to extend the monorail to Sea-Tac airport.

Seattle Monorail, passing through EMP.

Houseboats on Lake Union near Terry Pettus Park.

■ LAKE UNION *map page 165, B-1/2*

In the center of town, between Queen Anne and Capitol Hills, lies Lake Union. Once a center of shipbuilding and repair, the lake still has commercial shipyards, marina space, and hundreds of houseboats, as well as waterfront restaurants. A trail runs along the southern waterfront past lawns, restaurants, and docks where large yachts are moored.

Views from the lake include the clapboard houses of the Wallingford neighborhood on the north shore, sailboats crossing the lake's quiet waters, and floatplanes picking up passengers bound for Victoria, the San Juan Islands, or remote fishing spots in the mountains.

The **Lake Washington Ship Canal,** leading west from Lake Union to Puget Sound and east into Lake Washington, is a commercial waterway. Restaurants, shipyards, office buildings, and marinas crowd the shore, and fishing boats, yachts, and houseboats bob in the water. The houseboats moored along the eastern shore, once something of a floating low-rent district, have gone upscale in recent times.

■ **BALLARD LOCKS AND BALLARD** *map page 165, A/B-1*

You can while away an enjoyable afternoon at the **Hiram M. Chittenden Locks,** known locally as the Ballard Locks, watching boats pass through. The locks were completed in 1917. Of the 75,000 boats that use them each year, most are pleasure craft, but research vessels, commercial ships, and sightseeing boats also "get a lift." On the way to the locks from the parking lot is the splendid **Carl S. English, Jr. Botanical Garden,** which contains more than 500 species and 1,500 varieties from around the world. On the south side of the locks, salmon and steelhead trout heading to their spawning grounds swim up the 21-level **fish ladder** that runs parallel to the locks. The ladder allows them to make the steep trip gradually. *3015 NW 54th Street; 206-783-7059.*

Beyond the palm trees at Chittenden is the Ballard neighborhood, home port for most of the Alaskan fishing fleet, whose vessels have cruised north every year

(above) Asahel Curtis photographed the launching of the lumber schooner Minnie A. Caine *in 1900. (Washington State Historical Society)*
(opposite) Customers practice climbing at the REI flagship store near Lake Union.

Dale Chihuly (foreground, right) creates one of his glass sculptures.

since the end of World War I to catch salmon. Halibut boats, crabbers, and big-bottom trawlers make the northward voyage too.

The Ballard area has attracted artistic types, the most famous being the innovative glass sculptor Dale Chihuly, who was born and raised in Tacoma. Chihuly studied glass-blowing at the Venini factory in Venice in the late 1960s and in 1971 cofounded the Pilchuck Glass School in Washington.

Chihuly's studio is closed to the public, but you'll find his works all over Seattle. Benaroya Hall (200 University Street) contains two light sculptures, and several works are usually on display at the Foster/White Gallery (123 South Jackson Street) in Pioneer Square. The lobby of the Seattle Aquarium (Pier 59) holds one of Chihuly's *Seaform* installations, and the lobby of the Sheraton Hotel (1400 Sixth Avenue) is a showcase for his white *Floral Forms #2*. Additional works can be seen at, among other places, City Centre (1420 Fifth Avenue) and at the Washington State Convention Center (800 Convention Place).

■ FREMONT   *map page 165, A/B-1*

The motto of colorful Fremont, across the Ship Canal from Queen Anne Hill, is "De Libertus Quirkus," meaning "the freedom to be peculiar." Its restaurants, pubs, stores, and giddy street sculpture make the small neighborhood well worth a stop. To get here, take Mercer Avenue off I-5, turn right at the first light, then left at the second light. Follow Westlake Avenue until you pass under the Aurora Avenue Bridge. Cross the Fremont Avenue drawbridge and you've arrived.

The bronze pedestrians in **Waiting for the Interurban** (Fremont Avenue North and North 34th Street) have been waiting for a bus since Seattle artist Richard Beyer's sculpture went up in the late 1970s. Look close and you'll see a dog's head popping out between one passenger's legs. Look even closer and you'll see that the pooch's face is a human one, said to be that of the artist with whom Beyer competed for the sculpture's commission.

The **Fremont Troll** (North 36th Street under the Aurora Avenue Bridge), a two-ton rock sculpture of a figure crushing a Volkswagen Beetle in his left hand, is a city icon. Locals tend to love or hate the goofy behemoth, but mostly the former.

The Fremont Troll *snacking under the Aurora Avenue Bridge.*

Equally eye-catching is the **statue of Lenin** (North 36th Street at Evanston Avenue) a businessperson "acquired" from a defunct Eastern Bloc country.

Locals say the *Fremont Rocket* (Evanston Avenue and Fremont Place North), a 53-foot sculpture created out of a surplus 1950s rocket, marks the center of the universe.

Redhook Ale stopped producing its ales in Fremont in the late '90s, but the area-based outfit kept open the **Trolleyman Pub** (3400 Phinney Avenue North, at North 34th Street). Inside a former trolley-car barn you can sip brews and nosh on burritos and other fare.

Near Fremont are three attractions of note. The **Woodland Park Zoo**

Vladimir Lenin, liberated from a former Eastern Bloc country, holds forth in Fremont.

(5500 Phinney Avenue North; 206-684-4800) has won awards for its habitats, in which animals roam free. The Asian Elephant Forest is worth a look, as is the African Savanna. The Northern Trail is a well-designed refuge for brown bears, wolves, mountain goats, and otters. **Green Lake** (East Green Lake Drive North and West Green Lake Drive North) contains jogging and bicycling trails and supports a variety of recreational activities. **Gasworks Park** (North Northlake Way and Meridian Avenue North), where summer concerts take place, occupies the site of a former gas plant. The 20-acre park is prettier than its name suggests.

■ FIRST AND CAPITOL HILLS   *map page 165, B-2*

East of downtown, across the freeway, rise First and Capitol Hills. One pleasant way to walk across to either is to follow paths through the shrubbery, flowers, and waterfalls at Freeway Park, a garden sanctuary built atop I-5.

The more southerly First Hill is sometimes called "Pill Hill" because it holds the city's largest concentration of hospitals, clinics, and medical offices. One building that stands out in this jumble of shapes is the handsome edifice of the **Frye Art Museum,** on the western slope. The Frye has a strong collection of 19th-century American and European paintings. In recent years, the museum has expanded its focus to include works by contemporary American realist painters in addition to 20th-century European and Alaskan art. *704 Terry Avenue; 206-622-9250.*

Capitol Hill, north of First Hill and reached by taking Denny Avenue uphill and turning left on Broadway, has old mansions and tree-lined residential streets, and some of Seattle's best espresso shops. Broadway is, for several blocks, the city's liveliest thoroughfare.

The Capitol Hill faithful line up for pastries at La Batelle Bakery & Café in the Broadway Market.

The **Seattle Asian Art Museum** in Volunteer Park has an old brick water tower that provides great views west over Puget Sound. The museum, inside a renovated art-deco building, has an admirable collection that emphasizes Chinese, Japanese, Korean, and Southeast Asian art. *Volunteer Park, 1400 East Prospect Street; 206-625-8900; also downtown at 100 University Street; 206-654-3100.*

Martial arts movie star Bruce Lee is buried in the large **Lakeview Cemetery** (north side of Volunteer Park). Buried next to him is his son, Brandon Lee, also a martial arts movie star. Lakeview, built in 1887, is also the final resting ground for many of Seattle's pioneers—Denny, Maynard, Mercer, Yesler, Boren, and Renton.

The **Grand Army of the Republic Cemetery** (12th Avenue East and East Howe Street) is a Civil War cemetery for Union soldiers, their wives, and families. During World War II, the 2.3 acre-cemetery was used by the military for barracks.

St. Mark's Episcopal Cathedral, a blocky brick-and-concrete fortress with high, arched windows and a shiny copper roof, looks over the northwest edge of Capitol Hill. It is not one of the most beautiful gothic cathedrals in the country. Its bare, cavernous interior—vaulted ceilings, walls of raw concrete—was left unfinished to preserve the brilliant acoustics. *1245 10th Avenue East.*

The **Museum of History and Industry,** on the southern bank of the Ship Canal, preserves pioneer artifacts that reveal much about life in Washington from the 1700s to the present. Historic pictures of 19th-century Seattle, jewelry from Indian reservations, and Boeing's first aircraft are just a few of the items on display here. *2700 24th Avenue East; 206-324-1126.*

More than 40,000 native and exotic trees, shrubs, and vines live on the 230 acres of the **Washington Park Arboretum,** whose collective greenery comprises a living museum. Oaks, conifers, magnolias, camellias, Japanese maples, hollies, and at least 130 endangered plants are protected here. Mountain ash, pine, cedar, fir, and rhododendron also grow here. *2300 Arboretum Drive East; 206-543-8800.*

The **Seattle Japanese Garden**, on 3 acres within the arboretum, has a delight-ful water lily–studded koi pond, waterfalls, shaded woodland walks, secluded benches, and seasonal flowers. At this rarely crowded hideaway, you can walk at a leisurely pace or sit back on a bench and relax. Despite nearby Lake Washington Boulevard, it's so quiet you can hear waterfalls splashing and koi bubbling to the surface of the pond. There's an authentic teahouse, not open to the public but reserved for *chanoyu,* or Japanese tea demonstrations. *1000 Lake Washington Boulevard; 206-684-4725 or 425-861-9109.*

■ UNIVERSITY DISTRICT *map page 165, B-1/2*

West of Lake Washington and north of the Ship Canal lies the University District, home to the **University of Washington.** "U-Dub," as it's commonly called, is said to rake in more federal research and training money (for the marine sciences, cancer research, and urban horticulture) than any other public university in the United States. It's also known for big-time college football and highly publicized athletic scandals. Husky Stadium is near the Ship Canal, so fans arrive by boat.

With its small shops, restaurants, bookstores, and pubs, this neighborhood offers sharp contrast to the quiet, tree-shaded campus. Locals, not all of them affiliated with the university, hang out here till late at night.

Lake Washington was carved by the same glacier that gouged out the Puget Sound basin. The Ship Canal to Puget Sound, completed in 1916, was supposed to make Lake Washington a hub for building and repairing ships. It didn't, although wooden ships were built here during World War I and even later, and a small fleet of Alaskan whalers wintered in Kirkland for a number of years.

(above) University of Washington crew team practices on Lake Washington.
(preceding page) Japanese Garden in the Washington Park Arboretum.

Boeing's Museum of Flight.

■ **MUSEUM OF FLIGHT** *map page 165, B-3*

One of Seattle's most engaging attractions lies south of the city between I-5 and U.S. 99 at the former headquarters of Boeing, one of the world's largest aircraft manufacturers. The company was started in 1916, when William Boeing, an heir to midwestern lumber money who had come to Seattle to finish a yacht, decided to build airplanes. His first craft was a seaplane that made its maiden flight from Lake Union. Though Boeing, much to the chagrin of locals, moved its headquarters to Chicago in 2001, much of the development and manufacturing of its products still takes place at its plant here.

The Museum of Flight is centered around the red barn in which William Boeing built his first airplane. A huge hall inside contains airplanes—ranging in size from a biplane to a B-47—suspended from the ceiling. Also here is the original *Air Force One,* in which U.S. presidents from Eisenhower to Nixon flew. All the fancy trimmings are in place, like Jackie Kennedy's makeup parlor and Lyndon Johnson's custom-made temperature controls. *9404 East Marginal Way South; 206-764-5720.*

OLYMPIC PENINSULA
& WASHINGTON COAST

■ HIGHLIGHTS

■ OVERVIEW

THE NORTHWESTERNMOST PART of the contiguous United States, the Olympic Peninsula, extends north between the Pacific Ocean and Puget Sound. Heavily glaciated and not crossed by any road, the Olympic Mountains form the peninsula's 7,000-foot-high spine. Short, swift rivers tumble from the mountains to the Pacific in the west, the Strait of Juan de Fuca to the north, and Hood Canal to the east. In west-facing valleys, temperate rain forests grow within a day's hike of glacial ice and the surf-thrashed rocks of Pacific beaches. The northeastern portion of the peninsula lies in the rain shadow of the Olympic Mountains and has some of the lowest rainfall in western Washington, which explains why the region's major towns—Port Townsend, Sequim, and Port Angeles—are popular with artists and retirees.

The human history of the Olympic Peninsula goes back at least 3,000 years, and the oldest building foundations in the region are 800 years old. Other objects show that the Makah people had a stable culture for centuries. The Makah and other Native Americans, namely the Quillayute, Quinault, and Clallam tribes, hunted seals and whales, fished for salmon and halibut, gathered wild berries, and

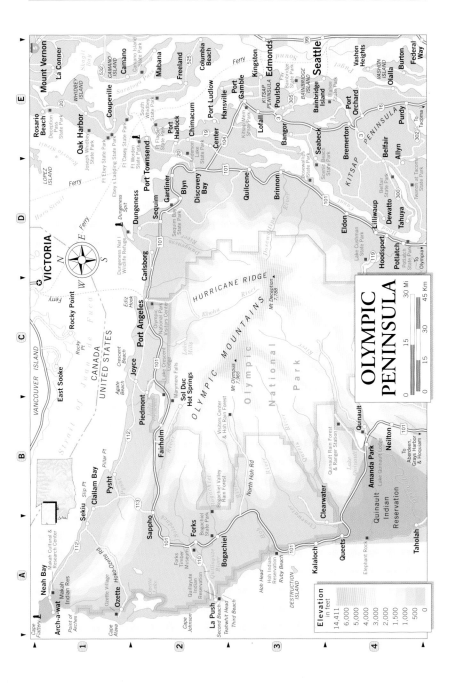

built cultures rich in myths and rituals. During the 20th century, inhabitants of this territory have also lived off the land, but to the extent that heavy logging and salmon fishing have made natural resources scarce. Fortunately, the heart of the peninsula, which includes acres of forests and rivers, has been protected from exploitation since Congress created Olympic National Park, which encompasses mountains, valleys, and rain forests, in 1938.

■ KITSAP PENINSULA   *map page 199, D/E-3/4*

If you travel to the Olympic Peninsula from Seattle, a car ferry will take you to the **Kitsap Peninsula,** where a fleet of gray warships rides at anchor in Bremerton, a navy-yard town since the late 19th century. The peninsula is a low, fjorded region of dense woods, picturesque harbor towns, and the U.S. Navy's largest West Coast shipyard and submarine base.

Makah Indians land a whale through the surf at Neah Bay. Sealskin floats hinder the whale from diving and keep it afloat after death. (Washington State Historical Society, Tacoma)

The grave of **Chief Seattle,** for whom Seattle was named, overlooks Puget Sound at Suquamish on the Port Madison Indian Reservation. As a boy, the future chief saw Capt. George Vancouver's ship, *Discovery*, sailing down Puget Sound in 1792; in 1850, as tribal leader, he welcomed the first white settlers to Alki Point.

This was also where, in 1854, Chief Seattle is said to have delivered what is considered the greatest speech ever given in the Northwest. Chief Seattle was speaking primarily to territorial governor Isaac Stevens. His speech was translated on the spot into the simplified Chinook jargon, from which it was translated into English 33 years later by Dr. Henry Smith, who had heard the original. Presumably, the ideas were Seattle's, but most of the language was Smith's.

"Undeniably majestic as it is," historian David Buerge has written, "Seattle's speech does not conform to what we know of the native speaking style of the Puget Sound region." Nevertheless, the speech attributed to Seattle is a masterpiece. One of the best-known passages reads:

> Every part of this soil is sacred in the estimation of my people. Every hillside, every valley, every plain and grove, has been hallowed by some sad or happy event in days long vanished. Even the rocks which seem to be dumb and dead as they swelter in the sun along the silent shore, thrill with memories of stirring events connected with the lives of my people, and the very dust upon which you now stand responds more lovingly to their footsteps than yours, because it is rich with the blood of our ancestors and our bare feet are conscious of the sympathetic touch....

Nearby, along Liberty Bay, the town of **Poulsbo** plays up its Norwegian immigrant history. Its name means "Paul's Place" in Norwegian, and, fittingly, the town sponsors the Viking Fest in mid-May, the Skandia Midsommarfest in June, and the Yule Log Festival in November.

The old mill town of **Port Gamble** overlooks the mouth of the Hood Canal, a glacial fjord on the far side of the Kitsap Peninsula. The many white buildings that dot the landscape evoke the Maine backgrounds of the founders of the Pope & Talbot Company, which sold lumber in gold rush San Francisco and built the first mill in Port Gamble in the 1850s.

(following pages) Point Wilson Lighthouse in Port Townsend has a fine view across the straits. Mount Baker is visible in the background.

As you drive over the floating bridge across the blue water of Hood Canal, try not to remember that 80-mile-per-hour winds sank the bridge's predecessor in 1979. Even the new bridge is closed during particularly severe storms. The bridge is opened by pulling aside a float to let large ships pass through, and you may be delayed by black, ominous-looking Trident submarines slipping out to sea from the Bangor base to the south.

■ NORTHEAST OLYMPIC PENINSULA

■ **PORT LUDLOW** *map page 199, E-2*
North of the bridge is the resort town of Port Ludlow, famous for its boat harbor, golf course, and the **Heron Bay Inn** (1 Heron Road; 360-437-0411) across the harbor on a sandy bar. The inn's restaurant serves the best food on the Olympic Peninsula. As you drive north toward Port Townsend, look around you. The woods and fields of this region were made famous by Betty McDonald in *The Egg and I.* Stop in Chimacum and ask where local heroes Ma and Pa Kettle lived.

■ **PORT TOWNSEND** *map page 199, E-2*
A special place, with its bookstores, restaurants, brick buildings downtown, and ornate Victorian homes on the bluff above, Port Townsend has a literary reputation and often hosts writer's workshops. At the decommissioned military post of Fort Worden—setting for the 1982 movie *An Officer and a Gentleman*—the officers' quarters and parade ground overlook the Strait of Juan de Fuca and trails lead through the woods to lonely bluffs and beaches.

The **James House** (1238 Washington Street; 360-385-1238 or 800-385-1238), an antiques-filled Victorian-era inn, sits on the bluff overlooking Port Townsend's waterfront district. This house is listed on the National Register of Historic Places and is just about everyone's favorite Port Townsend bed-and-breakfast. The decor of the spacious **Palace Hotel** (1004 Water Street; 360-385-0773 or 800-962-0741) reflects the building's history as a bordello. You can easily imagine the exposed-brick-wall lobby filled with music and men waiting for the ladies whose names now grace hallway plaques. The large rooms have 14-foot ceilings and worn antiques. The outstanding corner suite, Miss Marie's, has full views of the bay and the original working fireplace from Marie's days as a madam.

On the road west from Port Townsend, stands of massive old cedar and fir still crowd the highway. In autumn, the red and yellow leaves of vine maple glow among the evergreens. Other spots along this road resemble Christmas tree lots, with signs proudly proclaiming model tree farms. Clear-cut and reseeded a decade ago, these patches of fir and alder are choked with salal and bracken, where deer and black bears browse. Rain-soaked pastures are punctuated here and there with ancient stumps 6 feet in diameter.

■ SEQUIM AND DUNGENESS SPIT *map page 199, D-1/2*

The highway town of Sequim ("SKWIM") is noted for its burgeoning retirement population and its dry climate (it sits in the rain shadow of the Olympics). Dungeness Spit, possibly the largest natural sand spit in the world, juts into the Strait of Juan de Fuca, curving northeast for 5.5 miles to the lighthouse at its tip like the claw of a giant crab. Seabirds bob in the sheltered waters of the bay, and sea lions cruise along the exposed western shore. The coastal forest near the base and adjacent tidal zones are protected as part of the **Dungeness National Wildlife Refuge,** home to some 250 bird species.

■ PORT ANGELES *map page 199, C-2*

Talk about a town that has pulled itself up by the boot straps. The waterfront has undergone a transformation. A former railroad bed has been converted into a paved trail with benches and some truly splendid views across the Strait of Juan de Fuca, all the way to Mount Baker on a clear day. The small **Fiero Marine Life Center** (360-417-6254), on the public pier, has touch tanks with several species of sea creatures collected in local waters and docents on hand to answer questions. The center's viewing tower at the end of the pier is worth climbing for the views, especially when a full moon rises over the strait. This former mill town and commercial fishing port sits directly across the Strait of Juan de Fuca from Victoria, British Columbia. The actor John Wayne berthed his boat here; short-story writer Raymond Carver lived here; and poet Tess Gallagher still lives here.

Ediz Hook, at the western end of Port Angeles, is a long natural sand spit that protects the harbor from big waves and storms. The hook is a fine place to take a walk along the water and watch shore- and seabirds, and to spot the occasional seal, orca, or gray whale. From downtown, take Front Street west and follow it as it meanders past the shuttered lumber mill.

■ **OLYMPIC NATIONAL PARK** *map page 199, B/D-2/3*

Olympic National Park's grandest entrance winds 17 miles from Port Angeles to Hurricane Ridge, where you can look out over the Elwha Valley into the heart of the Olympics, or north to the Strait of Juan de Fuca. The area encompasses more than 1,300 square miles of wilderness in the heart of the Olympic Mountains. The surrounding land was set aside as forest reserve in 1897. Twelve years later, President Theodore Roosevelt established the Mount Olympus National Monument as a sanctuary for the later-named Roosevelt elk, which had been hunted nearly to extinction for its teeth, which were used as ornaments for watch fobs. Under pressure from logging and mining interests, President Woodrow Wilson reduced the protected area by half in 1915, opening much of today's park to logging and homesteading, activities that ended in 1938, when Congress created Olympic National Park. Since then, the park has expanded to include the Queets and Hoh River Valleys. Congress recently added the coastal strip, the longest stretch of wilderness beach in the United States outside Alaska.

Olympic National Park is the most geographically diverse park in America. In addition to 7,965-foot Mount Olympus, the park encompasses 57 miles of seacoast, temperate rain forests, and an array of wildlife that includes black bears, mountain sheep, bald eagles, and at least 5,000 Roosevelt elk. With more than 600 miles of trails, the park reveals itself best to travelers on foot or horseback. For auto-bound travelers and campers, a few spectacular roads probe fleetingly (never more than 20 miles) into its interior.

Typically, the region experiences more rain and fog than sunshine. Beaches, tide pools, and rain forests embellish the west side of the peninsula, where heavy rains irrigate massive forests of immense red cedar, Sitka spruce, and Douglas fir. The main roads to the rain forest trailheads follow the Hoh River near Forks; the Queets River near the town of Queets; and the Quinault River, beyond Quinault Lake in the southwestern corner of the park. Access roads to the beaches lead to Ozette Lake, La Push, and the southern stretch of coastline between Ruby Beach and Queets. The park keeps the road plowed in winter, and people drive up here for cross-country and downhill skiing.

Farther west, U.S. 101 passes through low forests to scenic **Lake Crescent,** surrounded by hills and beloved by trout fishermen. Nearby are the comfortable cottages of the **Lake Crescent Lodge** (416 Lake Crescent Road; 360-928-3211),

Avalanche lilies carpet Hurricane Ridge in Olympic National Park.

built for a visit by President Franklin Roosevelt in 1937. The lodge is a classic national park hostelry. Another favorite area pastime is "taking the waters" at **Sol Duc Hot Springs** (Sol Duc Hot Springs Road; 360-327-3583), which have been popular since pioneer days. Three sulfur pools boil and bubble here. Their temperatures are hot, hotter, and hottest.

■ ALONG THE WESTERN STRAITS
Beyond Port Angeles, narrow Route 112 winds west along the Strait of Juan de Fuca. South and east, a blanket of snow caps the crumpled ridges of the Olympic Mountains, rising starkly from their surrounding forests. As you follow the road along the coastline, curving around rocks and trees, don't rush—this is one of the finest coastal drives in the state. Near Pysht, huge, mossy spruce trunks crowd the blacktop, and along the Pysht River look for epiphytes—air plants that grow on other plants, not in soil—dripping from maple limbs. Farther west, you'll see rocky headlands and waves breaking on stony beaches.

An aerial view of Tatoosh Island (above). It is the northwesternmost point of the coterminous United States, resting just off Cape Flattery. Hobuck Beach (right) in Mukkaw Bay is on the Makah Indian Reservation.

■ **NEAH BAY** *map page 199, A-1*

Neah Bay is a sport-fishing and whaling village where the occasional totem pole reminds you that this is a centuries-old Makah settlement. It's also where the state's first European settlers came to build a home. In 1792, Spanish colonists from Mexico arrived aboard a frigate. They built a fort and a bakery, and planted a small garden, but they abandoned the area after five months. The first Americans here were traders, arriving in 1850. The Makah are still here.

The Makah Tribe requires hikers and others touring the reservation to purchase a $7 permit, good for the calendar year, but check the news if you are planning to visit the village during the annual migration of California gray whales. The resumption of whaling in Neah Bay has led to protests by environmental groups and clashes between protesters and the Makah. Neah Bay is not a fun place to be during these confrontations. (You might also want to miss the spectacle and stench of a huge whale being cut up on the local beach.) *Route 112 from U.S. 101 at Port Angeles, or Route 113 from U.S. 101 at Sappho.*

■ **MAKAH CULTURAL AND RESEARCH CENTER** *map page 199, A-1*

On display here are artifacts recovered from the Ozette Village site at Cape Alava. On the whole, the objects form a kind of hymn to cedar, which the Makah used to make just about everything, including their longhouses, woven mats, blankets, hats, canoe paddles, and canoes. The museum contains replicas of the smaller cedar canoes used for seal hunting and the long canoes used for whale hunting.

The most startling display case holds knife blades made of slate, shell, and rusted metal. Where did Makah craftsmen 500 years ago get metal to make blades? Presumably from shipwrecked Japanese vessels that were carried by currents into the peninsula's waters. It is unclear how often wrecked boats from other continents drifted ashore, but there is evidence that Japanese sailors survived a shipwreck here in the early 1800s. *Route 112, 1880 Bay View Avenue; 360-645-2711.*

West of Neah Bay, **Cape Flattery,** the northwesternmost point of land in the coterminous United States, extends into the Pacific. From high ground, you can look south along the misty coast, over the dark forest and white line of breakers at the edge of the continent, to the distant sculpture garden of sea stacks at Point of Arches. *After the Makah museum, travel west 1.5 miles to town and follow signs to Makah Tribal Center. A quarter-mile beyond the tribal center is a gravel road that leads to Cape Trail and Cape Flattery.*

■ OZETTE LAKE AND NORTH OLYMPIC COAST

West of Sekiu, on Route 112, a branch road winds southwest, following the Hoko River through heavily logged hills toward Ozette Lake. Most of the land along this road is clear-cut to low stumps and slash piles as far as the eye can see. The road ends at a ranger station on the north end of 10-mile-long Ozette Lake. You have just entered the coastal section of Olympic National Park.

■ AHLSTROM PRAIRIE   *map page 199, A-1/2*

One hundred years ago, the land around Ozette Lake was settled by homesteaders, mostly Scandinavian families who built dwellings here using wood cut from old-growth forests. Lars Ahlstrom, a homesteader who arrived in 1902, worked his claim alone until 1958. His decades of toil are commemorated in Ahlstrom Prairie, a broad marsh crossed by the Cape Alava trail. Around the lake, the forest has swallowed all traces of the farms that once thrived here. Even on Ahlstrom Prairie, seedling evergreens are beginning the long work of reclamation.

Two 3-mile-long boardwalk trails from Ozette Lake to the long wilderness beach cut through thick rain forests, where columns of sunlight split the dense canopy high overhead, and where a soft, green light seems to emanate from trees and the earth itself.

Between the Makah Reservation, which occupies the extreme northwestern tip of the peninsula, and the big Quinault Reservation, south of Kalaloch, the whole Pacific coastline is part of the Olympic National Park, except for three small pockets of land occupied by the Ozette, Quillayute, and Hoh Reservations. The ancient forests grow down to the shore. Near the water, pale lichens beard the scaly boughs of Sitka spruce. At low tide, the beach stretches out to small, wooded islands where surf-sculpted rocks dot the shore. Some of these landforms would look more at home in the Arizona desert than in the shallows of the Pacific Ocean.

Waves deposit spongy beds of sea grass along the tide line and scatter stiff stalks of bullwhip kelp in the sand. Deer and raccoon tracks show clearly in the sand, and black cormorants spread their wings to dry in the sun atop wave-shaped sea stacks—the weird-looking hives and spires of dark basalt that form close to water. The hoarse cry of a great blue heron splits the air as the bird rises with a few impossibly slow beats of its enormous wings. Mats of slick, red kelp pop underfoot, and a young bald eagle flies northeast with a fish hanging limp in its talons, a pleading gull in pursuit.

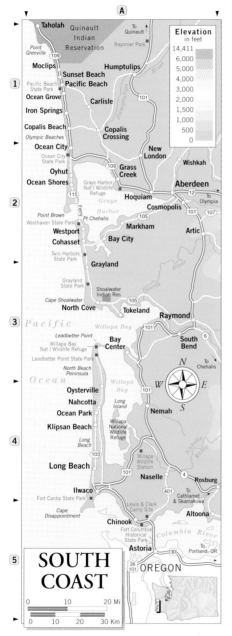

Elevation
in feet

14,411	
6,000	
5,000	
4,000	
3,000	
2,000	
1,500	
1,000	
500	
0	

SOUTH COAST

0	10	20 Mi
0	10	20	30 Km

■ **CAPE ALAVA** *map page 199, A-1*

The site of a Makah village for at least 2,000 years, Cape Alava was abandoned in the late 19th century after the U.S. government ordered village children off to school in Neah Bay. Like many places that have been long inhabited, Ozette Village was built in succeeding layers. An early layer, sealed by mudslides centuries ago and exposed by winter storms in 1970, provided one of Washington's most important archaeological sites—a Pompeii of the Northwest coast. Wooden artifacts and woven baskets dating to the 1400s, perfectly preserved in their airless tomb, gave a clear picture of traditional Makah life. The archaeological excavation of the Ozette Village eventually ran out of money, but the artifacts are preserved at the Makah Cultural and Research Center in Neah Bay, and a replica cedar longhouse now marks the village site.

■ **LA PUSH**
map page 199, A-2

Fourteen miles west of U.S. 101 and the town of Forks is the quaint village of La Push, close to the mouth of the Quillayute River on **Quillayute Indian Reservation.** The coast here, accessed by Route 110, is magnificent:

(right) Hall of Mosses Trail in the rain forest of Olympic National Park.

wind-warped cedar and hemlock and stands of lichen-whitened alder stand on steep clay banks overlooking the Pacific. **Second Beach** and **Third Beach** are reached by half-mile trails leading down from the road about a mile before town. La Push itself is on First Beach, a site occupied by the Quillayute for centuries. The town is a collection of shabby, weathered houses, an old Shaker church, and a small harbor where fishing boats bob. Salmon fishing is the chief livelihood of the Quillayute people, as it has been for millennia. Gray whales are known to play off-shore during their annual migrations, and most of the year the waves are great for surfing and kayaking.

■ RAIN FORESTS *map page 199, B-2/3*

People come from all over the world to see the enchanting rain forests of the Olympic Coast. Everything here is green—innumerable hues, shades, and over-lapping layers of green. Tree roots create ripples in the green, and waves of moss seem to flow toward the trees. In fall, you might hear the high "bugling" of Roosevelt elk or see one of the big creatures slip through the trees.

Multiple layers of tree limbs, vines, and moss create a canopy overhead, and where light is able to penetrate, a tangled undergrowth of brush and small plants flourishes on the forest floor. Some old trees die and remain standing as gray, weather-bleached snags. Others fall and decay slowly, releasing nutrients for centuries. These nutrients eventually develop into nurse logs that grow above the forest floor. Because nurse logs thrive away from the suffocating duff and aggressive fungi of the forest base, they allow less hardy species, like Sitka spruce and western hemlock, to survive. The western hemlocks that hitch rides on western red cedars can grow into substantial trees themselves, reaching diameters of 9 feet and heights of almost 200 feet. They are counted among the "Big Four" of the temperate rain forest, along with western red cedar, Douglas fir, and Sitka spruce.

Plant and animal life in the Washington rain forests equals that of tropical rain forests, though it is not as diverse. Only a few conifer species are found here, and there are even fewer deciduous ones. But the sheer size and number of these conifers, and the density of their over- and undergrowth, puts them among the tallest and thickest trees on earth. Willaby Creek Nature Trail, on the southern shore of Lake Quinault, passes through a grove of impressively lofty Douglas firs, some of them 300 feet high. Washington's rain forests are so dense with growth it's easy to get lost while hiking through them. Stick to established trails.

On U.S. 101, just south of Forks at Bogachiel State Park, head east into the **Bogachiel Valley Rain Forest.** Past the Bogachiel River, North Hoh Road leads inland to the **Hoh Rain Forest** (off U.S. 101 at Upper Hoh Road; 360-374-6925), where the best-known rain forest trails begin. Farther south, U.S. 101 leads east to **Lake Quinault,** where you will find trailheads, campgrounds, and the **Lake Quinault Lodge** (345 South Shore Road; 360-288-2900), an impressively handsome 96-room hotel built on the shores of Lake Quinault in 1926.

■ SOUTHERN WASHINGTON COAST *map page 212*

The Washington coast south of the Olympic Peninsula is dominated by three large river estuaries (and by the sand dunes and spits shielding them from the ocean)—that of the Chehalis, Willapa, and Columbia Rivers. All three have wide, "drowned" river mouths that were flooded when sea levels rose after the last ice age. They are backed by the Willapa Hills, a chunk of oceanic crust pushed up by tectonic forces, and their swampy shores are densely forested.

Northerly inshore currents deposited huge quantities of silt and sand carried seaward by the Columbia, all but blocking off the mouths of the Willapa and Chehalis. These deposits created two large, shallow bays: Willapa Bay, also known as Shoalwater Bay; and Grays Harbor. The sand spit running north from the rocky headlands abutting the Columbia has the longest beach on the west coast. It is aptly called Long Beach. Like the Olympic Peninsula to the north, this coast gets a lot of rain, but the air is moist even when the sun shines, making for a blurring of focus, a soft merging of land and sea, earth and water.

Nor is the land as firm as it might appear at first glance. The beaches of hard-packed sand are backed by ever-shifting sand dunes, cranberry bogs, and marshes. The bays and their tidal channels, tributary rivers, creeks, sloughs, and salt- and freshwater marshes are a maze of waterways—the closest any area of the West Coast comes to Louisiana's bayou. In some embayments, shallow marshes of marine grasses and reeds stretch as far as the eye can see; in others, tangled forests of moss-and-lichen-covered trees grow right up to the edge of meandering creeks. Like gray-clad highwaymen, great blue herons lurk in the shadows, patiently waiting for an unsuspecting fish, frog, or muskrat to swim by. Bald eagles drift through the fog like white-headed ghosts; ospreys plunge, feet first, into the water to snatch at fish. From their perches on waterside snags, kingfishers dive head first into the water in pursuit of their prey. Because these waters are shallow and calm, they are ideal for canoeing and kayaking (though many shores can also be explored on foot). Don't be surprised if you come upon the home of a fisherman on a remote islet, or see houses built on barges bobbing in the gentle swell of a backwater. Here, as in the bayous, some folks like their privacy.

The rocky headlands of the Willapa Hills reach tidewater in only a few places, most notably along southern Willapa Bay, where U.S. 101 runs almost at bay level, twisting in and out of small, marshy coves past cliffs covered with a dense growth of brush and trees. Oyster farms are tucked into many of these coves, their oyster beds marked by tall stakes rising from the water; the shucking sheds marked by heaps of bleaching oyster shells. The few rocky islets rising from the mud are topped by a dense tangle of conifers and salal scrub.

Bird-watchers flock to these shores and bays in fall and spring. The state's southwest coast has some of the best shorebird watching in the nation. Dennis Paulson writes in *Shorebirds of the Pacific Northwest,* "At times shorebirds in Grays Harbor feed as if choreographed: Short-billed Dowitchers in the water, Dunlins at the waterline, Western Sandpipers on the wet mud, Semipalmated and Black-bellied Plovers on the drier mud, and Least Sandpipers adjacent to the salt marsh."

(above and opposite) The Pacific coastline of Washington is foggy, wild, windy, and beautiful.

■ **GRAYS HARBOR** *map page 212, A-2*

Curving inland around the Quinault Indian Reservation, U.S. 101 connects the estuary and mill towns of Grays Harbor. The ocean beaches to the west have razor clams and are a popular resort destination for tourists and locals.

Grays Harbor has one of the largest estuaries on the Pacific Coast north of San Francisco. The towns of **Aberdeen** and **Hoquiam,** which stand beside the estuary, have always had plenty of lumber mills, and old pilings driven into the seabed to hold log booms still rise from the water's edge. The two towns are so close you can hardly tell when you leave one and enter the other, which might explain why they have never gotten along. Once, when the Chehalis River flooded, the city of Hoquiam built a dike across the main street to "keep the floodwaters in Aberdeen." In recent years, Aberdeen has maintained its downtown business core while also attracting retailers to several malls, the largest of which is south of the Chehalis River. Hoquiam, with its old extractive mills still standing along the Chehalis River waterfront, seems more interested in reliving the past.

A tall, masted ship may sail across the bay, a replica of Capt. Robert Gray's other nautical charge, *Lady Washington.* It was built for the Washington Centennial in 1989. Occasionally, rides are offered. Oysters grow in the waters on the south side of the estuary.

Up to one million shorebirds flock to **Grays Harbor National Wildlife Refuge,** at the northern edge of the estuary in the Bowerman Basin, during the spring birding season before flying off to northern breeding grounds. Dozens of species of shorebirds land here, but mostly sandpipers, dunlin, short-billed and long-billed dowitchers, and, of course, the semipalmated plover. Grays Harbor is a designated Western Hemisphere Shorebird Reserve, and hundreds of bird-watchers show up here each year in late April for the Shorebird Festival (360-495-3289). The best months to visit the refuge are April and May, and the best times of day to come are an hour before and an hour after high tide. *100 Brown Farm Road, Olympia; 360-532-6237 or 360-753-9467.*

Copalis Beach, a pleasant huddle of roadside stores and motels, serves visitors to the easily accessible beach and picnic areas. There is also a pleasant state park at the estuary, with beach access through the dunes and a bluff-top picnic area that overlooks the estuary. Great bird-watching abounds.

Westport, at the southern edge of the estuary's mouth, has a fishing and crabbing fleet, and charter boats for catching salmon and bottomfish, or for viewing

Buying Northwest Seafood

You are driving down the coast, blissfully gazing out the window—salt water as far as the eye can see—and since the coast is where seafood comes from, you might as well stock up and send some of that good, fresh stuff home.

That's the idea, at least. Reality can be a bit different. Just a few years ago, it was pretty difficult to find fresh seafood on the coast, unless you caught, dug, or gathered it yourself. That's not because there weren't any fresh fish, clams, crabs, or oysters. There were. But they went from the boat to the packing house, from the packing house to the big-city distributor, and then from the distributor back to coastal fish markets and supermarkets. Which means that you might find fresher seafood in Vancouver or Seattle than you could hope for in fishing harbors like Bellingham or Astoria.

The locals didn't care. Not because they didn't know fresh from stale, but because they didn't have to buy seafood at a market. They'd catch it themselves or get it free from friends. Even today, they rarely order seafood when they eat out. They have enough of that at home. When the locals go out to eat, they order steak. Which is why, more often than not, the steak served in restaurants up and down the coast is better than the seafood.

But all that's been changing for at least a decade. Fewer people have time to go fishing or dig for clams, which means that even many of the locals now have to buy their seafood at a market. And that means that the quality is up, since seashore residents know what fresh seafood is supposed to taste like.

■ British Columbia

Some of the freshest seafood in British Columbia is sold in **Chinatown fish markets** in **Vancouver** and **Richmond.** In **Steveston,** at the mouth of the Fraser River, you can buy fish, shrimp, and crab directly from the fishermen. In summer, this is the best place to buy freshly caught **Fraser River** sockeye salmon. Just look for boats with awnings stretched over their main decks. That's the sign that they have seafood for sale. But beware. Unfortunately not all fishermen are honest. Some will try to pawn off old fish, which they may or may not have caught themselves. Others sell farm-raised salmon. Look the fish in the eye. Is it clear? Are the gills red, not brown? Does the flesh bounce back when you press the skin? Or does it leave a dimple? Does the fish smell fresh? Fresh fish has clear eyes, red gills, and resilient flesh, and it does *not* smell fishy. These rules apply to U.S. fishmongers as well.

■ **Washington**

Chuckanut Drive is a narrow road that winds south from Bellingham between steep sandstone cliffs and the tide flats of Samish Bay. **Taylor Shellfish Farm** has the most scenic of all oyster farm locations in Washington, sprawling at the foot of a densely forested bluff, where wild roses bloom in spring. To the west, the mountainous San Juan Islands rise from the sea. The farm's small store sells not only different types of oysters (if you're lucky, they'll have Kumamotos, Olympias, and European flats), but also fresh crab (live and cooked), pink scallops in the shell, clams, and mussels. *188 Chuckanut Drive, Bow; 360-766-6002.*

A bit off the beaten path, on Samish Island, is the **Blau Oyster Company.** You can buy fish, crab, and other seasonal seafood here as well. If you order a day ahead, you get a 10-percent discount. *919 Blue Heron Road, Bow; 360-766-6171.*

On your way to the outer coast, if you're going by way of Fidalgo and Whidbey Islands, is the small roadside shack of **Strom's Shrimp**. The locally caught shrimp are very tasty and make for a great snack while you're waiting for the Keystone ferry to take you to Port Townsend. *1481 Route 20, Anacortes; 360-293-2531.*

Staked salmon is barbecued during the Makah Days festival held every August on the Makah Indian Reservation in Washington.

Piles of oyster shells discarded after shucking are recycled as fertilizer.

Driving south along the Hood Canal, look for the processing shacks and oyster shell piles of the **Hamma Hamma Oyster Company.** Here shellfish are kept fresh in live tanks. Besides the oysters, which here have an uncommonly delicate flavor, there are excellent clams for sale, as well as geoduck (pronounced "gooey-duck"), the uncouth-looking giant clam of the Northwest. But never mind the way it looks. Its meat is delicious. The Puget Sound inlets south of the Hood Canal have oyster farms, but these are difficult to find and prefer to sell wholesale. *Just south of the Hamma Hamma River; 360-877-6938.*

Jessie's Ilwaco Fish Co. is a big place on pilings on the waterfront. It has everything fishy or clammy or crusty you might want, and you can't miss it. *West of Ilwaco, on the way to Fort Canby; 360-642-3773.*

As you head down the coast, stop in Westport for shellfish. Northwesterners consider it a great pleasure to sit on the beach, sheltered from the sea wind by huge driftwood logs, and eat oysters on the halfshell and freshly cracked crab. Two good places to try are **Brady's Oysters** (3714 Oyster Place East; 360-268-0077) and **Nelson Crab** (3088 Kindred Avenue, Tokeland; 360-267-2911).

On the eastern shore, at the **Ekone Oyster Company**, you can buy absolutely delicious smoked oysters. *192 Bay Center Road, Bay Center; 360-875-5494.*

Look for **Jolly Roger Oyster Company** (360-665-4111) at the Nahcotta dock, and **Oysterville Sea Farms** (360-665-6585) at the Oysterville dock.

■ **OREGON**

South of the Columbia River, in Oregon, you have to stop at **Josephson's Smokehouse,** a local favorite for its smoked fish. Best of all, they ship, if you don't want to carry all that seafood around with you. If you're lucky, they'll have Columbia River sturgeon caviar, which is as good as the best imported roe. *106 Marine Drive; 503-325-2190.*

Look for **Norm's Fish & Crab** (8425 U.S. 101 North, Bay City; 503-377-2799), which sells smoked fish and fresh Dungeness crab. Also try **Bay Ocean Oyster** (603 Garibaldi Avenue, Garibaldi; 503-322-0040) and **Tillamook Oyster Company** (1985 Bay Ocean Road NW, Tillamook; 503-842-6921).

You'll have to drive out to the fishing harbor docks to visit **Smith Pacific Shrimp.** The shrimp are great and so is the smoked fish. *608 Commercial Drive, Garibaldi; 503-322-3316.*

You can't miss the **Tillamook Cheese Factory.** It's just north of Tillamook, and a two-masted schooner sits out front. The large store sells not just cheese but a variety of Oregon food products. *4175 U.S. 101 North, Tillamook; 503-842-4481.*

South of Tillamook Bay, U.S. 101 leaves the coast and runs inland. Take Three Capes Loop if you want to drive along the scenic cliffs.

At Pacific City, fishermen go down to the sea in dories launched through the surf. You can watch them launch and bring in the boats, but beware the four-by-fours pulling the boat trailers—they really move. Sometimes there's just a split second between a safe launch and a swamped boat. Buy some of the fishermen's catch at **Doryman Fish Company Market** (33315 Cape Kiwanda Road; 503-965-6412).

Barnacle Bill's Seafood Market (2174 NE U.S. 101; 541-994-3022) is a good place to stock up on the local catch. Few people know that southern Oregon grows oysters, perhaps because the farms are off the beaten path. Look for **Umpqua Aquaculture** (Ork Rock Road, Winchester Bay; 541-271-5684) at the far end of the harbor. **Qualman Oyster Farms** (4898 Crown Point Road; 541-888-3145) is across the slough from Charleston harbor.

The best place for fresh fish in southern Oregon is **Bandon Fish Market** (250 First SW Street; 541-347-2851). Stock up on cheese and other local foods at **Bandon Cheese** (680 East Second Street, U.S. 101; 541-347-2456).

whales that migrate up the coast in spring. A drive south from Westport takes you past dunes and cranberry bogs. In spring, look for wild strawberries growing in the dunes; in fall, search for wild cranberries growing in moist, boggy depressions among the sand hills. In season, you may dig for razor clams on the beaches. Westport is an active town with boating, bicycling, clam digging, and lots of fishing. There's a great boardwalk here, at the end of Neddie Rose Drive, and the town has miles and miles of beaches.

■ WILLAPA BAY   *map page 212, A-3*

Willapa Bay, just south of Grays Harbor, is the cleanest estuary anywhere in the United States outside Alaska. The area produces more oysters than any other place in the United States and ranks among the top five oyster-producing spots in the world. You can't miss the town; most of it is covered under huge piles of oyster shells, which rise beside packinghouses at the water's edge.

A quick drive south from Grays Harbor takes you to the old riverside logging town of **Raymond,** where a tall wooden statue of a logger stands in a little park. Farther south, U.S. 101 runs along the waterfront of **South Bend,** known to some as "the oyster capital of the world." After passing through South Bend, U.S. 101 follows the Willapa River to Willapa Bay. A historical plaque here marks the site of **Bruceport,** from which oysters were first shipped to San Francisco in the 1850s.

Parts of Willapa Bay have been protected since 1937 as a national wildlife refuge. Near the refuge's headquarters, just south of South Bend, **Long Island** supports a 4,000-year-old grove of western red cedar. The remainder of the refuge is across the bay, at the northern tip of **Long Beach Peninsula,** which separates Willapa Bay from the Pacific Ocean. This is a low, fenny land of slowly meandering rivers, of reedy marshes and damp forests, of old docks and piles of oyster shells on the shore.

Gray whales pass by Long Beach Peninsula two times a year: from December to February, on their migration south from the Arctic to their winter breeding grounds in the saltwater lagoons of Baja, California; and from March to May, on the return trip north. One good place to view the whales is the **North Head Lighthouse,** north of Cape Disappointment in Fort Canby State Park.

Oysterville, once the center of the local oyster industry, has houses from the 1860s and a 1906 schoolhouse. Quaint is the operative word here. Don't miss the 1892 Oysterville church, with its shingled steeple. A sign marks the site of the first

Pacific County Courthouse—the seat of local government until South Bend boosters stole the records and built their own courthouse. This small coastal community was settled in 1854, when it became a major oyster producer for San Francisco. But this was an oyster town long before that, going back to the days when Chinook Indians harvested oysters from Willapa Bay.

Leadbetter Point State Park, just beyond Oysterville but before the refuge at the extreme tip of the peninsula, gives you a chance to walk along a bay that looks unchanged from a century ago. Snowy plovers breed on the sandy beaches of Leadbetter Point, and shorebirds rise, skim the water, flash white undersides as they turn, and settle up the beach. Their twittering fills the air.

■ THE COLUMBIA RIVER   *map page 212, A-5*
Below the steep cliffs of Cape Disappointment, the Columbia River and the Pacific Ocean growl at each other across a barrier of sand where tall breakers pound the beach. Many ships have wrecked here in the last 200 years, even though a lighthouse clinging to the sheer rock has signaled the dangers of these waters since 1856. This is the beach on which Lewis and Clark first walked beside the Pacific in 1805.

Fort Canby was built on a rocky headland during the Civil War to protect the coast from Confederate raiders. The **Lewis and Clark Interpretive Center** here contains journal excerpts from the Lewis and Clark expedition and photo murals of places on the explorers' route. Despite the construction of two lighthouses and a few military bunkers, these wild headlands are little changed since Clark stood here on November 18, 1805, and recorded in his journal:

> This spot, which was called Cape Disappointment, is an elevated circular knob, rising with a steep ascent 150 or 160 feet above the water, formed like the whole shore of the bay, as well as the seacoast, and covered with thick timber on the inner side but open and grassy in the exposure next to the sea.

The woods certainly remain as tangled as they were when Clark traversed them. You can walk through the crumbling concrete gun emplacements or hike to the north jetty, which guards the mouth of the river. Waves smash against the black boulders, throwing spray to the uppermost rocks, as gulls screech overhead. *Fort Canby State Park, 2.5 miles west of Ilwaco; 360-642-3078.*

■ EAST UP THE COLUMBIA *map page 212, A-4*

If you drive from Fort Canby up the Columbia River (follow U.S. 101 to Route 401 then to Route 4), you'll notice dark rock—a basalt flow older than the mountains—pushing through the soggy ground along the riverbank. From the abandoned gun batteries at **Fort Columbia State Park,** you can look straight down the river to the ocean. This is a delightfully rustic backwater of old sloughs, churches, and the green superstructure of the bridge to Astoria. A sign indicates the site at which Lewis and Clark camped for 10 days in November 1805, and evidently first saw breakers driven upriver from the open sea.

Abandoned cannery towns like Altoona, with tall pilings rising from the shore, are all that's left from the salmon traps and canneries that once lined the river. Across the Columbia, Cathlamet Bay is a maze of marshy islands and sloughs, where river folk live in floating homes, their boats tied up out front.

Be sure to wander through **Skamakowa,** a picturesque small town just off Route 4. Skamakowa is squeezed into a canyon so narrow that some of the houses are built on stilts over the water. You may also want to stop a bit farther on in **Cathlamet,** a charming hamlet with white clapboard Victorians and storefronts, rising on a wooded bluff above low-lying pastures and the fishermen's shacks of Puget Island. From here, if you are so inclined, you can take a ferry across the narrow channel separating the island from Oregon.

■ TRAVEL AND CLIMATE

■ GETTING THERE AND AROUND

Even though the Olympic Peninsula is quite close to Washington's metropolitan centers, it is separated from the more settled part of the state by saltwater channels and thus remains sparsely settled. In recent years a rise in tourism has led to a corresponding increase in good lodging facilities and restaurants.

By Car

From the south you can drive to this region via U.S. 101, which here is a narrow, winding two-lane highway skirting eerie bogs, moss-festooned forests, and clear-cuts overrun with alder and ferns. Even narrower roads lead from this parameter highway into the mountains and to quiet beaches. Route 8 and U.S. 12 link the coast at Grays Harbor to Olympia on Puget Sound. The road between Chehalis and Raymond is slow, winding, forest-lined Route 6.

By Ferry

You can take a car ferry to the Olympic Peninsula from Seattle, Anacortes, and Victoria *(see pages 176-177 for more information).*

■ CLIMATE

The coastal areas of the Olympic Peninsula are wetter but warmer than the lowlands of western Washington; the northeastern section of the peninsula lies in the rain shadow of the Olympic Mountains, and in some years the area receives little precipitation. But the Olympic rain forest has one of the highest annual rainfalls in the United States.

Snow falls in the mountains every winter but rarely reaches the shore, even when Puget Sound is shrouded in white. Storms rolling in from the Pacific can be fierce, with huge waves slamming into the shore and shooting driftwood high into the air. Calm, balmy winter days are fine times for walking the deserted beaches.

(above) Fishing boats in the harbor at Westport.
(opposite) Cape Disappointment Lighthouse overlooks the mouth of the Columbia River.

SOUTHERN LOWLANDS

■ HIGHLIGHTS

■ LANDSCAPE

SOUTH OF SEATTLE, THE LOWLANDS become much divided by saltwater inlets of Puget Sound cutting peninsulas into convoluted puzzle shapes and separating islands from the mainland. For this reason, this is a region of bridges and ferries. The latter connect Vashon Island to Seattle and Tacoma, and the Kitsap Peninsula to Seattle.

South of Olympia, the lowlands continue as a wide trough, between the Cascades and the Coast Range, all the way to the Columbia River. To the southeast rise the stately Mount Rainier and the broken-off top of Mount St. Helens, once the most beautifully symmetrical of all Cascade volcanoes.

■ SOUTHERN PUGET SOUND   *map page 229*

Traveling through the southern Puget Sound country is a delight. In much of the southern lowlands, roads shaded by trees alternate with green pastures where cattle graze contentedly; in southern Puget Sound, you never know when the trees lining your road will drop away to reveal views of idyllic saltwater inlets. Peninsular roads are quiet enough to allow for enjoyable exploration by bicycle. Because few ferries

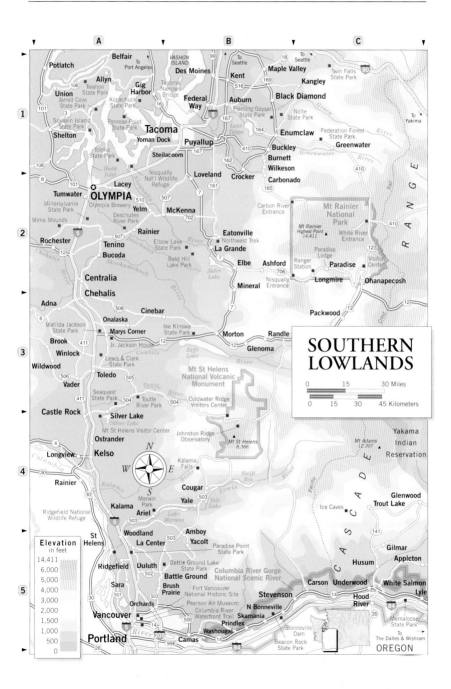

SOUTHERN LOWLANDS

0   15   30 Miles

0   15   30   45 Kilometers

travel on the southern inlets, you'll have to bring or charter a boat to explore the intricate waterways. Many local mariners do that in the same canoes they use on lowland rivers. But be aware that tidal differences are greater the farther south you travel. At Olympia, they can be more than 16 feet, and high tides create strong currents at ebb and flood.

When Capt. George Vancouver named Puget Sound in 1792, he made it clear he was referring only to its southern end: "...to commemorate Mr. Puget's exertions, the south extremity of it I named Puget's Sound." The name has since become applied to a much greater region, encompassing Admiralty Inlet to the north and even Washington Sound (Bellingham Bay and the San Juan Islands).

The bay Vancouver named after Mr. Puget was most likely Commencement Bay, where the city of Tacoma is now located. Puget's party made note of the people living along the water's edge:

> They seemed not wanting in offers of friendship and hospitality; as on our joining their party, we were presented with such things as they had to dispose of: and they immediately prepared a few of the roots, with some shell fish for our refreshment, which were very palatable. (Journal, May 20th, 1792)

Which is just what might happen to a modern-day visitor coming upon a clambake on the beach.

■ TACOMA *map page 229, B-1*

Tacoma, draped dramatically over a waterbound headland between Commencement Bay and Puget Sound, offers great views of Mount Rainier, excellent parks, and a downtown with some interesting and ornate late-19th-century buildings.

Visitors will find much beauty in Tacoma, and many things to admire. To see the city from its best angle, travelers should arrive by ferry from Vashon Island to the north (take the ferry from Fauntleroy Cove in Seattle to Vashon, drive down the island, and take the ferry from Vashon to Tacoma). You'll be facing the tree-clad slopes of Point Defiance as you arrive, with the port stretching to the east.

But most visitors arrive in town via I-5 and take I-705 downtown, a spur that ends on A Street. **Old City Hall** and the headquarters of the **Northern Pacific Railway** are the portals of the north end of downtown. Up the hill, the Broadway Center for the Performing Arts, a complex of historic and new theaters, presents plays, concerts, and films in three fine venues: **Pantages Theater** (901 Broadway; 253-591-5894), a restored vaudeville house; the **Rialto Theater** (301 South Ninth Street; 253-591-5890); and the newer **Theater on the Square** (Broadway and South Ninth Street).

At the south end of downtown, look for the old, domed Union Station, now part of a federal courthouse. The **Washington State History Museum** (1911 Pacific Avenue; 888-238-4373) tells the state's story with artifacts and high-tech video displays and interactive computers. The **Museum of Glass** (1801 East Dock Street; 253-396-1768), which opened in 2002, exhibits glass and other media, with an emphasis on the contemporary. The **Tacoma Art Museum** (1123 Pacific Avenue; 253-272-4258) houses a small collection of European and American art.

If Tacoma's Stadium-Seminary and Hilltop Districts seem to have more than their share of stately Victorian homes, that's because of the building boom of the 1880s, when the Northern Pacific Railway picked Tacoma over Seattle as the Pacific Northwest endpoint for its transcontinental railroad. Fancy new homes sprouted all over town until the nationwide depression of 1883, when construction came to a screeching halt. The depression was over by the 1898 gold rush, but by then Seattle had its own railroad connections and momentum shifted away from Tacoma.

Most of the Victorian-era homes decorating hills around Tacoma can't be toured, but a few are open to the public, including **Chinaberry Hill** (302 North Tacoma Avenue; 253-272-1282), a Queen Anne–style dwelling with stained-glass windows, original fixtures, and a garden. Also worth a look is the **E. R. Rogers Mansion** (1702 Commercial Street; 253-582-0280) in Steilacoom, south of Tacoma. Built in 1891, the house, which is also a popular restaurant, has views of the Tacoma Narrows Bridge and is tastefully decorated with lace valances, brass fixtures, and antiques.

Point Defiance Park is one of the most rewarding parks you'll ever visit anywhere in the United States. On a wooded peninsula that projects into the sound, the park has miles of tree-shaded roads that wind through idyllic glens. A beach runs along the shore, and there are rose gardens, grassy slopes, and brushy ravines echoing with the song of birds. The outdoor **Camp Six Logging Museum** (253-752-0047) displays old logging equipment and has the original granary from the Hudson's Bay Company's old **Fort Nisqually** (253-591-5339). **Point Defiance Zoo & Aquarium** (5400 North Pearl Street; 253-591-5337) has a shark tank, aquariums, and elephants. *From downtown Tacoma, take Ruston Way north along the waterfront (follow signs).*

The state capitol in Olympia.

■ NISQUALLY NATIONAL WILDLIFE REFUGE
map page 229, B-1

On the shore of Puget Sound between Tacoma and Olympia, the fields and marshes of the spreading Nisqually Delta are preserved as the Nisqually National Wildlife Refuge. Walk through the refuge to the water's edge. To the north, beyond the sprays of purple daisies and the brown marsh grass beaten flat by high water, the gray-green Nisqually River, lined by dense stands of trees, flows toward Puget Sound.

A wooden boardwalk runs in a loop from the visitors center through the marshes to the river and back to the visitors center. This is a great place to observe marsh birds, dabbling ducks, and, in spring, wetland wildflowers like skunk cabbage. Primeval-looking giant horsetails also grow here. Ask the ranger to point out the resident great horned owl, which perches in a black cottonwood during the day. Ponds to the west of the parking area are home to uncommon ducks even during the non-migratory season. (The refuge also has the only public restrooms on the freeway between Seattle and Olympia.) *I-5 Exit 114; 360-753-9467.*

■ OLYMPIA *map page 229, A-1/2*

The first territorial legislature met here in 1854, in a room above the Gold Bar Store and Restaurant. At the time, the town was little more than a few scattered cabins and a patch of land above a muddy bay. The domed marble capitol that stands above the modern city wasn't completed until 1928. For 74 years before that, legislators met in the Masonic Temple, a humble wooden hall, and (from 1901 to 1928) in the old Thurston County Courthouse, currently known as the Old Capitol.

You can see the current capitol dome from the freeway, rising above the trees. Up close, it's an unusually handsome building set in a nicely landscaped campus—quite beautiful in spring, when the trees are in bloom. Downhill from the capitol and state office buildings east of Capitol Way lie downtown Olympia and the old center of political gravity at **Sylvester Park.** The turreted stone mass of the **Old Capitol** building, between Franklin and Washington Streets, overlooks the park from the east. On the north stands the former **Olympian Hotel** (116 Legion Way SE), where generations of lobbyists bought politicians lavish meals, deals were made,

Paradise Inn in Mount Rainier National Park. The ranger station here records more snow annually than any other place on earth—over 100 feet in a recent year.

big-time legislators set up housekeeping, and old pols hung out in the lobby. The Olympian suffered major structural damage in the Nisqually earthquake of 2001.

The **Japanese Garden,** a symbol of the sister-city relationship Olympia shares with Yashiro, Japan, opened in 1989. Within the garden are a waterfall, bamboo grove, koi pond, and stone lanterns. *Union and Plum Streets, east of the Capitol campus.*

Olympia's downtown is low-key but interesting, replete with used bookshops, cafes, and record stores. Old brick buildings—many a bit rundown and some of them stripped of their cornices by a fierce earthquake in 1949—line the streets. The town's vitality shines in the scruffy bars where the worlds of middle-age working stiffs and college kids with green hair overlap. But even around its dilapidated edges, Olympia is never threatening.

■ **MOUNT RAINIER** *map page 229, C-2*

Mount Rainier National Park lies 92 miles (a two-hour drive) south of Seattle and 143 miles (a three-hour drive) north of Portland. Embracing the slopes of the 14,410-foot volcano, the park contains broad tracts of old-growth forest, waterfalls, glaciers, and meadows carpeted in summertime by wildflowers. Roads lead to vantage points on all sides of the mountain, each with its own celebrated views (when the clouds lift), lodges and campgrounds, and hiking and cross-country ski trails. You don't have to walk far to enjoy Rainier's wild beauty: even near a much-traveled entrance road a brief uphill walk from the pavement can leave you standing all alone, contemplating the sharp outline of a bear's fresh paw print.

Mount Rainier can be approached by road from the west, the northwest, and the east. That said, keep in mind that the southwestern and one of the eastern approaches actually take you to the southern slopes of the mountain.

The **park headquarters,** including a visitors center and an inn, is located in the southwestern corner of the park at Longmire, 2,761 feet above sea level. From there, the road climbs 13 miles to **Paradise,** at 5,400 feet.

You can drive through a forest of huge trees to the **Paradise Inn** at any time of year—in summer to enjoy the hiking, in winter for the cross-country skiing. The inn looks exactly the way a mountain lodge should. With its hand-carved cedar logs, burnished parquet floors, stone fireplaces, Indian rugs, and glorious mountain views, the 75-year-old inn is loaded with atmosphere. *Nisqually Entrance, Route 706 off I-5; 360-569-2211.*

(preceding page) Alta Vista Trail winds through fields of wildflowers in the Paradise area.

■ MOUNT ST. HELENS *map page 229, B-4*

A trip to Mount St. Helens is a bit like a visit to a war zone. Although more than two decades have passed since the volcanic eruption that destroyed the mountain's top, scars of that event are still prominent everywhere you look. Until 1980, Mount St. Helens was a serene-looking 9,677-foot volcano. Visitors to nearby Spirit Lake enjoyed the reflection of the peak's perfectly symmetrical cone in the lake's blue water. Then, in the spring of 1980, geologists noticed some ominous rumblings and warned that an eruption was inevitable.

Few were prepared for what happened on the morning of May 18. More than 1,300 feet of its top simply disappeared. Instead of going straight up, the blast went north, destroying everything in its path. Old-growth forests were vaporized. Big trees a little farther from the blast were scattered across the hillsides like straw or were simply killed where they stood. Soil was incinerated and nearby slopes were scoured down to bedrock. Volcanic ash fell on 22,000 square miles of land, including much of eastern Washington.

The sky in many eastern Washington communities darkened at midday, and ash piled up like drifted snow on the streets and sidewalks. Snow and glacial ice melted by the blast poured down the mountain, creating rivers of mud that swelled the Toutle River, which rose 66 feet above its normal level, sweeping away homes and bridges. Mud flowed down to the Cowlitz and the Columbia Rivers, where millions of tons had to be dredged from the shipping channel. Fifty-seven people died. The devastation appeared complete.

But pocket gophers living underground survived the blast, and fireweed and other plants started recolonizing some of the blast area within a year. Soon, herds of huge brown elk wandered comfortably across the mud and the ridges above. Much of the area remains a moonscape, but life is returning. Weyerhaeuser, which owned most of the land in the path of the blast, traded some to the federal government, which included it in a Mount St. Helens National Volcanic Monument.

Before making the long drive to the mountain along Route 504, stop at the **Mount St. Helens Visitor Center at Silver Lake** (360-274-2100), where you can learn about the eruption by walking through a giant model of the volcano. You can also pick up maps and information for touring and hire guides to lead you into the blast zone.

Mount St. Helens smolders above Coldwater Lake (left).

The 1980 eruption leveled everything for miles around. Now fireweed grows among the trees blasted by the eruption.

■ FALL COLOR

Few people outside this region know that the low hills and the mountains surrounding Mount Rainier and Mount St. Helens have some of the most spectacular fall color in the West. Most of the color in the mountain meadows is provided by the red and pink leaves of huckleberry bushes and by the golden leaves of mountain ash. As an extra bonus, ripe blueberries often stay on the bushes until well into October. On the lower slopes, the yellow and brown leaves of bigleaf maples, the gold of mountain maples, and the fiery reds of vine maples brighten the hillsides.

The fall colors are in their prime before the first killing frost and fade shortly after. You will find the best color in open areas and along creeks and rivers, where deciduous trees dominate the landscape and in clear cuts. Near Mount St. Helens National Volcanic Monument, along Forest Road 81, fall color should be best by mid-October. Other prime areas run from the town of Cougar along Forest Roads 90/25 to their junction with Forest Road 93; from Elk Pass north to Randle on Forest Road 25; and the entire length of Forest Road 90, especially from Swift Dam to the Pine Creek Information Station and the east end of Swift Reservoir.

■ VANCOUVER *map page 229, A-5*

Vancouver lies more in the economic orbit of Portland, Oregon, than of any place in Washington State. The city's downtown buildings rarely rise above two stories, and its tallest ones resemble sawed-off corncobs. Unlike most cities, you never feel like you can find the center of things. Vancouver contains a handful of beautiful art deco structures built during the 1930s, like the elegant **Telephone Exchange** (112 West 11th Street) and the **Elks Building** (916 Main Street).

Vancouver may not be the most exciting city in the world, but the people who live here are friendly, and the city demonstrates unusual ethnic diversity. If you like pawn shops, you'll love Vancouver. There must be more of these places per capita than just about anywhere else in the state—there are three of them in the 600 block of Main Street alone. Though it may be short on modern attractions, Vancouver has plenty in the way of history, much of it at the **Fort Vancouver National Historic Site.**

Vancouver developed as a city on the site of the Hudson's Bay Company's Fort Vancouver in the early 19th century. The Hudson's Bay Company was originally a British fur-trading monopoly that established a network of forts, farms, and way stations, and served as an arm of His Majesty's government in the Oregon Country. The company built Fort Vancouver on the river's flat north bank in 1824. After the British left, the fort was taken over by the U.S. Army.

During World War I, Fort Vancouver served as headquarters for the army's Spruce Production Division, and a mill on the site cut Sitka spruce into lumber for wood-and-fabric military aircraft. Army barracks built in 1849 adjoin the Fort Vancouver National Historic Site and are still in use. And the Hudson's Bay Company is still in business, making its famous point blankets and maintaining stores in shopping malls throughout Canada.

The last building of the original fort burned to the ground in 1866, but since the mid-1960s, most of its buildings have been reconstructed on the fort's original site (east of I-5, off Exit 1C). Old Fort Vancouver stood at the edge of the Columbia River, but a more modern avenue of commerce, Route 14, now runs between the reconstructed fort and the river. Outside the stockade are an apple orchard and an orderly garden full of flowers and vegetables. Inside the stockade, park rangers dressed in period costume offer demonstrations in the bakery and the smithy.

The original fort owed its importance to early-19th-century geopolitics. After the War of 1812, Great Britain and the United States set the U.S.–Canadian border east of the Rocky Mountains at the 49th parallel, but failed to agree on a border west of the Great Divide. After much deliberation, the two countries agreed to a joint occupation of the disputed Oregon Country, a wilderness stretching from the Alaska panhandle to California, and bounded east and west by the Rockies and the Pacific Ocean respectively.

In the early years of joint occupation, Fort Vancouver was the vast territory's sole bastion of Anglo civilization, and orders from the Hudson's Bay Company were law. Indeed, the company strove for self-sufficiency, building farms, sawmills, and smithies to supply its forts and outposts. It guaranteed protection to anyone traveling to or from its forts with furs, and forbade its employees to trade liquor to the Indians (who did most of the trapping).

Pacific Northwest historian Carlos Schwantes wrote that within its 20-foot-high stockade, "Fort Vancouver constituted a small, almost self-sufficient European community." Also here were a hospital, storehouses, workshops, mills, a shipyard, a dairy, orchards, and a farm of several hundred acres. "Ships from distant ports called at Fort Vancouver bringing news, books, and periodicals to stock the post's library."

John McLoughlin ran the fort on the Columbia in a truly imperial manner. "Nightly," writes Peter C. Newman in a history of the Hudson's Bay Company, "the Company's traders and visiting dignitaries gathered at the officers' mess to trade tall tales in the warm light of candelabra, lolling at tables laden with crested cutlery, crystal glasses and blue earthenware dishes…with McLoughlin leading spirited exchanges of ideas that spun on long into the convivial nights."

McLoughlin's virtues as a host did not mean that he was soft on the people who worked for him or on those who strayed into the Company's sphere of influence. "What impressed the Indian chiefs who came to call was McLoughlin's sense of justice," Newman writes. "Anyone—white or Indian—caught breaking the Chief Factor's concept of permissible behavior was sentenced to be lashed while tied to the fort's cannon." Nevertheless, McLoughlin fed American trappers who showed up hungry on his doorstep, and he gave supplies on credit to American settlers who came over the Oregon Trail, ignoring company policy against helping Americans, who rarely paid him or the company back. Although McLoughlin was later called "the Father of Oregon," he died in Oregon Territory unappreciated and bitter.

By that time, Vancouver had become part of the United States. Hudson's Bay Company governor George Simpson had foreseen the outcome of the boundary struggle between the United States and Great Britain and had relocated Company

(opposite) Jonathan Campbell-Lewis dressed as Lt. Henry Warre, Fort Vancouver.

headquarters to Vancouver Island, in Canada, in 1843. Three years later, Britain gave up all claim to what is now Washington and Oregon. *Fort Vancouver National Historic Site, East Evergreen Boulevard and East Fifth Street; 360-696-7655.*

The 4-mile **Columbia River Waterfront Trail** follows the river from the Captain Vancouver Monument, near the I-5 bridge, to Tidewater Barge, passing Waterfront Park, Renaissance Promenade, and the plaza and a statue dedicated to Ilchee, daughter of Concomly, a famous Chinook Indian chief of the 19th century. The oldest apple tree in the state, the Marine Park Wetlands, and Kaiser Viewing Tower and Shipyards are a few of the passing points worth noting along the trail.

East of Fort Vancouver is Pearson Air Field, the oldest active airfield in the western United States. It's the site of several famous aviation feats, including the 1937 trans-polar flight from Moscow to Vancouver (63 hours and 16 minutes). The **Pearson Air Museum,** in the M.J. Murdock Aviation Center on the north side of the field, reveals this history with a 25,000-square-foot museum that includes vintage airplanes, exhibits, a cockpit simulator, and photographs of planes and their pilots. *1115 East Fifth Street; 360-694-7026.*

■ TRAVEL AND CLIMATE

■ GETTING THERE AND AROUND

By Car
This region lies between southern Puget Sound and the Columbia River, which divides Oregon and Washington. The main north-south route, I-5, connects Seattle to Portland. Off the freeway, this is a region of quiet farms and forests. Narrow two-lane highways connect the lowlands to the coast and to the high country of the southern Cascades. Mount St. Helens and Mount Rainier rise above the deeply green foothills to the east. U.S. 12 skirts the lower slopes of Mount Rainier before descending into the fertile Yakima Valley to the east.

■ CLIMATE

Weather in this area can be highly variable: the Coast Range intercepts much of the rain coming in from the ocean. Skies are often sunny or covered with broken clouds. Summer temperatures range from 65 to 80 degrees F. Winters can be quite cold, and the lowlands can be covered with snow for days at a time.

YAKIMA VALLEY FOOD AND WINE TOUR

The Yakima Valley is Washington's food basket and wine vat. Most people either travel here via Portland and the Columbia Gorge, coming up U.S. 97, or begin the trip in Seattle, crossing the Cascade Mountains on I-90. Interstate 82, which starts in Ellensburg, runs the length of the Yakima Valley. Or you can reach the valley on U.S. 12, which skirts the southern flanks of Mount Rainier.

■ COUNTRYSIDE

The Yakima River flows southeast from its source in the Cascades, cutting steep canyons through serried basalt ridges. After merging with the Naches River, it crosses the Ahtanum Valley as it passes the city of Yakima. At Union Gap, the river breaks through Ahtanum Ridge and enters the long valley bearing its name. Throughout its course, the Yakima is a rocky river, with many rapids. It was once a major salmon stream. A few salmon, undefeated by dams, still ascend the river to spawn.

Grass-covered hills, where the Yakama people freely roamed little more than a century ago, rise above green fields, orchards, and vineyards. Horses still run wild in the Horse Heaven Hills on the Yakama Indian Reservation.

Apples and other fruits took hold in valley orchards in the 1890s, with the first irrigation schemes. Grapes came much later. Concord grapes were planted first, and finally vinifera grapes used in making fine wines. Three decades ago, there were virtually no vinifera vineyards in the valley; today, they dominate the local wine industry. This is more than just another wine valley, though. The Yakima Valley grows most of the nation's hops,

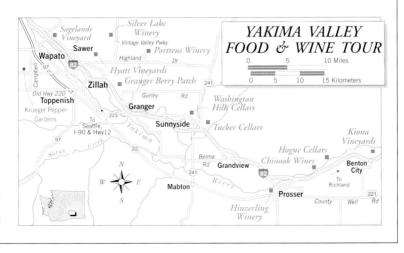

and some of its best asparagus—it's so tender you can eat it raw, straight from the field. Tomatoes and chilis ripen to perfection in the long, hot summer days, and melons take on extra sweetness.

There are apricot, cherry, peach, and apple orchards as well. Their quality is good, though not as outstanding as the fruit grown in the east-facing valleys of the North Cascades. Yakima Valley apples get better farther west, in the foothills of the Cascades. Which is why Selah, west of Yakima, is the apple capital of south-central Washington.

Conversely, the grape quality improves the closer you get to the mitigating influence of the Columbia River. Which is why Prosser and Benton City are at the heart of the Yakima Valley wine country.

■ TOURING THE VALLEY

Because the valley's vegetables are as good as the wines, we'll start at a Wapato farm before visiting our first vineyard. The serious wine touring starts just beyond Union Gap at I-82, Exit 40, about 7 miles east of the town of Yakima.

Krueger Pepper Gardens

This exceptional farm is known for high-quality peppers—more than 60 varieties are grown here. Bring your own container, though, it's strictly u-pick. The peppers are at their peak when the grape harvest starts, as are the tomatoes, eggplant, squash, and melons. Pick up a free recipe booklet at the farm office. *3491 Branch Road, Wapato; 509-877-3677.*

Sagelands Vineyard

The valley's westernmost winery occupies a beautiful spot on a south-facing slope. Sagelands' umbrella-shaded picnic area frames great views across the valley and nearby hills. While sipping an excellent cabernet or merlot, you can watch turkey vultures, hawks, and eagles soar against the backdrop of snow-capped Mount Adams. In a valley where most wineries have adopted a utilitarian, rustic style that makes it difficult to distinguish them from barns and farm sheds, Sagelands is most definitely an architectural high point—a feast for the eyes as well as the palate. *71 Gangl Road, Wapato; 509-877-2112.*

Silver Lake Winery

In August 2001, Silver Lake acquired the former Covey Run Winery building adjacent to Silver Lake's Roza Hills Vineyard. This winery is famous for its panoramic views of the Whiskey Canyon vineyards, the Yakima Valley, and Mount Adams. The cabernet sauvignons and merlots are uniquely flavorful. *1500 Vintage Road, Zillah; 509-829-6235.*

Hyatt Vineyards

Hyatt Vineyards has earned national attention, especially for its zesty merlots and flavorful cabernet sauvignons. The late-harvest Riesling is also worth tasting. Hyatt sits on 97 acres and has spacious grounds for picnicking. On clear days, you can take in views of Yakima Valley and the Cascades. *2020 Gilbert Road; Zillah; 509-829-6333.*

Portteus

Before making its own wine, Portteus gained fame as a grape grower, its grapes going into some of Washington's best reds. Taste the cabernet and merlot as well as the spicy zinfandel—yes, zinfandel. Portteus was the first Washington winery to vinify this noble grape. *5201 Highland Drive, 5 miles north of Zillah; 509-829-6970.*

Granger Berry Patch

This farm sells many different varieties of berries, including uncommon tayberries, blackcaps, and yellow raspberries. The farm also grows raspberries that ripen in fall, just as the grape harvest gets underway. *1731 Beam Road, Granger; 509-854-1413.*

Washington Hills Cellars

Brian Carter of Washington Hills has a reputation second to none. His winery divides its products into three brands: Apex for the top of the line wines; Washington Hills for varietals and blends; and W. B. Bridgman for quaffing wines. Any respectable wine cellar should have some Apex wines, especially the cabernets, merlots, and chardonnays. *111 East Lincoln Avenue, Sunnyside; 509-839-9463.*

Tucker Cellars

Tucker produces refreshingly fruity Rieslings and chenin blancs. The red varietals and reserve chardonnays are sold only at the winery. In spring, you can buy delicious asparagus; in summer, perfect melons and vegetables; and in fall, incredibly sweet corn. At any time of year, you can sample Tucker's white popcorn, pickled vegetables, and wines. *70 Ray Road, Sunnyside, east of Route 24, Exit 69; 509-837-8701.*

Hinzerling Winery

Mike Wallace, a Washington wine industry pioneer, has produced some superb wines, particularly reds and port-style wines. He also has a talent for bringing out the complex flavors of gewürztraminer. *1520 Sheridan Avenue, Prosser; 509-786-2163.*

Hyatt Vineyards in Zillah.

Chinook Wines

The happy marriage of viticulturist Clay Mackey and wine-maker Kay Simon has resulted in fine chardonnays, sauvignon blancs, semillons, cabernet francs, cabernet sauvignons, and merlots. Unfortunately, these wines are always in short supply. But chances are you'll find some at the winery when they're unavailable anywhere else. *Wine Country Road off I-82, Prosser; 509-786-2725.*

The Hogue Cellars

Besides grapes, Hogue grows hops and vegetables and produces excellent pickled asparagus and beans, all for sale at the winery. The Hogue fumé blanc has gained a regional reputation, the dry chenin blanc is everyone's favorite summer afternoon wine, and the reds go well with most foods. *Wine Country Road off I-82, Prosser; 509-786-4557.*

Kiona Vineyards Winery

At one of the state's most respected red wine producers, the cabernet sauvignons and merlots have deeply complex flavors, and late-harvest wines made from Riesling, chenin

A picture-perfect Yakima Valley vineyard near the town of Zillah.

blanc, and gewürztraminer grapes are top-notch. Bring the fixings for a picnic, and spend the afternoon. *44612 North Sunset Road Northeast, Benton City; 509-588-6716.*

Other Wines of Note

Be sure to taste the Gordon Brothers' merlots from their **Snake River Vineyards** and the semillons by **L'Ecole No. 41,** made from Walla Walla Valley grapes. The Walla Walla cabernet sauvignons made by **Leonetti Cellar** and **Woodward Canyon** are good too. And by no means neglect the delicious cabernets of **Quilceda Creek.** Look for them in wineshops or ask for them in restaurants. (The restaurant at Yakima's Birchfield Manor Inn has an excellent selection of rare local bottlings.)

One last note: summer days in the Yakima Valley can get very hot. Don't leave wine or fresh produce in your car. The produce will cook, and the wine bottles may pop their corks.

P O R T L A N D

■ **SETTING**

PORTLAND IS ONE OF the most beautiful cities in the West, its downtown snuggled between the Willamette River and tree-clad hills. Mount Hood, rising up majestically in Portland's backyard, adds to the city's ambiance and seems to anchor it in its lush green home.

Between springtime showers, Portland sparkles. The entire city greens up in an instant, and there's a heady burst of cherry trees, dogwoods, and daffodils, all damp from the last shower and pulsing with growth.

Metropolitan green spaces, access to rivers, and lively neighborhoods are important to Portland's sense of place. The touches of old-fashioned statuary and what's now called public art, from the elk at SW Third Avenue and Main Street to the umbrella man on Pioneer Courthouse Square or the Electronic Poet near 10th Avenue and Morrison Street, show that this is a city with a civic spirit. Among the best-loved graceful touches are the "Benson bubblers," non-stop water fountains on downtown streets. Simon Benson, an early timber king, reputedly donated the four-pronged fountains to divert employees from the evils of whiskey.

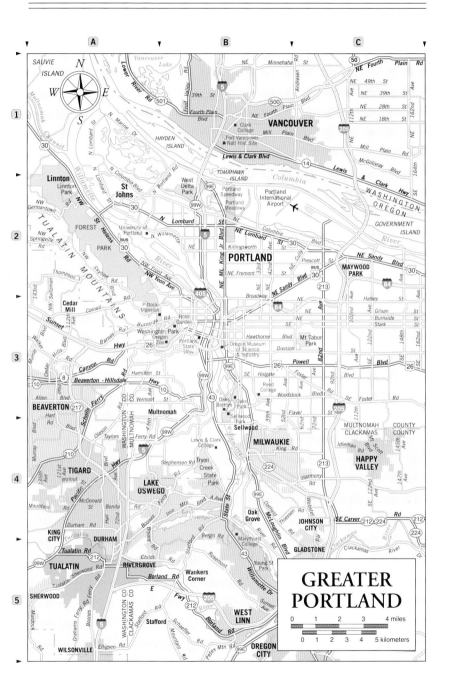

GREATER PORTLAND

0   1   2   3   4 miles

0 1 2 3 4 5 kilometers

■ HISTORY AND CULTURE

The west bank of the Willamette River was a canoe stop for Indians traveling between the Willamette Valley and the Columbia River trading markets well before Portland's first settlers took a shine to it in 1843. Portland rose to become an important river port and seaport. It supplied the mines of Idaho and Montana and shipped out wheat from eastern Oregon and Washington farms.

But if you saw Portland in the middle of the 19th century, you might not have given the fledgling community on the lower Willamette much of a chance. Oregon City, the Northwest's first city, was fortuitously located at the falls of the Willamette, which meant not only waterpower to drive mills but also translated into an advantageous proximity to the rich agricultural lands of the Willamette Valley. Therefore, at the time, it was the territorial capital. But Portland's founders were not discouraged. For one thing, Portland was connected to the rich wheat fields of the Tualatin Plains by a primitive but serviceable road; for another it had something Oregon City did not have: deep water. Captain John H. Couch, one of Portland's founding fathers, is said to have pointed at the Willamette River bank and remark, "To this very point, I can bring any ship that can get into the mouth of the Columbia River. And not, sir, one rod farther."

Upon such slight encouragement, the Portlanders improved the wagon road to the Tualatin Plains by paving it with wooden planks. With the new road, the farmer's trade transferred from Oregon City to Portland. Oregon City faded into the twilight zone of just another mill town. (The capital was moved to Salem in 1859, when Oregon became a state.) After that, Portland had an eye out for the main chance. A few years later, it snagged the lucrative trade to the Idaho gold fields, leaving Fort Vancouver high and dry. Portland entrepreneurs got control of the Columbia riverboat lines, and when the first railroads came through, they snagged those, too. It wasn't until late in the 19th century that other upstart cities, like Seattle, were able to catch up.

But it wasn't all smooth sailing. Portland, derisively called "Stump Town" by its many detractors, was not designed to be a regional metropolis. One problem was the Willamette River, which insisted on its ancient right of spreading out over its floodplain—Portland's downtown. Flooding became an almost annual spring event. And while setting aside land for forested Washington Park back in 1871 was most certainly a visionary move, it also meant that elk and even black bears regularly meandered downtown to drink from public fountains and to nibble on municipal grasses, shrubs, and fruits. Building a higher and higher seawall along the riverfront finally kept floodwaters at bay. Infilling, through the construction of brick and granite mercantile emporiums and office buildings, coupled with population growth, eventually drove the wild animals back into the hills.

As Portland grew, the north end of First Street was chockablock with sailors boarding in rooming houses, drinking in bars, and sleeping with the pros. When a ship needed more crew members, drunk or drugged men sometimes woke up below deck, shanghaied to serve as sailors.

Growth, based largely on the shipment of lumber and Willamette Valley farm products, continued. Even though Portland did not have the airplane and ship-building industries of Seattle, its rival to the north, the city prospered during World War II and has never looked back. In recent years, high-tech industries based in the suburbs (most notably Intel) have contributed to Portland's well-being. And, of course, Portland's shops, theaters, museums, and parks attract large numbers of visitors.

■ DOWNTOWN PORTLAND

■ PIONEER COURTHOUSE SQUARE *map page 249, B-3*
Office workers and street kids carve out their territories on the inscribed bricks of Pioneer Courthouse Square, and it's a rare summer afternoon when "downtown's living room," as it's called, doesn't feature a concert or rally. The square, reclaimed from a parking lot in 1983, is a good place to start a walking tour of downtown.

Before its tenure as a parking lot, Pioneer Courthouse Square was the site of the Portland Hotel, an elegant building that, were it still standing, would turn heads today. The eponymous courthouse, across Sixth Avenue from the square, was Portland's earliest sign of civilization. When it was built in 1869, it was considered too distant from the city's waterfront hub. Traffic patterns changed, and for a century, the Pioneer Courthouse has marked downtown's center.

■ NIKETOWN *map page 249, B-3*
Niketown, at SW Sixth Avenue and Salmon Street, offers up a more pedestrian culture. The vault-like shoe store is a celebration of professional sports, a reliquary for the runner Steve Prefontaine's letter jacket from the University of Oregon, a Wheaties box signed by basketball star Michael Jordan, a football jersey that Brett

Favre wore, and Scottie Pippen's 1995 NBA All-Star Game shoes. To shop, cross the Willamette to the Nike outlet at 3044 NE Martin Luther King Boulevard.

■ **PORTLAND BUILDING**   *map page 249, B-4*
At the postmodern Portland Building at SW Fifth Avenue and Main Street, city bureaucrats complain about the tiny windows in architect Michael Graves's "birthday cake" of a building. This was Graves's first big public commission and the nation's first postmodern public building, a triumph of theory over the shapes and spaces that comfort human beings. Wander into the lobby, visit the balcony gallery, or sit in on a public meeting, and see whether you're pleased or appalled.

Portlandia, the 36-foot-tall, 6.25-ton copper statue of a woman kneeling over the front door of the Portland Building gets as much attention as the building itself. The elk statue in the middle of SW Main Street between Third and Fourth Avenues is a whimsical favorite. The plaza next to the statue was once a meadow where elk grazed. Today, pigeons and courthouse workers feed here. (All manner of people use the benches; the bathrooms are not a safe bet.)

The Portlandia statue outside the Portland Building on Fifth Avenue.

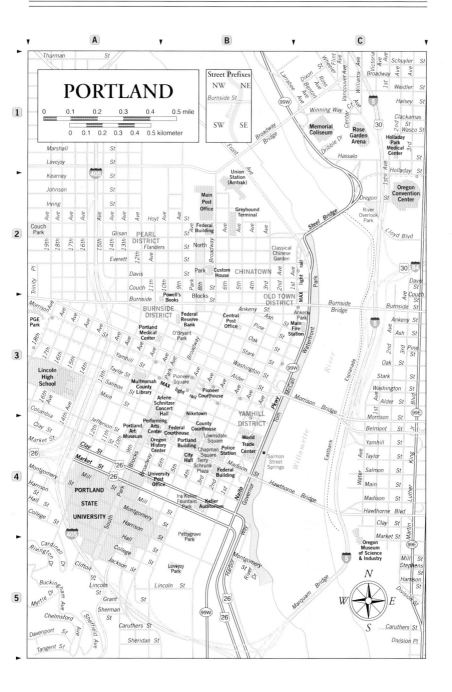

PORTLAND

| 0 | 0.1 | 0.2 | 0.3 | 0.4 | 0.5 mile |

| 0 | 0.1 | 0.2 | 0.3 | 0.4 | 0.5 kilometer |

Street Prefixes

NW NE

Burnside St

SW SE

■ PORTLAND CENTER FOR THE PERFORMING ARTS

map page 249, A-4

The fancy brick buildings just north of the History Center make up the Portland Center for the Performing Arts, the city's premier spot for live theater. The Center comprises three main buildings. The "Schnitz," **Arlene Schnitzer Concert Hall** (SW Broadway at Main Street), is a grand Portland vaudeville house, host to the Oregon Symphony and the popular Portland Arts and Lecture Series. Watching plays performed by the Tygres Heart Shakespeare Company is worth a special visit to Portland. This lively group has taken Shakespeare to heart, putting on dynamic performances on a par with those of Ashland's Shakespearean troupe. **The Keller Auditorium** (222 SW Clay Street at Third Avenue) and the **New Theater Building** (SW Broadway at Main Street), which contains the Dolores Winningstad Theater, the Newmark Theater, and the Brunish Hall, present a vast array of performances. But there's more to these theaters than the state-of-the-art facilities. Portland is a theater town and watching the audience respond to good acting is as enjoyable as watching the actors perform on stage.

Free tours (503-248-4335) are offered on Wednesdays at 11 A.M., Saturdays every half hour from 11 A.M. to 1 P.M., and on the first Thursday of every month at 6 P.M. Tours leave from the lobby of the New Theater Building at SW Broadway and Main Street.

■ PARK BLOCKS

In 1852, as tree stumps were being pulled from the muddy streets, civic leaders were thinking about preserving corridors of trees and grass in the fast-growing city. The stately Park Blocks are a strip of downtown city streets set aside as a park, an oasis of tree-shaded lawns, walkways, and benches (with an occasional statue and fountain) one block west of Broadway. With the exception of a seven-block stretch, the Park Blocks remain intact.

■ PORTLAND ART MUSEUM AND OREGON HISTORY CENTER

The elm-shaded Park Blocks are flanked by the Portland Art Museum (1219 SW Park Avenue; 503-226-2811) and the Oregon History Center (1200 SW Park Avenue; 503-222-1741). The art museum draws raves for its Northwest Coast Indian collection and for its Wednesday evening "Museum After Hours" concerts (from October to April). Exhibits change seasonally at the History Center's museum, which faces onto Broadway.

■ WATERFRONT *map page 249, B/C-2/5*

The waterfront, once lined by wharfs, then overrun by a freeway, is now a pleasant park. **Salmon Street Springs**, a fountain whose flow is timed to be highest when the city is bustling, is a great place to pause and people-watch.

Stroll north past men fishing for sturgeon with giant hooks (occasionally one is pulled onto the seawall) to the **Japanese-American Historical Plaza**, north of the Burnside Bridge. It's a quiet spot, where stone-carved words recall the lives and contributions of Portland's Issei, Japanese immigrants who were forced into internment camps in eastern Oregon during World War II.

■ TOM MCCALL WATERFRONT PARK *map page 249, B/C-2/5*

The reclamation of the west bank of the Willamette River between 1974 and 1982 gave the city the **Tom McCall Waterfront Park**. The 3-mile swath of green is shared by visitors, transients, joggers, and bicyclists. From late spring through the summer, a different festival takes place on most weekends.

■ OLD TOWN *map page 249, B-3*

In Old Town, near the Burnside Bridge, cast-iron facades on old brick buildings hint of a grand past. The pilaster-fronted **New Market Theater** (SW First Avenue and Ankeny Street) was the reputable place to spend an evening in the 1880s, though second-floor theatergoers had to put up with the din and muddle of first-floor greengrocers and butchers. Outside, the four graceful bronze women of **Skidmore Fountain** hold an overflowing basin aloft. The fountain was built in 1888 for "men, horses, and dogs," and remains a lovely rendezvous for men, women, children, and dogs (the occasional horse, bearing a cop, still comes by).

■ SATURDAY MARKET *map page 249, B-3*

On Saturdays and Sundays, Portland's justly famous Saturday Market is held in several adjacent parking lots between First Avenue and Front Street near the Skidmore Fountain. It's said to be the nation's largest crafts fair, with more booths than you can possibly stop and shop at in one weekend. Ethnic food booths serve a great variety of different cuisines, from American barbecue to Latin American, African, and Southeast Asian specialties. It's the perfect place for a quick and inexpensive luncheon or snack. A tent protects diners from sun, rain, or snow.

■ **BURNSIDE**   *map page 249, A/B-3*
Nightlife and comparatively wild times thrive around Burnside district. Local pundits like to say Portland has three genuine tourist attractions: Darcelle's drag shows, Powell's Books, and the Church of Elvis.

According to some Portlanders, the popular drag show at **Darcelle's XV Showplace**, established in 1967, has some of the best dancers in town. Nearly everyone enjoys the female impersonators, donned up with rhinestones, wigs, and falsies. These "girls" know how to entertain. The decor is largely given over to glossy photos of performers and guests plastered onto black-matte walls, charting Darcelle's 30-year history in Portland. (Darcelle, by the way, is known as a witty and outspoken community activist, who regularly participates in Old Town hall meetings.) The show, led by Darcelle, includes a dozen different musical performances. On Friday and Saturday nights, a male dance revue serves as the big finale; reservations are an essential. Darcelle's appears to be popular for "bachelorette" parties. Beware: the drinks are potent! *208 NW Third Avenue; 503-222-5338.*

At 720 SW Ankeny Street near the Benson Hotel is the **Church of Elvis**, where 25 cents will get you an interesting fortune. If drag shows and Elvis lose their thrill, try **Powell's Books,** at SW 10th Avenue and West Burnside Street, crammed with new and used books. It is open till 11 P.M. on most nights.

Powell's is on the southern edge of the Pearl District, a post-industrial neighborhood of lofts, galleries, and brewpubs. If you're here on the first Thursday evening of the month, check out the gallery openings. Wind up at Portland's first brewpub, the **BridgePort Brewpub** at 1313 NW Marshall Street, and sit on the loading dock for some of Portland's best pizza and microbrewery beer. For a younger scene try **La Luna** at SE Ninth Avenue and SE Pine Street off Burnside Street. The bar offers microbrews and the music is usually alternative rock at least three times a week, with big names and local artists playing regularly.

■ **WINERIES AND MICROBREWERIES**
Vineyards grow up to Portland's suburbs, and the downtown is only a short half-hour drive from the wineries of the northern Willamette Valley. Portland is said to have more microbreweries and brewpubs than any other city in the United States—several dozen at last count. Portlanders claim that no part of their thirsty city is more than 15 minutes from a brewpub or brewery outlet. You don't have to mix drinking and driving. You can explore the breweries on the **Portland Brewbus** (888-244-2739), which takes visitors on a three- to four-hour guided tour.

■ **CLASSICAL CHINESE GARDEN**   *map page 249, B-2*

Vancouver, British Columbia, is no longer the only West Coast community with a classical Chinese garden built by master craftsmen from Suzhou, China's garden city. Portland's new Classical Chinese Garden is the largest urban Suzhou-style garden ever crafted outside China. The serene garden provides a contrast to Portland's urban bustle. Rugged rocks and serpentine walkways skirt a pond, and banana leaves waft in the breeze. Depending on the season, flowers, shrubs, and trees bloom among the rocks. The garden's aptly named Courtyard of Tranquility is a perfect place for meditation. According to a story in the *Oregonian* newspaper, many hope the Classical Chinese Garden will help revitalize the Old Town/Chinatown neighborhood, but other residents fear gentrification and an increase in rent. *NW Third Avenue and Everett Street; 503-228-8131.*

Tea house at the Portland Classical Chinese Garden.

Washington Park's Rose Garden.

■ NORTHWEST PORTLAND *map page 249*

Though some contend that Portlanders are, by nature, a little distant from their neighbors, this modern malady may be at least partly ameliorated by the local coffee culture. **Northwest 23rd Avenue,** between Burnside and Thurman Streets, is a great place to dip into the scene and stroll through trendy shops.

Northwest Portland took off in 1905 with the Lewis and Clark Exposition, an orgy of boosterism. John Olmsted, son of Frederick Law Olmsted, who codesigned New York's Central Park, came to town and designed a fairground with most of the buildings in Spanish Renaissance style. The building everybody talked about for years to come was decidedly different—a gigantic log "cabin" housing a forestry exhibit.

Portland must have gotten the hang of putting on a fair back then because it wasn't long before the city decided to celebrate its gardeners' penchant for roses by staging a **Rose Festival** (503-227-2681) in 1907. The event has been going strong ever since—it takes place in the spring—the crowning event of an old-fashioned Oregon subculture. High schools elect Rose Princesses and one becomes the good

A view of Mount Hood and downtown Portland from Washington Park.

city's Rose Queen—even if queens are a bit out of fashion these days. Business people aspire to become Royal Rosarians, who dress up in white suits and wave straw boaters during parades. Military vessels line the Willamette, and sailors flood the town, taking advantage of the (officially sponsored) date-a-sailor hotline.

■ **WASHINGTON PARK** *map page 253*

A short uphill walk from Northwest Portland or an easy bus ride from downtown leads to well-manicured Washington Park, home of the **International Rose Test Garden.** Here, Portland's mania for the Rose Festival begins to make sense. From the Rose Garden's hillside perch, where the names of Rose Festival queens are enshrined in a cement path, downtown is framed by shiny green leaves and deep, rich blooms. *400 SW Kingston Avenue; 503-227-7033.*

Uphill from the Rose Garden are the peaceful **Japanese Gardens**, where water trickles through bamboo chutes. A shuttle bus and hiking trail climb the steep grade. *611 SW Kingston Avenue; 503-223-1321.*

The **Oregon Zoo** (formerly known as the Washington Park Zoo) had humble beginnings at the back of a downtown Portland pharmacy. In 1887, Richard

Knight, a local pharmacist who collected animals as a hobby, officially presented his menagerie to the city and the zoo was created. The zoo has several major exhibits, representing various geographic areas of the world (with about 200 species of birds, mammals, reptiles, amphibians, and invertebrates). These include an African rain forest, an Amazon flooded forest, an insect zoo, a piece of Alaskan tundra (with short-eared and snowy owls, musk oxen, and wolves), a section on native animals of the Cascade Mountains, and a Northwest coastal cove (with Steller's sea lions and sea otters). *4100 SW Canyon Road; 503-226-1561.*

West of downtown and next to the zoo, the **Portland Vietnam Memorial** is a bit unusual as far as war memorials are concerned, but it is very "Northwest" in concept and execution. The entrance opens onto a gravel path, which curves around in a loose spiral, and a circular lawn and hedge are set in a peaceful, tree-bordered meadow. Stone panels along the path break the war into major epochs. Each panel list the issues and events of a particular time period, and displays the last names of local soldiers who died in the war.

The **Hoyt Arboretum** was founded in 1928 by representatives of the timber industry, the U.S. Forest Service, and Portland Parks. Initially developed on 80 acres designed to serve as a "municipal arboretum for conifers," the scope of plantings soon expanded to include flowering trees. The new arboretum was set on a steep slope a few miles west of downtown on land that had been homesteaded and logged in the 1850s and 1860s. Though the Hoyt Arboretum is still known for its conifer collection, it has more recently gained recognition for its magnolias, which include several rare and exceptionally beautiful trees.

The first magnolias—*Magnolia accuminata* (Cucumber Tree), *Magnolia grandiflora*, and *Magnolia soulangeana*—were planted in 1934. Since 1955, the Portland Men's Garden Club has planted a new magnolia each year to help gradually build the collection. The Hoyt Arboretum is located two miles west of downtown Portland. The visitors center is in the heart of the arboretum on Fairview Boulevard. Park here to get information about trails, classes, and events. *503-228-8788.*

Hoyt Arboretum trails join the **Wildwood Trail** and continue north to Forest Park, which on a drizzly Sunday afternoon proves itself the lifeblood of Portlanders. The 50-some miles of trails are well-used, but rarely clogged. Before the park was established in 1947, the 1,100-foot hills rising straight from the Willamette had been heavily logged; most of the trees are second growth, with hardy red alder eclipsing the young Douglas fir and western hemlock.

■ FOREST PARK   *map page 253*

At 7.5 miles long and 1.5 miles wide, Forest Park, in the city's northwest corner, is one of the country's largest city parks. There are no manicured gardens or swing sets in Forest Park, and even though it abuts the state's most densely populated neighborhood, it's remarkably wild. Wildlife, including deer, coyotes, and warblers, use it as a corridor to the Coast Range to the west. *Skyline Boulevard, on the west side, leads to parking areas and trailheads; 503-823-7529.*

■ SAUVIE ISLAND   *map page 253*

Determined berry-pickers skip the trailside thickets and drive out on U.S. 30 to Sauvie Island, a flat agricultural island known for pick-it-yourself berry patches, bird-watching, and Columbia River beaches, including a nude beach. A highly productive bottomland since well before Lewis and Clark stopped here in 1805, this was a favorite trading spot of the Chinook Indians. They swapped tuberous wapato lily, which women pulled from marsh bottoms with their toes, and fished with huge cedar-bark nets that they sank to the bottom of the river with rocks.

■ EASTSIDE PORTLAND   *map page 253*

For a breath of fresh air, and a different view of the city, walk over one of the nine bridges spanning the Willamette—the Hawthorne and the Broadway are best for strolls from downtown. The Willamette River bisects Portland, with most of the wealth falling out on the hilly west side and a funky charm and rapid gentrification surrounding the shopping streets of **SE Hawthorne** (used-book stores are the neighborhood specialty) and **NE Broadway.** The area around Burnside contains a slew of new restaurants.

Sellwood, at the city's southern edge, has had an antique row for years. Its riverside park is worth a picnic or a swim in the outdoor pool. Oaks Park, an antiquated, slightly down-at-the-heels amusement park, abuts Sellwood Park and is adjacent to Oaks Bottom, a wetland crisscrossed by trails ideal for bird-watching. From the west side of the Sellwood Bridge, a greenway for cyclers and hikers runs 3 miles along the Willamette to downtown's Waterfront Park.

The Eastside has another distinction: Mount Tabor makes Portland the only U.S. city with a dormant volcano within city limits. If you thought the eruption of Mount St. Helens was catastrophic, wait until Mount Tabor blows its top.

■ TRAVEL AND CLIMATE

■ GETTING THERE AND AROUND

By Car

Portland is easy to reach, located at the junction of major freeways (I-5 and I-84) and railways. One of downtown Portland's charms is its compact size. It's easy for most folks to tour downtown, the Pearl district, and Northwest Portland on foot. Ambitious walkers can even go from downtown to the Rose Gardens (it's not far, but it is uphill). If walking's not your thing, then hop on a streetcar, bus, or light rail train. They're all free within the downtown core. One of the city's biggest assets is its proximity to beautiful and diverse outdoor areas. Many visitors will use Portland as a hub for day trips to the Columbia Gorge and Mount Hood, the northern Oregon coast, and the Willamette Valley wine country. All are wonderful, with each place offering an entirely different look at the state.

Portland's downtown is very compact—a walker's delight. Within prescribed downtown borders, public transportation is free. The transit mall was built on SW Fifth and Sixth Avenues and is served by light rail (MAX) trains. Stop by TriMet Customer Service in Pioneer Courthouse Square for bus and MAX information. For **Amtrak** travel information call 800-872-7245.

By Air

Portland International Airport (PDX, 7000 NE Airport Way; 877-739-4636) has numerous daily national and international flights, as well as flights to other Oregon towns, like Bend and Eugene. At the airport it's easy to rent cars or get vans into town.

■ CLIMATE

Portland's weather can be wet (pioneers called themselves "webfeet"), but the weather is often sunny and balmy in spring and fall and can be quite warm in summer. In winter, icy storms blowing down the Columbia River Gorge can chill things down in a hurry. Like other metropolitan areas of the Pacific Northwest, Portland is paralyzed by snow, which, luckily, does not fall very often or stay long.

Author's Favorites:
Portland Food and Lodging

■ Lodgings

Fifth Avenue Suites Hotel. Right in the heart of downtown, this grand hotel is in a converted department store. The rooms are quiet and luxurious. *506 SW Washington Street; 503-222-0001 or 800-771-2971.*

Imperial Hotel. The recently renovated hotel has large, comfortable rooms and a friendly ghost. Wine is served in the lobby every afternoon and the staff is friendly and helpful. *400 SW Broadway; 503-228-7221 or 800-452-2323.*

Portland's White House. This stately old home in the tree-shaded northeast Portland neighborhood is one of the great inns of the Pacific Northwest. The rooms are luxuriously comfortable and the breakfasts are sumptuous. *1914 NE Second Avenue; 503-287-7131.*

■ Restaurants

Alexis. Locally popular for its home-style Greek food, Alexis has an unpretentious atmosphere, tacky 1980s decor, belly dancers, and Greek wines. *215 West Burnside Street; 503-224-8577.*

Bistro Montage. Cajun spices accent everything: catfish and macaroni-and-cheese alike. Formal white tablecloths contrast with the tattooed servers and capture the spirit of Portland. *301 SE Morrison Street; 503-234-1324.*

Bluehour. This is Portland's most recent hot spot for the young, upscale dining crowd—and crowded it is, with tables less than an arm's length from each other. The design is elegant, and the cuisine is regional Italian with some continental touches and influenced by Northwest ingredients. *250 NW 13th Avenue; 503-226-3394.*

Dan & Louis Oyster Bar. This old-time place near the waterfront is a favorite visitors' hangout, but locals come here too, though they may not tell their yuppie friends. Try the old-fashioned oyster stew and the fresh seafood salads. *208 SW Ankeny Street; 503-227-5906.*

Esplanade. The quiet, old-school restaurant overlooks the Willamette River and has an ambitious menu of seasonal Northwest ingredients prepared with a French touch. A Portland classic. *1510 SW Harbor Way, Riverplace Hotel; 503-295-6166.*

COLUMBIA GORGE
& MOUNT HOOD

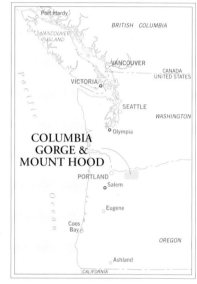

■ **OVERVIEW**

THE COLUMBIA RIVER GORGE east of Portland is not only the most beautiful stretch of a very scenic river, it is beautiful whether you traverse it on the north or the south bank of the river. Even hurried drivers rushing through the gorge on the I-84 freeway can't escape the almost overpowering beauty of the scenery, since the freeway runs close to the level of the river.

The entire river is 1,245 miles long. It springs from the Columbia Glacier, an ice field in the Canadian Rockies, and at first runs north, through the Rocky Mountain Trench, then turns south to northeastern Washington. Here it first flows south, then swings west to the eastern foothills of the North Cascades, turns east at the Rattlesnake Mountains, and, after joining the Snake River flowing in from the east (the Snake rises in Yellowstone Park), it breaks through the Wallula Gap and flows west toward the Pacific Ocean. The fact that the river runs through its gorge at almost sea level attests to the fact that the Columbia is older than the Cascade Mountains and cut its way through the range as it slowly rose from the earth's crust. As the river forces its way west, through a fairly level, narrow passage, its deep waters are hemmed in by the steep rock walls of the Cascade Mountains, densely covered by Douglas fir and larch forest to the west, and by grasslands and ponderosa pine and oak woods to the east on the "dry" side of the Cascades. Much of the narrow sliver of land at the foot of the cliffs is taken up by road and railroad beds. Here and there is enough arable land for a farm or two, though there are orchards on the benchlands of the Washington side and in the fertile Hood River Valley, which branches off to the south near the eastern end of the gorge. It is towered over to the south by Mount Hood, one of the most beautiful and symmetrical of the Cascade volcanoes, and to the north by broad-shouldered Mount Adams. If you look closely, you may even spot a vineyard or two.

The scenery of the gorge is truly spectacular, with its views of dark basalt cliffs, and the winding river sparkling in the sun, or half hidden by mists, depending on the weather. Mists may envelop the river, but rainbows stretch across almost every shoulder along the Columbia Gorge. That's because of the difference in the climate at the east and west ends of the gorge. Even if it's rainy on the west side, the east side generally has blue skies. The dark layers of basalt dominating the rock walls of the gorge are ancient lava flows, some of which cover the plateaus to the east to a depth of more than 3,500 feet. About 10,000 years ago, an ice dam in northern Idaho backed up a huge lake stretching over much of what is now western Montana. Periodically, the dam would pop up, like an ice cube in a drink, releasing torrents of water across eastern Washington and through the Columbia River channels. The floodwaters scraped the basalt so clean that, even today, no topsoil has established itself on many of the steep walls, leaving them bare of vegetation.

Explorers Lewis and Clark took this route as they traveled west to the mouth of the Columbia and back, and they were the first explorers to note that the river runs almost at sea level. Pioneers followed in their wake, braving fierce rapids now submerged by the waters of Bonneville and other dams.

Interstate 84, a major east-west freeway, passes through the canyon following the route taken by the old Oregon Trail. Portlanders love to take visitors on "the loop," a long day's drive up the Columbia to Hood River, then south for a sunset at Mount Hood's Timberline Lodge, and back to Portland in the dark. Or you can make it a shorter loop trip by driving up the Washington side of the river in the morning and returning via the Oregon side in the afternoon.

(following pages) The view from the Portland Women's Forum Park looking east up the Columbia River Gorge to Crown Point.

■ OREGON SIDE OF THE COLUMBIA *map page 272*

Begin a Columbia Gorge drive from Portland at Exit 17 off I-84. For the **Columbia Gorge Scenic Highway,** turn left at the first light past the outlet mall, where the sign says "Corbett." (A right turn here leads to the Edgefield complex, the former county "poor farm," now the most expansive of the McMenamin's brewpubs.) The scenic highway follows the Sandy River, known as "Quicksand R." to Lewis and Clark. Stop at **Dabney State Park,** with riverside trails, fishing, and boat launches. When the water warms up, the Sandy's swimming holes fill up with local kids, and its modest rapids host floaters in inner tubes. Past Dabney, the scenic highway cuts away from the Sandy and heads through upland orchards to Corbett. The Columbia first becomes visible at the **Portland Women's Forum Park;** roundish, green hills give way to blocky, dark basalt upstream. The **Crown Point Vista House** is on the next bluff upstream, and the Women's Forum Park is a great vantage point for photographers. The Vista House, built in 1918, offers great views up the gorge. The stocky stone octagonal house has picture windows topped by stained glass and a copper-green dome. Between Crown Point and Multnomah Falls, the old highway is at its best. The arched stone guardrails are softened by moss, and ferns grow in every interstitial niche.

Everybody stops at **Multnomah Falls,** for good reason. The falls drop 620 feet, and they are unfailingly impressive. It takes an hour to hike to the top of the falls, and the trail continues on to Larch Mountain (another 5 miles uphill). Little effort is required to see naturalist John Muir's favorite bird, the American dipper, here. Even in icy weather, the birds plunge into the stream at the base of the falls.

If you don't have time for more than a two-hour hike, try the **Horsetail Falls/Oneonta Trail loop,** which has waterfalls and river views. From the tall spray-spitting plume at the scenic highway, it's half a mile uphill to the step-behind Upper Horsetail Falls. In spring the trail is lined with springtime trilliums and lavender bleeding heart. False Solomon's seal reaches long lily-leaved, flower-tipped arms toward shafts of light. The trail then follows a sun-struck ridge above the Columbia, where pikas squeal from their rockslide homes. The short descent into the next drainage offers a look down through the narrow Oneonta Gorge and a return to the highway. On the roadside walk back to the car, it's tempting to wander back into the Oneonta Gorge. If it's warm enough for wet feet, go with the urge; there's no place quite like this dramatic and dark chasm, which is home to rare shade-loving plants.

River Through Time

As a river cutting through the Cascades at almost sea level, the Columbia at the gorge has been an important trading route since ancient time. Resident tribes controlled trade on the river between inland and coastal tribes.

When American explorers Lewis and Clark floated down the Columbia in 1805, cedar plank longhouses up to 200 feet in length dotted the riverbanks. Cedars were also crafted into long canoes, and Chinook Indians (including Cascades, Wascos, and, on the Washington side, Wishrams) took the rapids in canoes.

Oregon Trail immigrants portaged their belongings past the river's roughest section on an 1842 wagon road built around the 5-mile-long Cascade rapids, followed by a mule-drawn tramway along the north bank of the river. Soon the south shore also had a portage railroad. Since the Columbia River tightly squeezes through basalt cliffs at several points along the gorge, it leaves little room for a roadway. In 1872, the Oregon legislature called for a wagon road between Troutdale and The Dalles, and a few stretches of the narrow road are still visible at Shellrock Mountain near Milepost 52. Portage railroads around rapids were spliced together, often using the wagon road as a railbed, and in 1883, they formed part of a transcontinental line.

Stern-wheelers that could "float on mist" made it through some dodgy rapids and shoals, but railroad portages around the Cascades were essential until 1896, when the Cascade Locks, a 3,000-foot-long canal, cleared a path for boats. It's still possible to ride a stern-wheeler along the Willamette and Columbia Rivers, but it's strictly a party boat now. Barges and tugs took over most of the river work in the 1940s, when being a tug captain was as glamorous a job as any Oregonian could hope for.

Sam Hill, son-in-law of the Great Northern Railway's James J. Hill, began scheming to build a road through the Columbia Gorge in the early 1900s. He hired Samuel Lancaster to build a riverside highway, and together they went on a European tour to study ancient road patterns. They traveled through the Alps, drove on Roman roads, and thought of the rustic natural designs of the American Craftsman movement. When construction started, Lancaster worked with Italian-American stonemasons, whose arched guardrails gracefully line the road. The road was finished in 1916, and its remaining stretches are nearly as popular now as they were then.

Bonneville Dam, a few miles upriver and just off I-84, was one of the great Depression-era public works projects and has been a source of pride for decades. Bonneville and the other Columbia River dams generated huge amounts of electricity and spawned the region's aluminum industry, a notoriously power-thirsty business. Head to the sub-basement fish-viewing window in the dam's visitors center. Official fish-counters sit in their own darkened cubicle, counting each fish swimming past their window. **Eagle Creek** trailhead is about a mile east of Bonneville and is, after Multnomah Falls, the gorge's most popular stop. In the spring, water streams down in dozens of makeshift falls, turning portions of the trail into a refreshing shower. Hikers measure the spring's wetness by the number of falls and the intensity of the wildflower display.

At **Cascade Locks,** just upriver from Bonneville Dam, the focus shifts back to the river. Cascade Locks Marine Park is a grassy, relaxing riverside spot. A footbridge spans the now-obsolete 1896 locks. Below it, Indian dip-net platforms hang from guy wires like a window-washer's rigging above rushing water. The stern-wheeler *Columbia Gorge* (541-374-8427 or 800-643-1354) departs from the Marine Park several times daily from mid-June until early October (during the winter, it's based at Portland's Waterfront Park). The **Bridge of the Gods** spans the Columbia at Cascade Locks.

Even when the west end of the gorge is clouded over, the sun often breaks through in the town of **Hood River**, a sleepy fruit-shipping center near the eastern entrance to the Columbia River Gorge. The climate here is nearly perfect for fruit trees, and the steep gorge walls funnel winds into a fury near Hood River, making it the windsurfing capital of the Northwest, if not the nation. The sport really does permeate the local culture. Wind reports are regular features on every radio station, and it's a great place to shop for a sailboard or wetsuit. An uncommon number of "boardheads" have settled here, and make good livings peddling windsurfing gear. To watch the boardheads in action, drive to the **Columbia Gorge Sailpark** or follow Second Street to the waterfront. The best action is during the middle of the day, when the winds are at their best.

Because it has a strong local following, as well as members from across the nation, Canada, and Europe, the **Columbia Gorge Windsurfing Association (CGWA)** is one of the largest and most successful windsurfing associations in the United States. One of the organization's goals is to work for improved access along both the Washington and Oregon shores of the Columbia River to allow members to take full advantage of the best daily wind conditions. The organization also has a Community Windsurfing Program, which provides introductory windsurfing lessons to local residents at affordable rates. The CGWA holds an annual event called **Windfest** (usually in late June), billed as "a windsurfing celebration of fun on the water." It includes a Pray for Wind Party, with windsurfing clinics and dancing to live music. *202 Oak Street, Suite 150; 541-386-9225.*

The **Columbia Gorge Hotel** (400 Westcliff Drive; 541-386-5566 or 800-345-1921), northwest of town was built in 1921 by the timber baron Simon Benson. Some rooms have nice views of the gorge, but the hotel can be noisy because it is squeezed between the freeway and the railroad tracks. The **Hood River Hotel** (106 Oak Street at First Street; 541-386-1900) is a nicely restored old downtown hotel with small but comfortable rooms. The **Full Sail Brewing Company Tasting Room and Pub** (506 Columbia Street; 541-386-2247) is one of the Pacific Northwest's oldest microbreweries. You can sit on the deck of the pub, look down onto I-84 and the Columbia River, sip a Full Sail ale, and enjoy tasty chow.

■ MOUNT HOOD LOOP   *map page 272, C/D-2*

From Hood River, Route 35 heads south up Mount Hood, and I-84 continues east. A surviving stretch of the old highway splits off the freeway at Mosier (17 miles east of Hood River) and climbs past cherry orchards, through scattered oak and pine trees, to the Rowena Plateau, where the transition from a wet west-slope habitat to a drier east-side environment is manifest. From the wildflower-fringed high plateau, it's all mounds and swales down to the river. Yellow balsamroot and deep blue-violet lupine grow on meadows spread out on top of basalt flows.

Route 35 heads south and uphill from Hood River's laid-back trendiness into orchard country—the Hood River Valley is famed for its apples, pears, and dark red cherries. The **Mount Hood Railroad** (110 Railroad Avenue; 541-386-3556 or 800-872-4661) runs from Hood River south to Parkdale; it's a popular springtime trip, when snowy Mount Hood is the backdrop for pink and white blossoms. The road wastes no time before beginning the long pull up Mount Hood. Stop at a fruit stand for a trunkload of apples and pears. **River Bend Organic Farm** has tours and a store at 2363 Tucker Road, near Odell. Turn off at **Parkdale** toward a perfect canoeist's view of the mountain from the middle of Lost Lake. The little lakeside resort has cabins, a restaurant, and canoe rentals.

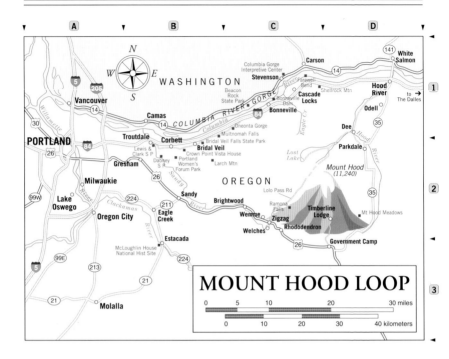

map page 272, C/D-2

■ MOUNT HOOD   *map page 272, C/D-2*

Mount Hood erupted sporadically through the 1800s, though not with the force of the 1980 Mount St. Helens blast. An 1859 *Oregonian* article reported:

> It became hot about midday . . . in the evening occasional flashes of fire were seen. On Thursday night fire was plainly visible . . . . A large mass on the northwest side of Mount Hood had disappeared, and an immense quantity of snow on the south side was gone.

Oregon Trail emigrants who chose the Barlow Road route from The Dalles to Oregon City enjoyed a close-up of the mountain, and learned, on the steep slopes, how to hold back a wagon to prevent it from nipping the heels of the animals.

Perhaps it's the ancestral memory of the Barlow Road, perhaps it's that wonderful vision on the eastern skyline, but Portlanders have long looked to Mount Hood when they have felt intrepid. Four Portlanders climbed the 11,240-foot mountain in 1857, and it caught on. Two hundred people climbed through sleet and thunder in 1894, the inaugural climb of the Mazama Club. This mountain club is restricted to those who have climbed a glaciated Cascade peak. The Portland-based Mazamas still sponsor mountaineering classes and climbs.

Developers have long eyed Mount Hood; in the 1920s, the Mazamas fought against a tramline up to the peak. By 1937, there was nothing but applause for **Timberline Lodge** (off Route 26; 503-622-7979 or 800-547-1406), built as a WPA project. Unemployed artisans were put to work fashioning beams from giant trees, carving newels into owls and bears, and weaving rugs and chair covers. There's now a separate, 1980s, concrete-bunker-style day lodge filled with contemporary crafts, ski-rental shops, and snack bars. But Mount Hood savants know the second-floor bar in the old lodge has comfortable sofas, great sunset views down the Cascades, and a happy blend of rusticity and comfort for weary hikers and skiers. **Silcox Hut** (503-219-3192), a sturdy stone cabin just up the mountain from the lodge, houses guests wanting more of a rustic overnight experience. Guests are transported to the hut via snow-cat or chairlift.

It's safe to climb the mountain only from May to early July. Climbers start from Timberline Lodge around 2 A.M., aiming to reach the top by midmorning and be off the mountain when the afternoon sun increases the chance of an avalanche.

For those who prefer to see the horizon a little bit at a time, a 40-mile trail circles the mountain at timberline; pick up the trail at Timberline Lodge and walk the loop (allow a few days). Or light out west to Paradise Park, an exuberant alpine meadow 5 miles from the lodge. Continue another 5.5 miles past a deep V of a chasm holding the cascading headwaters of the Sandy River to Ramona Falls, where basalt terraces split the creek into a multitude of thin falls, then funnel them back together at the bottom of the 100-foot drop.

Downhill skiing and snowboarding runs through the summer at Timberline's above-timberline Palmer glacier snowfield. During the winter, **Mount Hood Meadows** overtakes Timberline in popularity—it's just east of the pass (on Highway 35), which frequently means good weather in Oregon's westside/eastside precipitation sweepstakes. Many cross-country skiers enjoy the groomed Teacup Lake trails, just across Route 35 from Mount Hood Meadows.

The Trillium Lake trail, about a mile east of Government Camp, is, after an initial slope, a flat and easy loop. More advanced cross-country skiers head for Bennett Pass and the great views from the "Terrible Traverse." Rent cross-country ski gear in Government Camp. For ski reports call Timberline at 503-222-2211, or Mount Hood Meadows at 503-227-7669.

COLUMBIA GORGE & MOUNT HOOD 275

■ **WASHINGTON SIDE OF THE COLUMBIA**
map page 272, A-D/1

The Columbia River Gorge marks the spot at which the river flows west through the Cascades between basalt cliffs that are older than the mountains themselves. Route 14 follows the north bank of the river all the way through the gorge, although most visitors take the freeway on the Oregon side.

The road along the gorge's Washington shore provides more dramatic views but slower driving than the freeway on the Oregon side. It winds around rock walls and bores through the rock in short tunnels, passing fruit warehouses, small sawmills, and outcroppings softened by moss. On the opposite shore, you can see mountains plunging straight to the river, their forested slopes split by ravines. In winter, snow dusts the upper slopes.

One interesting stop along the way is the **Columbia Gorge Interpretive Center,** off Route 14 in Stevenson. On exhibit are a replica of a native fishing platform, a 19th-century fish wheel, and a display of seismic activities. *990 SW Rock Creek Drive; 800-991-2338.*

For a long view up and down the river, you can climb a series of ramps and steps up 848-foot-tall **Beacon Rock.** Beacon Rock State Park offers campsites and a chance to swim in the Columbia.

■ **TRAVEL AND CLIMATE**

■ **GETTING THERE AND AROUND**

Portland is the best starting point for visiting the gorge. Interstate 84, a major east-west freeway, passes through the canyon following the route taken by the old Oregon Trail. Besides the popular loop from Portland, you can also make a shorter trip by driving up the Washington side.

■ **CLIMATE**

At the western end of the gorge, skies are frequently gray. Around Hood River the sun often breaks through the clouds and spring days can quickly warm to 80 degrees Fahrenheit. As you go higher, the temperatures get cooler. Up at Timberline Lodge snow can fall almost any time of year, although July and August are usually sunny and warm, with temperatures in the 70s.

(opposite) Mount Hood rises above Lost Lake in the Mount Hood National Forest.

CENTRAL OREGON

■ LANDSCAPE

CENTRAL OREGON IS A TAPESTRY of volcanic rocks, edged with towering peaks and basalt cliffs, and textured with perfect cinder cones. Forests, mountain lakes, and rivers dab the landscape with blues and greens. Skiers, floaters, and anglers skid and cast across the rugged quilt. The lava underfoot may not even have a dusting of soil covering it, though most of it was laid down 14 to 16 million years ago during a burst of volcanism so intense that volcanic flows covered all but the tips of the Blue and Wallowa Mountains.

The volcanic spine of the Cascades rose when the oceanic plate dove beneath the North American continental plate. Friction generated heat, and lava poured forth. Mount Hood, Mount Jefferson, Three-Fingered Jack, Mount Washington, the Three Sisters, Broken Top, Mount Bachelor, Mount Thielson, Mount Mazama (now Crater Lake), and Mount McLoughlin are the volcanic high Cascade peaks. They are ages younger than the low western Cascades, worn-down piles of ash and lava, just off their western shoulders.

Central Oregon's Cascades form a backdrop of quintessential Western scenery right out of a movie. On clear days, the Metolius headwaters or the Crooked River Canyon at Smith Rock are as mesmerizing as any place on earth. Summers are hot, winters are cold, and flash floods can follow drought on the east side of the Cascades. Tourist bureaus say the sun shines 310 days a year, but plenty of snow falls from these supposedly cloudless skies, especially at higher elevations. There are more resorts here than in any other part of the state, and they run the gamut from funky little log cabins on a mountain lake to upscale Sunriver condos.

■ HISTORY

At central Oregon's northern edge, the Columbia River divides Oregon from Washington as it cuts a low, almost sea-level, path through the Cascade Mountains. Back before French Canadians named the Columbia's basalt-walled narrows "Les Dalles," after giant Gallic flagstone gutters, The Dalles was called Winquatt, a "Place Encircled by Rock Cliffs." For Indians, this was a prized fishing area. Salmon resting in eddies and pools were easy dip-net or spear targets, and traders were drawn from all over Oregon, bringing items from afar: Minnesota pipestone, Southwestern turquoise, Vancouver Island dentalium, Alaskan copper, and Puget Sound dried clams. Two groups lived on the Columbia's south shore, Sahaptin-speakers and Chinook-speakers. To supplement their salmon diet, they gathered roots and berries and hunted.

The tribes of north-central Oregon stayed on good terms with early white settlers, and Indians did a brisk business ferrying Oregon Trail pioneers through the Columbia River rapids. But as settlers from the East wanted even more land, the Indians were forced to move to the Warm Springs Reservation in 1855. The lands taken from the Indians were occupied by cattle ranchers, sheepherders, and wheat farmers. You can spot their homesteads by the tall black locust trees the pioneers planted to provide shade. Look for hawk nests atop tall trees just off the highway.

■ THE DALLES *map page 278, B-1*

When steamboats plied the Columbia, during the late 1800s, The Dalles was a bustling port, where wheat from eastern Oregon was transferred onto Portland-bound boats. Rudyard Kipling, in high tourist mode, rode a steamer up the Columbia to The Dalles in 1898 and reported that "all the inhabitants seemed to own a little villa and one church apiece."

Stop by **The Dalles Visitor Information Center** (401 West Second Street; 541-296-2231 or 800-255-3385). Cherry canneries, quiet most of the year, whir

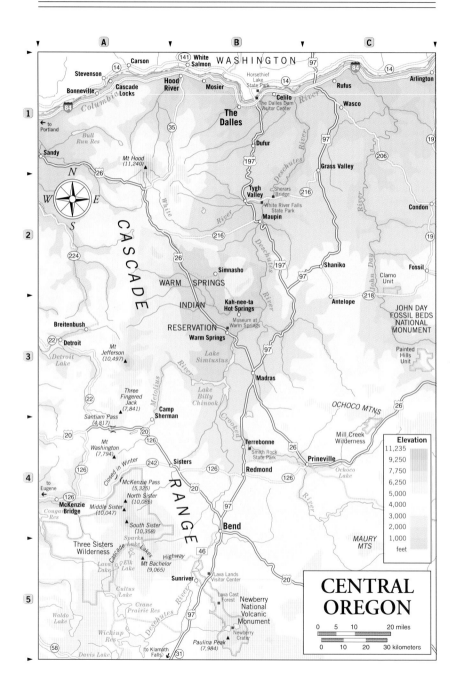

A   B   C

WASHINGTON

Carson · Stevenson · White Salmon · Horsethief Lake State Park · Arlington

Bonneville · Cascade Locks · Hood River · Mosier · Celilo · Rufus · Wasco

to Portland · Columbia · The Dalles · The Dalles Dam Visitor Center

Bull Run Res · Dufur

Sandy · Mt Hood (11,240) · Grass Valley

Mt Hood · Tygh Valley · Sherars Bridge · Condon

White River Falls State Park · Maupin

Simnasho · Shaniko · Clarno Unit · Fossil

WARM SPRINGS · Deschutes River · John Day River

INDIAN · Kah-nee-ta Hot Springs · Antelope · JOHN DAY FOSSIL BEDS NATIONAL MONUMENT

RESERVATION · Museum at Warm Springs

Breitenbush · Warm Springs · Painted Hills Unit

Detroit · Mt Jefferson (10,497)

Detroit Lake · Lake Simtustus · Madras

Three Fingered Jack (7,841) · Lake Billy Chinook · OCHOCO MTNS

Santiam Pass (4,817) · Camp Sherman · Mill Creek Wilderness

Mt Washington (7,794) · Crooked River · Terrebonne · Smith Rock State Park · Prineville · Ochoco Lake

to Eugene · Sisters · Redmond · MAURY MTS

McKenzie Pass (5,325) · North Sister (10,085)

McKenzie Bridge · Middle Sister (10,047) · Cougar Res

South Sister (10,358) · Bend

Three Sisters Wilderness · Sparks Lake · Highway · Mt Bachelor (9,065) · Sunriver · Lava Lands Visitor Center

Lava Lake · Elk Lake · Lava Cast Forest · Newberry National Volcanic Monument

Cultus Lake · Crane Prairie Res · Newberry Crater

Waldo Lake · Wickiup Res · Paulina Peak (7,984)

Davis Lake · to Klamath Falls

Elevation	
11,235	
9,250	
7,750	
6,250	
5,000	
4,000	
3,000	
2,000	
1,000	
feet	

CENTRAL OREGON

0 5 10 20 miles

0 10 20 30 kilometers

into action in early summer, and The Dalles hums with business from migrant pickers who come to town. The Dalles has escaped the gentrification that's crept up the gorge—it's a no-nonsense place, stuck tight to the basalt.

A fine side trip from the Dallas lies across the river, on the Washington side. At **Horsethief Lake State Park,** a trail leads to petroglyphs that escaped the floodwaters of the dam. Vandalism has forced the closure of the trail, but the park ranger still leads tours in Fridays and Saturdays; for reservations call 509-767-1159. Many rock carvings are now displayed at the **Dalles Dam's Visitor Center** (north and east of I-84, Exit 87). Here, the petroglyph called *Tsagigla'lal,* or "She Who Watches," forever stands guard over the waters.

■ COLUMBIA PLATEAU *map page 278, B/C-2*

From The Dalles, U.S. 197 climbs south to the Columbia Plateau, where the sun bounces off wheat fields with a high, bright glow, and the spaces get big in a hurry. Drive south as far as the crossroads town of Tygh Valley, overlooked by rimrock and home of the All-Indian Rodeo, which takes place in mid-May.

A bull rider hangs on during the All-Indian Rodeo Days Celebration at Warm Springs Reservation.

To the east is **White River Falls State Park**, where a triple-tier waterfall splashes down to the stony bones of a hydroelectric power plant. It's lovely in an eerie, ruined way, as though a river finally won a round in its match with technology. The road descends through dry canyons to the **Deschutes River** to Sherar's Bridge. It then crosses the frothing waters at the bottom of high canyon walls at one of the few remaining Indian dip-net fishing spots, where rickety-looking platforms reach out over furious rapids. In season, tribal fishers snare salmon with long-handled nets.

Maupin, built on a mesa-like bench above the river, is a close-to-perfect place to fish, float, or sit and watch the play of light on the Deschutes. Steelhead, wild trout, and salmon keep anglers busy year-round. In the summer, Maupin's river outfitters run white-water trips down the Deschutes.

Try **High Desert Drifters** (541-389-0562) or **Ouzel Outfitters** (800-788-7238), which also runs trips on the McKenzie, Rogue, Owyhee, and North Umpqua Rivers.

■ WARM SPRINGS AND VICINITY *map page 278, B-3*

In 1855, the **Warm Springs Reservation** was allotted to the Tenino, Tygh, John Day, and Wyam people. These tribes are now, together, called Warm Springs. The Confederation of Warm Springs Indians includes the Warm Springs, Wasco, and Paiute tribes. They have bought out all the private holdings within the reservation, including the hot springs at the Kah-Nee-Ta Resort (see below).

Traditional activities, both spiritual and economic, still go on. Fishing platforms at The Dalles and Sherar's Bridge are used, though they yield fewer salmon every year. The season's first salmon are feted, blessed, then eaten at a ritual dinner. The First Salmon Feast is supplemented by a Root Festival. Honored tribal members dig the tuberous *piyaxi* (bitterroot).

After several days' preparation, the roots are cooked, as dances are performed. When the meal is presented, initial sips of water and bites of food are taken as the name of each food is called out. After these first ritual bites, everybody chows down. In June, *Pi-Ume-Sha* celebrates the 1855 treaty with a pow-wow and rodeo. Nontribal members are welcome at these events, but remember that they are not "shows" put on for entertainment.

Kah-Nee-Ta (root-digger), was named after a woman who once lived in the Warm Springs Valley. The **Kah-Nee-Ta Resort** (6823 Highway 8; 541-553-1112 or 800-554-4786) has an enormous swimming pool with naturally warm water. Even a golf course cannot hide the raw beauty of the land, towered over by Mount Hood and Mount Jefferson, and awash with the scent of pine and juniper.

The **Museum at Warm Springs** (541-553-3331), on U.S. 26 in the town of Warm Springs, started buying cultural artifacts from tribal members in the late 1960s. By the time the museum opened in 1993, an unparalleled collection of beadwork and basketry had been amassed. Symbolism of the reservation's three tribes is present in the building's feather-bustle door handles and basketweave wall panels. The high-tech video and audio displays keep the Warm Springs culture vital and accessible. For a non-tribal visitor, this is a great introduction.

East of **Antelope,** off U.S. 97 and Route 218, are the **John Day Fossil Beds**— beautifully sculpted, colorful rocks with red, tan, and green striations—where many unusual fossils have been found, including those of sabertooth cats and hornless rhinos. *541-987-2333.*

■ SMITH ROCK *map page 278, B-4*

West of the town of Prineville, the Crooked River cuts through Smith Rock State Park. (From U.S. 97, turn east at Terrebone and follow the signs.) Half the fun at Smith Rock is the people-watching. From a distance, red-orange rock faces and pinnacles are traced against deep blue sky; closer in, the cliffs are speckled with rock climbers, inching upward through prisms of pure color. Somehow their sun-burned legs and muscular shoulders don't detract from the luminosity.

The network of trails here is good and nonclimbers will find some easy rock scrambles. Hike the riverbank trail to the base of Monkey Face and scramble up just until the Cascade peaks come into view. For information and gear for climbing at Smith Rock, visit **Redpoint Climbers Supply** (975 Smith Rock Way; 800-923-6207).

A railroad bridge over the 320-foot-deep Crooked River Gorge near Terrebone was a tough bit of engineering when it was built in 1911. Crews from both the Great Northern and the Union Pacific Railroads worked from opposite sides of the river to control the way to central Oregon markets. Sabotage was common. A truce called for the Great Northern crew to finish the span but for the two lines to share the use of the bridge. Today a rest stop along U.S. 97 provides a spectacular opportunity to peer into the dizzying gorge.

(following pages) A winter sunset over Smith Rock State Park.

■ SISTERS AND VICINITY *map page 278, A-4*

Sisters feels Western, with its namesake trio of snowcapped peaks, once called Faith, Hope, and Charity, now North, Middle, and South Sister, in the town's backyard. Real ranchers and cowboys stick out pretty easily from the tourists flocking to false-front shops. But they may raise llamas instead of cattle on the 30-some (and counting) llama ranches of the area. The Patterson Ranch, west of Sisters on Route 242, is the biggest llama outfit; the herd is usually visible from the road. The animals pack gear on wilderness trips. Some sheepherders keep llamas close to their flocks because they protect the herds from coyotes.

From Sisters, Route 242 climbs southwesterly to McKenzie Pass, intersecting the **Pacific Crest Trail.** In the summer you can follow it southbound along a ridge running along the west slopes of the lava-strewn, wildflower-lit, and glaciated Three Sisters peaks. North Sister is the oldest. The Middle and South Sisters are younger and less sculpted. South Sister, at 10,358 feet, is the highest peak; there's a crater with a small lake at the top. (The best trail to the peak starts from the Cascade Lakes Highway.)

U.S. 20, the Santiam Pass road, heads northwest through pine forests. A few miles from town, the **Metolius River** springs in a big rush from rocks at the base of Black Butte. With clear, piney air and Mount Jefferson in the background, this area is idyllically beautiful. The Metolius runs 30 miles through a glacier-scoured basin before it's swallowed up by Lake Chinook. Fish thrive in the clear, 46-degree water. Wild bull (Dolly Varden) and rainbow trout share the stream with brown and brook trout, whitefish, and kokanee salmon.

Stop for a snack at the Camp Sherman store and linger at the riverside deck, or venture downstream to the **Wizard Falls Fish Hatchery** (541-595-6611), renowned for its spectacular setting and tank of oddball fish.

■ BEND *map page 278, B-4*

Bend is the hub of central Oregon and a good place to pause before exploring the eastern flanks of central Oregon's Cascade peaks and the high lava plateaus.

People move here to be near the mountains and out of the rain. Rails were laid to Bend in 1911, and within five years, trains were shuttling ponderosa pines into and out of two big new mills on the Deschutes. Tracks went out to the logging sites, where loggers and their families lived in cabins trundled from site to site by rail. Scandinavian timber workers started skiing around town in the early 1920s, and the sport caught on. Outdoorsy Californians and western Oregonians began moving here in the 1970s, and the boom continues.

From the moment you arrive in Bend, people will ask if you've been to the **High Desert Museum**. Don't skip it—the museum provides a good introduction to central and eastern Oregon history and ecology. The natural history displays are as good as everyone claims, but the real surprise is the sophisticated diorama exhibit. No grade school shoe-box displays here; birdsongs and the scent of sage envelop a marshside Paiute wickiup, and the trapper's tent smells like dirt. Outdoor exhibits of river otters and porcupines get you out walking. *9800 South U.S. 97, 3.5 miles south of Bend; 541-382-4754.*

■ **MOUNT BACHELOR** *map page 278, A-5*

Mount Bachelor was first called "The Bachelor" and then "Bachelor Butte" before the Chamber of Commerce decided to elevate its status. The mountain, 9,065 feet high, has alpine slopes and cross-country ski trails. Skiers know Bachelor as the ultimate intermediate mountain, with lots of tree skiing, though the resort has expert terrain as well. Separate lodges for downhill and cross-country skiers provide food and warmth, but there are no overnight accommodations. Most skiers stay in Bend—the Inn of the Seventh Mountain (Century Drive; 541-382-8711 or 800-452-6810), a condo-cum-motel 5 miles west of Bend, has the closest lodgings to the slopes. Bachelor's ski season is long and the snow powdery. *Century Drive (also known as the Cascade Lakes Highway); 800-829-2442, general information; 541-382-7888, ski report.*

The mid-May **Pole Pedal Paddle race** is one of Bend's defining cultural institutions. Several thousand contestants start out on Mount Bachelor's downhill ski slopes, swoosh down to a cross-country ski circuit, then hop on bikes for a 22-mile ride to the Deschutes, where it's a 5-mile riverside run to kayaks and canoes, which racers paddle to a final sprint through Bend's Drake Park. For most participants, it's a relay race, though individuals are welcome to race the entire course. *541-388-0002.*

(following pages) Fields of wildflowers form the foreground to a view of Iron Mountain in the western Cascades.

■ CASCADE LAKES *map page 278, A-5*

A road to the Cascade Lakes area southwest of Bend was started in 1912. Originally built to facilitate firefighting and forest ranger business rather than recreational pursuits, the road, Route 46, also known as the Cascade Lakes Highway, is a great long-cut alternative to busy U.S. 97. Or you can travel portions of both roads to make full day trip from Bend.

The Cascade Lakes Highway starts in downtown Bend near Drake Park, passes a thicket of condos and resorts, and begins climbing. During the winter, the road is plowed only as far as Mount Bachelor. After Bachelor, the mountain lakes, many formed by lava dams, really start in, and a new Cascade peak springs into view at every break in the lodgepole pines. Trails into the **Three Sisters Wilderness Area** sprout from the road; virtually every lake has a few campsites on its shores, and resorts at Elk Lake, Cultus Lake, and South Twin Lake have cabins.

One of the first lakes you'll see on the drive, Todd Lake, is right off the main road. From late spring through the summer, it is surrounded by violet lupine, pink penstemons, red Indian paintbrush, and red-and-yellow columbine, all crowned by the rugged beauty of Broken Top. For even closer views of Broken Top's caved-in crater and craggy peak, continue past Todd Lake on Forest Service Road 370, turn left onto Road 380, and then pick up the Ditch Trail. It follows a ridge around Broken Top to Green Lakes.

Strong hikers can climb 10,358-foot **South Sister.** It's a steep 5.5-mile hike to the top. Take off from Devil's Lake where the highway takes a sharp turn to the south, and follow the trail 'til it quits. Make sure to hike under sunny skies, and at the top you'll have all the central Oregon peaks as neighbors.

Farther along the Cascade Lakes Highway the Deschutes's headwaters spurt up from springs beneath Little Lava Lake. **Crane Prairie Reservoir,** which impounds the fledgling Deschutes, is home to a fascinating osprey colony. They nest on snags in the reservoir and dive for rainbows, brookies, kokanee, and largemouth bass. Ospreys are often mistaken for bald eagles, but the osprey's dive for fish is far more graceful than an eagle's feet-first snatch.

Road 42 joins the Cascade Lakes Highway just south of Crane Prairie and shoots east to Sunriver, passing Twin Lakes and Wickiup Reservoir before joining U.S. 97 at the base of Newberry Volcano.

■ **LAVA LANDSCAPES** *map page 278, B-5*

The slopes of bulky **Newberry Volcano,** 23 miles south of Bend, are riven with fissures. Vents and over 400 cinder cones have lined up along these weak spots. Most of the effluent from Newberry flowed from these vents. As lava oozed out, the volcano's top collapsed, leaving a 5-mile-wide caldera, **Newberry Crater.** The glassy, obsidian flow in the caldera is from Newberry's most recent eruption, some 1,300 years ago.

Newberry's most staggering view is from **Paulina Peak,** the high point on the volcano's rim. Visitors descending to the caldera with its two lakes learn that one of them, East Lake, comes complete with a stinky, milk-of-magnesia-textured, dig-it-yourself hot springs. Non-native trout and kokanee, the Big Obsidian Flow, down-home resorts, and a handful of campgrounds are there, too.

To reach the **Lava Lands Visitors Center** (58201 South U.S. 97; 541-593-2421) drive 16 miles north of the Newberry Volcano turnoff on U.S. 97. A trail leads from the visitors center to the base of Lava Butte over jagged 'a'a lava. A narrow, spiraled road leads careful, non-acrophobic drivers to a butte-top viewpoint. Scramble through the nearby Lava River Cave, where hot lava moved beneath the crusted-over surface, leaving caves and tubes. It's a rough ride to the stony tree-trunk molds in the Lava Cast Forest (9 miles east of U.S. 97), where basalt flowed into, then out of, a forest, leaving tree trunks coated with molten rock. The trees slowly burned from the hot lava, but the hollow black lava casts remain.

■ **TRAVEL AND CLIMATE**

■ **GETTING THERE AND AROUND**
U.S. 97, a two-lane highway that often runs straight through the pines, is the main north-south route; U.S. 20, a twisting, two-lane road, is the main route across the Cascade passes. **Horizon Air** flies to Bend from Portland and Seattle.

■ **CLIMATE**
It snows often in Central Oregon, though the region lies in the rain shadow of the Cascades. The snow is dry and powdery, making for ideal skiing. Spring, summer, and autumn are warm to hot—which is when local rivers and the numerous lakes seem particularly inviting.

WILLAMETTE VALLEY
& WESTERN CASCADES

■ **HIGHLIGHTS**

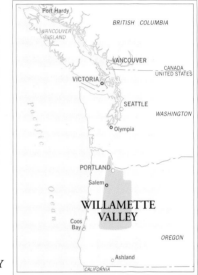

■ **LANDSCAPE AND HISTORY**

MUCH OF THE WILLAMETTE VALLEY is a serene, rustic place of meandering rivers, small farms and ranches, fields and meadows. Vineyards climb the gentle, south-facing slopes, and fields of multi-colored irises spread across the valley floor. Ancient groves of oaks border orchards and berry patches. Cattle and sheep graze in lushly green meadows. Side roads follow white-water rivers east into the Cascade Mountains and west into the Coast Ranges, past ancient barns and over pretty covered bridges, and through small towns little changed for a hundred years, with names like Sublimity and Sweet Home.

Bustling cinderblock malls and used-car lots blight their urban fringes, but the old quarters of the valley's cities—Salem, the state capital, and the college towns of Corvallis and Eugene—have also preserved a special charm. As you drive the valley's byways and relax by a river, you'll understand why 19th-century pioneers considered this the Eden at the end of the Oregon Trail.

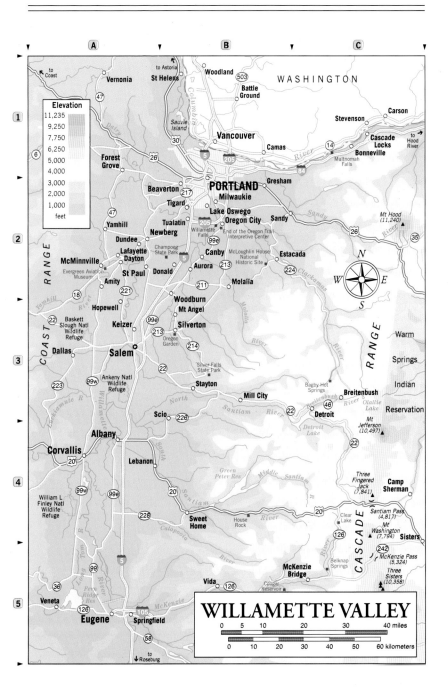

WILLAMETTE VALLEY

| | 0 | 5 | 10 | 20 | 30 | 40 miles |
| 0 | 10 | 20 | 30 | 40 | 50 | 60 kilometers |

■ NORTH WILLAMETTE VALLEY *map page 291*

Oregon City, 20 miles up the Willamette from the Columbia River and near a splendid falls, was the site of an 1829 Hudson's Bay Company settlement. Etienne Lucier was posted here, and he built three cabins and a store. Today, Oregon City is a suburb of Portland, a testament to urban sprawl, and there's something poignant in the idea that this spot was the end of the "rainbow."

The Oregon Trail, which began at Independence, Missouri, officially ended at Abernethy Green. At Oregon City, emigrants picked up land deeds from the federal office, where all the West Coast plats were held.

Abernethy Green is now the site of the **End of the Oregon Trail Interpretive Center,** whose exhibits trace Pacific Northwest history from the fur-trading era to the early days of the railroads. *1726 Washington Street; 503-657-9336.*

John McLoughlin, a British citizen and the director of the Hudson's Bay Company, joined the Willamette Valley settlers in the early 1840s. The **McLoughlin House National Historic Site** includes his house and the nearby Barclay House, both moved to their present locations in the early 1900s. McLoughlin was known as the Father of Oregon for his many accomplishments, which included helping new arrivals to the state and laying out the town of Oregon City (he also served as mayor of the town). *713 Center Street; 503-656-5146.*

At Willamette Falls, a dam generates power, and locks ease boat travel. For a good view of the dam and the scene around it, ride the city's pink elevator 90 feet up the basalt cliffs from the riverside business district to a roadway built on a bench above the river. The Seventh and Railroad elevator, which has operated since 1913, was hydro-powered until it was converted to electric power in 1954.

South of Oregon City, Route 99E winds past small farms and orchards in all hues of green. In **Aurora,** ornamental cherry orchards and endless fields of tulips and irises lead the way to a utopian community now taken over by antique shops. In 1857, a German communist/utopian/Christian colony migrated here from Bethel, Missouri, and settled halfway between Portland and Salem. Their leader, Dr. William Keil, espoused that, "No man owns anything individually but every man owns everything as a full partner and with an equal voice in its use and its increase and the profits accruing from it."

Despite such egalitarian ideas, Keil was pretty much an autocrat, and as young people began to question his dictates, the community foundered. After Keil died in 1877, the community property was divided up, and Aurora became just another well-heeled valley town, albeit one with a good utopian history museum, the **Old Aurora Colony Museum** (212 Second Street NE; 503-678-5754).

In Aurora, a turn right (west) on First Street and a turn right (north) on Main Street will take you on a pretty country drive across the valley. Turn right (north) onto Butteville Road (after crossing I-5), then left (west) onto Champoeg Road. After a few miles, you'll see a sign on the right directing you to **Champoeg State Park,** a beautiful area that looks much like the Willamette Valley the pioneers saw, with its wildflower meadows, streamside woods, and marshes filled with birdsong.

Champoeg Park marks the place where Joe Meek called Oregon's first political convention in 1843, to establish an American provisional government. At the time, Champoeg was an open prairie at the river's edge, used by fur-traders and farmers as a landing for trans-shipping furs, grain, and produce. Today the bank is overgrown with tall trees and dense brush. The world's largest black cottonwood tree towers above the riparian trees along one of the sloughs. Shaded trails invite visitors to take a walk or bike ride through walnut orchards or groves of native oak trees. The Willamette River is big and fast here, running between steep wooded banks. Raccoons and deer leave tracks beside streams, and harmless snakes slither away from sunny spots when they're disturbed (rattlesnakes are rare north of Eugene; none have been found north of Salem). Blue-flowered camas dot wet meadows.

St. Paul, to the southwest, was the site of the first church (a log building) within Oregon's present boundaries and also of the state's first vineyard where Jesuit padres planted Oregon's first grapevines. Now St. Paul is best known for its Fourth of July rodeo, a lively scene, and one of western Oregon's few big rodeos.

If you have the time, be sure to take the rustic **Wheatland Ferry** (503-588-7979) across the Willamette, near the town of **Hopewell.** The six-car ferryboat runs on an underwater cable. On the river's east side, there's a transition from vineyards to hop fields, where more than 14 different varieties of the bitter, aromatic herb are grown. Hop vines grow up trellised strings like giant pole beans, and by late summer form a green canopy. These hops go into some of America's best microbrews.

The **Evergreen Aviation Museum** exhibits the experimental Hughes Flying Boat, more commonly known as the *Spruce Goose.* Howard Hughes's cargo plane, designed to carry troops and material over great distances, remains the largest aircraft ever built. *Route 18, 1 mile east of McMinnville; 503-434-4180.*

■ **SALEM AND VICINITY** *map page 291, A-3*

Salem, the capital city, is a study in contrast between old, tree-shaded residential neighborhoods traversed by Mill Creek, which opens to unexpectedly idyllic vistas right in the center of town, and the greensward of the government office campus. As modern buildings were erected, old trees were spared, unifying the old and the new. Built in 1938, after the original capitol burned, the statehouse is an art deco marvel with a golden pioneer perched on top. The interior is decorated with striking WPA murals—a gargantuan, muscled logger and fisherman, and scenes from Oregon's history. The venerable buildings and tall trees of Willamette University, the oldest college in the West, rise just across the road from the capitol. The Willamette River flows by just west of downtown. The vineyards of the Eola Hills lie beyond. The Riverfront Park's main attraction is an old-fashioned carousel with an organ and carved wooden horses.

Salem has some truly execrable malls along Lancaster Drive and along the I-5 corridor, as well as ticky-tacky housing developments, but it also has a bustling downtown where old buildings, like Reed's Opera House, have been turned into modern shops and restaurants. Salem also has some very fine restaurants.

Though Salem is a city of trees, rhododendrons, and roses, nearby fields are planted with irises, one of the area's important floral products. East of town, the valley rises in a series of hills that rivers descend in white-water rapids. Driftboat fishing for steelhead can be very rewarding, in season.

At **Silver Falls State Park,** a 7-mile trail passes 10 waterfalls. One trail even leads behind a waterfall, where the air is refreshingly cool on a hot summer day. *From Salem, head east on Route 22 for 5 miles and then Route 214 for 20 miles.*

Head north on Route 214 to Silverton and visit the **Oregon Garden**, which opened in 2001. This public display garden and botanical complex is currently in its first phase of construction, with 60 acres of plantings open to the public. When finished, the garden will encompass some 240 acres. Highlights include the Signature Oak, a 400-year-old native oak—22 feet 10 inches in circumference and 99 feet tall—and other oaks whose ages range from 150 to 200 years. There's also a Water Garden and a Children's Garden. The Frank Lloyd Wright–designed **Gordon House** is nestled in the oak grove at the entrance to the Oregon Garden. The only house designed by Wright in Oregon, it was moved in sections from Wilsonville to its current home. *Off Route 213 via Westfield Street at the intersection with Main Street; 503-874-8100 or 877-674-2733.*

(preceding pages) Willamette vineyards. (opposite) South Falls in Silver Falls State Park.

Mount Angel, north of Silverton on Route 214, is one of the Willamette Valley's most interesting towns. A hilltop Benedictine abbey dominates Mount Angel, and the museum there is a fascinating mishmash, even for heathens. Where else can you find a Coke bottle collection, or a giant hairball under glass? The state-of-the-art library, designed by Finnish architect Alvar Aalto, houses a surprisingly good collection of ancient manuscripts. For some reason, Mount Angel celebrates Oktoberfest every September, and tries to maintain a Bavarian theme year-round.

Albany, upriver from Salem, is a treasure trove of historic homes. These Victorian and Craftsman houses are reminders of Albany's late-19th- and early-20th-century prosperity, when produce and flour were shipped out by riverboat. (To experience the flavor of the old town, pick up a map of historic homes from the kiosk in the Market Place, 300 SW Second Avenue.) Numerous covered bridges, the greatest number in the West, cross creeks and rivers east of Albany, off Route 26. Look for them on Crabtree and Thomas Creeks. The **Shimanek Bridge,** over Thomas Creek near Scio, is unique for Oregon: it is painted barn red, instead of the usual white.

Tiny **Scio** is a town frozen in time, with false-front buildings on its main street and a rustic museum. The 1890s **Depot Museum,** run by the Scio Historical Society, occupies the West Scio Depot. Exhibits include clothing, dishes, paintings, kitchen items, farm implements, and other articles that were donated by descendants of families that settled here from the 1880s. Family bibles, family heirlooms, old scrapbooks, pictures, and diaries that tell of life back in the early days of settlement are also on display. The museum has on file the weekly Scio newspapers from 1890 through 1984. There is also an old caboose kids can clamber over. The museum is in downtown Scio. *503-394-2199 or 503-394-2354.*

A road leads to the top of 4,097-foot-high **Mary's Peak,** west of the pleasant university town of **Corvallis.** The highest point in the Oregon Coast Ranges, the peak has a gorgeous display of unusual wildflowers in late spring and early summer.

■ WESTERN CASCADES   *map page 291, C-2/5*

East of the valley's broad agricultural floor rise the western, or old, **Cascade Mountains.** This tree-covered range is home to some of the last old-growth forest of the Cascades.

Several scenic highways lead from the Willamette Valley into the Cascades and across passes to central Oregon. From Salem, Route 22 follows the North Santiam

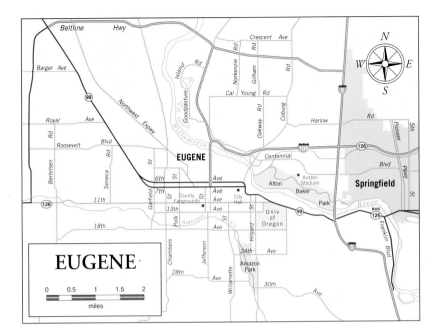

into the mountains. This river is dammed to form **Detroit Lake.** Just north of the Forest Service's Breitenbush campground, turn east to the **South Breitenbush Gorge** trail. The trailhead is not far from the main road, and it's as splendid an example of an old-growth forest as you'll find. Leggy rhododendrons and Oregon grapes break through the mossy floor; cedars and Douglas firs rise to the sky or lie fallen on the ground, nourishing young trees as "nurse logs." Keep an eye out for black bears scrambling up and down tree trunks. Consider it a special treat to come across a bear, but do keep your distance.

Turn off Route 46 about 27 miles north of Detroit for an 18-mile trip to **Olallie Lake**, with its no-frills resort and campground. It's worth the long, slow drive. In the Chinook jargon (19th-century trader's pidgin) "olallie" means huckleberry, and huckleberry bushes dominate the understory beneath the lodgepole pine and mountain hemlocks. Olallie is the largest of the many lakes in the area, most of which are small, shallow basins scooped out by glacial ice. From **Olallie Butte** there's a fine view of the lakes and of Mount Jefferson.

Past the Olallie turnoff, Highway 46 follows the Clackamas River. Pullouts and trailheads dot the road, and steam plumes rise from hot spots in the river.

BRIDGES OF LINN COUNTY

Oregon has more covered bridges than any other state on the West Coast—some 59 at last count. It's because rural Oregonians are fiscally conservative, and covered bridges, built with locally abundant logs, could be built at a lower cost than steel or concrete spans.

As old-fashioned as they look, these bridges are actually marvels of modern engineering. But that doesn't make them any less pretty to look at. Ounce by ounce, these wooden bridges are at least as strong as steel bridges. These bridges have roofs because it rains a lot in western Oregon. Rainwater collecting in exposed joints of wooden bridges makes them rot, and pretty soon an uncovered bridge falls down. On a covered bridge, the roof protects the joints, giving it a life expectancy five times that of an open bridge. But the roofs also protect people from the rain. Because they're on back roads with little traffic, the bridges sometimes close and community dances are held on their sturdy decks.

Covered bridges span creeks and rivers throughout western Oregon, from Josephine County north to Portland, and from the coast to the Cascades. But the easiest ones to visit on a day trip (or half a day, if you're in a hurry), stand south and east of Scio, in Linn County, just a few miles east of the I-5 freeway at Albany.

These covered bridges are only a few miles apart. You might want to start your tour with the **Hoffman Bridge** or **Gilkey,** proceed to the **Shimanek Bridge** (unusual because it's painted barn red instead of the common white) and the **Hannah Bridge,** and finish up with the **Larwood Bridge,** where you can rest and have a picnic in tree-shaded Roaring River Park.

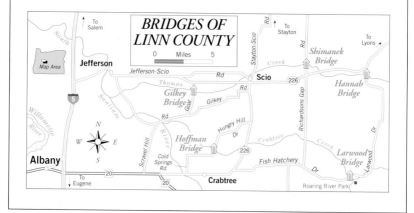

Hannah covered bridge.

From Albany, U.S. 20 follows the track of the **Santiam Wagon Road**, which once crossed the Cascades. Traces of it remain near the House Rock Campground, 24 miles east of Sweet Home, where a huge boulder sheltered early travelers. Old-growth trees now form a broad canopy; a short trail leads to a waterfall on the South Santiam River.

■ EUGENE AND THE MCKENZIE RIVER *map page 291, A-5*

Eugene revolves around the University of Oregon in a loose, elliptical orbit. This is one of the few towns in America where tie-dyed T-shirts have been in fashion for 30 solid years. It's certainly one of the few places in the state where the corner grocery stocks soy milk and nitrite-free sausage. But a culinary tour of Eugene won't disappoint those with more sophisticated and carnivorous tastes—the local restaurants are quite good.

There's as much partying here as in any college town—*Animal House* was filmed in Eugene. But what sets the town apart is the laid-back atmosphere at its fairs and markets: the weekly **Saturday Market** downtown; the **Oregon Country Fair** in Veneta in early July; and the **Eugene Celebration** in late September. The Saturday Market offers the expected mix of beads and dried herbs, and the Eugene

Celebration is lively, but not too giddily foreign for the unprepared visitor. The university itself is set on a gracious campus and is highly thought of. If you stop by the **University of Oregon Museum of Natural History** (1680 East 15th Avenue; 541-346-3024), you can see the 13,000-year-old Fort Rock sagebrush sandals, one of the oldest Paleo-Indian artifacts ever to be found.

A paved foot/bike path runs through town along the **Willamette River** (past riffles named Pietro's Pizza Rapids, after a local hangout above the shore). The river here was a navigational challenge for daring riverboat captains; today, locals run the rapids in rubber rafts. Bike paths line many streets and run to the hinterlands. A pleasant drive or bicycle trip takes you south to Spencer Butte, bounded by Willamette Boulevard and Fox Hollow, for good views of the Cascades and the Three Sisters.

Route 126 winds east into the Cascade foothills along the **McKenzie River** past hazelnut orchards into the mountains. On a sunny day you might want to pack a lunch and dawdle up the highway to the **Goodpasture Bridge** for a picnic.

Tokatee Golf Course (54947 Route 126; 541-822-3220), near Cougar Reservoir and McKenzie Bridge, is one of Oregon's loveliest and most celebrated. The nearer you get to the headwaters of the McKenzie (at Clear Lake, on Route 126), the more mysterious the river becomes. **Clear Lake**, formed by a lava dam, flooded a forest still visible underwater.

The scenery along winding **McKenzie Pass Highway,** Route 242, undergoes a startling transition, as it crosses from the ferns and trees near McKenzie Bridge to a moonscape of crusty, brown-black lava flow. Parts of the flow are only 400 years old. Just 30 years ago, these lava fields stood in for the moon, when astronauts practiced landing and walking on the lunar-like surface here. (Apollo astronauts left a central Oregon lava rock on the moon, in exchange for the moon rocks they ferried back to Earth.) This road is not plowed in winter.

■ Travel and Climate

■ Getting There and Around

The Willamette Valley is a long, green river valley dividing the southern Cascades from the Coast Range. Even though urban sprawl gnaws at its edges, it is still mostly agricultural, its rivers hidden behind dense stands of cottonwood, ash, and willow, its fields and meadows dotted with copses of ancient oaks. Corn, berries, plums, pears, apples, and nuts grow here; the wines made from local pinot noir, chardonnay, and muscat grapes are justly famous.

One freeway, I-5, runs the length of the valley, and because it's so easy to breeze along, going faster and faster, it's also easy to get a speeding ticket—highway patrol cars have a way of materializing out of blackberry bushes. There are two rustic and scenic alternatives to the freeway: Route 99W, which connects Portland to the Yamhill County Wine Country, Corvallis, and Junction City; and Route 99E, which connects Salem and Albany to Portland.

■ Climate

Willamette Valley weather is mild, with abundant rain in winter and sunny summer weather, but it varies considerably through the 110 miles of the valley. Because of the mitigating influence of the Columbia River, which channels cool marine air inland, Salem, near the northern end of the valley, is often cooler in summer and warmer in winter than Eugene, near the southern end. It's also more likely to snow in Eugene. But even in the coldest of winters and wettest of summers, the inclement weather never lasts long, and in a pinch you can always find a spreading oak or maple tree under which to hold your picnic.

WILLAMETTE VALLEY WINERY TOUR *map next page*

Wine-making in Oregon predates the Prohibition era, but it wasn't until Richard Sommer planted grapes in the Umpqua Valley in 1961 that wineries took off. Following Sommer's pioneering efforts, Charles Coury planted European grape varietals in the northern Willamette Valley. He was soon followed by David Adelsheim, Dick Erath, and David Lett, who established the first Yamhill County vineyards and wineries. Their first wines proved them right: this was prime wine country indeed.

Today, the valley's wineries are booming, and Yamhill County is turning into the Napa Valley of the Northwest. Fortunately for travelers, these vineyards are close to Portland and are easily reached by a short drive. Expect a steady flow of visitors, especially on weekends. Tasting rooms are generally open daily from 11 A.M. to 5 P.M., but call ahead for specific hours and days.

Pinot noir was an early favorite among locally grown grapes and makes great wines in the hands of master vintners like Ken Wright, Myron Redford, Dick Ponzi, and Dick Erath. But some vintages proved disappointing; others have not aged well. Recently there's been a boom in pinot gris plantings. This pink Alsatian grape does very well here. It is the perfect wine to accompany fresh salmon, crab, shrimp, or other seafoods. Chardonnays, Rieslings, muscats, and other grapes also do well here. You'll have to visit and taste to discover your favorites. We're listing some of the most important wineries on the following pages to give you a solid introduction to the tempting wines of a beautiful region.

■ TOURING THE VINEYARDS

Ponzi Vineyards

Ponzi, the winery closest to Portland, has earned acclaim for producing quality pinot noir, pinot gris, chardonnay, vino gelato, and Arneis. Dick Ponzi's name has been synonymous with Oregon wine since he produced his first four barrels in 1974. Today, Oregon is famous for its pinot noir and pinot gris—wines Ponzi helped pioneer. The tasting room is on Route 99W between Dundee and Lafayette. *14665 Southwest Winery Lane, Beaverton; 503-628-1227.*

Ponzi Vineyards: a family affair

Rex Hill Vineyards

This is the next winery you come to as you travel south on Route 99W from Portland. Shortly after you cross into Yamhill County, where the landscape changes from subdivisions to trees and vineyards, keep a sharp lookout for the blue sign marking the turnoff. The winery rises in landscaped grounds beneath vineyards. Rose arbors and beds of flowers frame a grassy picnic area. The wines to taste here are pinot noir, pinot gris, and chardonnay. *30835 North Route 99W, Newberg; 800-739-4455.*

Adelsheim 4	Chehalem 3	Lange 11	Sokol Blosser 13
Amity 20	Duck Pond 7	Montinore 18	Tyee Cellars 24
Archery Sum. 12	Elk Cove 16	OR Tasting Rm 23	Yamhill 21
Argyle 8	Eola Hills 22	Panther Creek 19	Youngberg 1
Brick House 6	Erath 10	Patricia Green 5	
Cameron 9	Ken Wright 15	Ponzi 25	
Chateau Benoit 14	Kramer 17	Rex Hill 2	

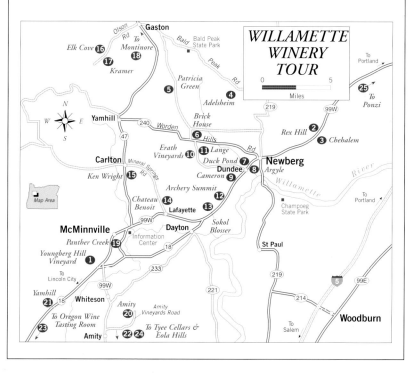

Chehalem

This winery is right across the highway from Rex Hill. The name translates as "valley of flowers," after the land where these grapes grow. The winery makes intense, hand-crafted pinot noirs, pinot gris, and chardonnays. Tasting is by appointment. *31190 NE Veritas Lane, Newberg; 503-538-4700.*

Adelsheim Vineyard

Adelsheim makes consistently good wines and is among the handful of wineries that have helped to put Oregon vineyards on the world map. Founded in 1971 by David and Ginny Adelsheim, the winery has remained small, producing a mere 20,000 cases of wine annually. There's a splendid pinot gris, a silky pinot noir, and a crisp chardonnay. The winery is only open on Memorial Day and Thanksgiving weekends. *16800 NE Calkins Lane, Newberg; 503-538-3652.*

Patricia Green Cellars

Patricia Green, wine-maker for Torii Mor winery, and her cellar master James Anderson bought Autumn Wine Vineyards in April 2000. Their goal is to make distinct pinot noirs that are both complex and enjoyable. Tasting room hours are noon to 5 P.M. on weekends through the summer. *15225 NE North Valley Road, Newberg; 503-554-0821.*

Brick House Vineyards

The grapes of this beautiful vineyard are organically grown among the hazelnut orchards of Ribbon Ridge. Pinot noir, chardonnay, and gamay noir all give excellent wine here. Production is small—less than a thousand cases of handcrafted wines annually. Visits are by appointment only. *18200 Lewis Rogers Lane, Newberg; 503-538-5136.*

Duck Pond Cellars

The grounds and well-stocked gift shop are reasons alone for visiting, but the wines made by this family-owned-and-operated winery and vineyard are also worth a special trip. Duck Pond concentrates on pinot noir and chardonnay, but also makes a superb (and reasonably priced) Columbia Valley merlot and chardonnay. The Columbia Valley wines come from family-owned vineyards on the Wahluke Slope. *23145 Route 99W, Dundee; 503-538-3199.*

Duck Pond Cellars tasting room

Argyle

The tasting room for Argyle is in a Victorian house surrounded by flowers. It's just off the highway and hard to miss. Argyle makes very good sparkling wine and enjoyable chardonnay, pinot noir, and dry Riesling. *691 Route 99W, Dundee; 503-538-8520 or 800-427-4953.*

Cameron Winery

The winery offers excellent pinot noir and chardonnay from three distinctive vineyards: Abbey Ridge, Brick House, and Clos Electrique. It's open to the public only on Thanksgiving weekend. *8200 Worden Hill Road, Dundee; 503-538-0336.*

From the town of Dundee, take Worden Hill Road to Erath and Lange Wineries (turn right on Ninth Street in Dundee). Follow the signs (the lane leading to Lange angles off to the right).

Erath Vineyards

Dick Erath is one of the true pioneers of Willamette Valley wine-making. Although the winery is best known for its complex, long-lived pinot noir, Erath also makes outstanding pinot gris, pinot blanc, chardonnay, and Riesling. The winery is high in the Dundee Hills and has a picnic patio with a view. Roaring River Park, next to the winery, is a great place for taking a walk and clearing your head before you drive back on the winding country road. *9409 NE Worden Hill Road, Dundee; 800-539-9463 or 503-538-3318.*

Lange Winery

Take Ninth Street off Route 99W in Dundee and follow the blue signs up into the Red Hills. The pinot noir, pinot gris, and chardonnay are wines you want to take home. There are splendid views of the Chehalem and Willamette Valleys from the winery's lofty ridge. *18380 NE Buena Vista, Dundee; 503-538-6476.*

The next winery can be reached via attractive Archery Summit Road, off Route 99W.

Archery Summit

Archery Summit is a surprisingly friendly place for a premium winery with snob appeal. To create distinctive pinot noir, the vineyards are planted with several clones of pinot noir on rootstocks designed to match the soils, 2,200 vines per acre. The wines are aged in caves. *18599 NE Archery Summit Road, Dayton; 503-864-4300.*

Sokol Blosser Winery

This winery is just off Route 99W, but it sits on a hilltop with spectacular views—on a clear day, you can look from the vineyards all the way to Mount Hood. Sokol Blosser makes first-rate pinot noir and chardonnay. The tasting room is well stocked with local foods. A shady picnic area beckons you to linger over a bottle of wine. Take the self-guided tour through the vineyard after your repast, to learn about vines and viticultural practices like trellising. There is a tasting fee. *5000 Sokol Blosser Lane, Dundee; 503-864-2282.*

Chateau Benoit Winery

Founded in 1979 by Fred and Mary Benoit, Chateau Benoit is located 1.5 miles off Route 99W near Lafayette, high above the valley. Among the wines made here, you should taste the brut sparkling wine, the sauvignon blanc, and the easily drinkable, delicious mullerthurgau, which is just right for a warm-weather picnic. *6580 NE Mineral Springs Road, Carlton; 800-248-4835 or 503-864-2991.*

Ken Wright Cellars

Ken Wright is a genius, a true artist of wine-making, and his wines are eagerly searched out by collectors. The winery is open to the public on Thanksgiving weekend only. *236 North Kutch Street, Carlton; 503-852-7070.*

Chateau Benoit

For the wineries north and northeast of Carlton, follow the map to the wineries, on (often narrow) roads winding in and out of the hills through a beautiful landscape of orchards, vineyards, meadows, and oak groves. Almost all Oregon wineries are well marked by blue highway signs. Keep a sharp lookout: You might come across a new winery so young it's not yet listed in any guide.

The turnoff for both Kramer and Elk Cove is at the southern city limits of Gaston, which is also the Yamhill County line, and can be difficult to spot.

Elk Cove Vineyards

Northwest of Newberg, near the farming hamlet of Gaston, the tasting room of Elk Cove Vineyards rises above a vine-covered "cove," actually a saucer-shaped valley surrounded by tall trees. On the drive in, the road, winding along the slopes of the Coast Range foothills, offers spec-tacular views of the Willamette Valley farmlands. The wines are as beautiful as the set-ting. Elk Cove produces excellent pinot noir and pinot gris, highly enjoyable chardon-nay, cabernet sauvignon, and, if the weather is right at harvest time, some nicely bal-anced dessert wines. All of these are "food wines," designed to enhance Oregon's meats, seafoods, fruits, and cheeses. *27751 NW Olson Road, Gaston; 503-985-7760.*

Kramer Vineyards

A short drive from Elk Cove brings you to Kramer Vineyards, a cliffhanger of a win-ery where wine-maker Trudy Kramer handcrafts splendid pinot gris, pinot noir, mer-lot, and syrah. *26830 NW Olson Road, Gaston; 503-662-4545.*

Montinore Vineyards

The Montinore story begins with a funny twist. Folks at the winery chuckle when vis-itors try to show off their sophistication by trying to pronounce the name in the French fashion. The estate, originally a ranch, was established by a tycoon who made money in the Montana mines and retired to Oregon. He decided to call his estate MONTana IN OREgon. The name stuck and was taken over by the winery established here a few years back. Highlights include crisp gewürztraminer, a lushly rich pinot noir, and a refreshing pinot gris, which happens to be a perfect wine for accompanying North-west seafood. The tasting room staff is among the most knowledgeable and friendliest in the Oregon wine country. *3663 SW Dilley Road, Forest Grove; 503-359-5012.*

From Montinore, you can head right back down Route 47 and drive south to McMinnville—unless you want to take a detour in Yamhill and drive west into the foothills to spend a night or two at the secluded **Youngberg Hill Vineyard** (10660 SW Youngberg Hill Road; 888-657-8668).

McMinnville is the "capital" of the northern Willamette Valley wine country. Held each July at Linfield College, the **International Pinot Noir Celebration** (503-472-8964), a bacchanalian event, stretches over a long weekend. The town has some of the Oregon wine country's best restaurants.

Panther Creek Cellars

Panther Creek Cellars, founded in 1986, occupies McMinnville's original and his-torical power plant. Pinot noir, melon

Montinore Vineyard

(a little-known French white wine grape), and chardonnay are Panther Creek specialties. The winery is open to the public on the Memorial Day and Thanksgiving weekends, and by appointment. *455 North Irvine, McMinnville; 503-472-8080.*

The next three wineries are south of McMinnville, along Route 99W, one of the main arteries running the length of the Willamette Valley. Except for briefly touching on towns, villages, or hamlets now and then, this is a rustic road, bordered by fields, orchards, berry patches, and the remnants of the oak grasslands that once covered much of the Willamette Valley.

Amity Vineyards

This small family-owned winery sits high on a hill, overlooking the village of Amity and the Willamette Valley. Since 1976, founder and wine-maker Myron Redford has concentrated on pinot noir, gamay noir (a rare grape in Oregon), dry and late-harvest gewürztraminer, and Riesling. He also makes a sulfite-free pinot noir made from organic grapes and a blush wine from pinot noir and pinot blanc. Redford is one of the true artists of Willamette Valley wine-making. His silky, full-flavored pinot noir is excellent with food, as is the dry Riesling. The winery's tasting room is closed in January. *18150 Amity Vineyards Road; 503-835-2362.*

Yamhill Valley Vineyards

On the way to the coast, just off Route 18, these premium vineyards are tucked into the foothills where the Coast Range meets the Willamette Valley. Try the full-bodied pinot noir and an intense pinot gris. Open May through November. *16250 SW Oldsville Road, McMinnville; 503-843-3100.*

Eola Hills Wine Cellars

To the south of the Eola Hills, just west of Salem, Eola Hills Wine Cellars makes great wines and has an excellent reputation for its Sunday brunch. Call to make reservations. *501 South Pacific Highway 1W, Rickreall; 503-623-2405.*

Oregon Wine Tasting Room

This is a terrific place for tasting and buying hard-to-find local wines. It's located in the Lawrence Art Gallery, before the coast at the Bellevue crossroads. *19706 SW Highway 18, McMinnville; 503-843-3787.*

As you head south on Route 99W, through Corvallis, look for a blue sign directing you to Tyee Wine Cellars. Watch for big hunting goshawks, descending from nearby Mary's Peak. Long, sinuous rows of trees mark rivers and watercourses. Large leaves of wild cucumber vines make much of this woodland look like jungle.

Tyee Wine Cellars

Tyee Wine Cellars is among the truly great wineries of this region. The setting, too, is special. The winery is part of a "century farm" that has been run by the same family for over a hundred years. The place is as rustic as ever: the tasting room is in an old dairy house. Highlights include the pinot noir, pinot gris, chardonnay, and gewürztraminer. The latter is among the best of this variety

Tyee Wine Cellars tasting room

produced in the Northwest. Ancient Oregon oaks in a pristine meadow shade a picnic area. This section of the farm has never felt the bite of a plow. Look for beavers in the marsh below, their pathways in the shoreside reeds and their tooth marks on riparian trees. *26335 Greenberry Road, Corvallis; 541-753-8754.*

SOUTHERN OREGON

■ **HIGHLIGHTS**

■ **LANDSCAPE**

BETWEEN EUGENE AND ASHLAND, 162 miles to the south, I-5, the great north-south road, runs through some of the prettiest scenery in the Pacific Northwest. The road skirts cliffs, climbs mountain passes, and winds through wooded river canyons and pastoral valleys. In Sunny Valley, a white covered bridge just east of the freeway adds to the charm.

In spring, purple-tipped grasses grow taller than the backs of grazing sheep. In summer, the meadows are dotted with white daisies, and the brushy edge of the woods glows bright blue with ceanothus blooms. Madronas, cedars, oaks, and manzanita line the road. In the southern corner, where U.S. 199 runs to the coast, you'll even see a few redwoods.

Crater Lake and the Oregon Shakespeare Festival are among regional highlights. Along the rivers, old-timers keep cabins and fill them with fishing rods, trophy heads, and furniture hewn from gigantic logs.

■ **UMPQUA RIVER VALLEY** *map page 313, A-2*

The Umpqua is a most unusual river. It is created by the lowland confluence of two main forks, North and South, which rise high in the western Cascades and are so different from each other that it seems odd they should end up conjoining.

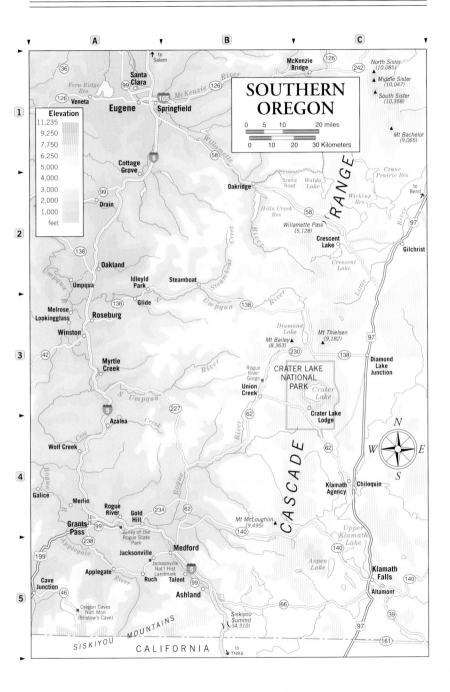

SOUTHERN OREGON

0   5   10   20 miles

0   10   20   30 Kilometers

The **North Umpqua** has its origin high up in the western Cascade Mountains. Its source is Maidu Lake (east of Diamond Lake), which is fed by the snowfields of Fairview Peak, Elephant Mountain, Mount Bailey, and Mount Thielsen. Its course is swift, as it tumbles for some 50 miles through deep chasms of basalt pillars, past hillsides densely clad with stands of tall fir, cedar, and hemlock. Here the waters of the river are deep blue-green and magical.

Trails, most leading to waterfalls, leave the road every few miles; riverside campsites are plentiful. **Steamboat Creek,** alive with trout, drains an area that was a major draw for placer miners in the 19th century. After rushing through the narrow defile of **Idleyld Park,** the silty Little River roils into the jade-colored waters of the North Umpqua near Glide, amidst a jumble of giant rocks, before sliding down in the eastern reaches of the Umpqua Valley.

The steep-walled gorge of the North Umpqua, gushing with waterfalls, is a popular place to fish for spring chinook and summer steelhead. Coho salmon travel upriver in fall to spawn; wild brown trout live in the river's upper reaches. To reach the best fishing holes, and the **Steamboat Inn** (42705 North Umpqua Highway;

White-water rafting on the North Umpqua River.
(opposite) Portions of southwestern Oregon are still blanketed by deep and wild forest.

800-840-8825 or 541-498-2230), a top-flight but unpretentious fishing lodge with a splendid riverfront location and great food, take Route 138, the North Umpqua Road, east of Roseburg into the mountains.

From Rock Creek (east of Idleyld Park) to Lemolo Lake (north of Diamond Lake, near the headwaters of the North Umpqua), the river is open to fly fishing only. Even so, you may have to fight for standing room near the shore, when the fish are biting.

The **South Umpqua** is a great place for dangling your feet in the water or for skinny-dipping in a cool pool on a hot summer day. The two forks of the South Umpqua (Castle Rock and Black Rock) rise in a landscape much drier than that of its northern sibling. Starting in the high country of the western Cascades, the river flows through subalpine meadows before gently dropping over a huge half-dome rock at **South Umpqua Falls.** From here the river continues down a narrow valley, which, unlike the valley of the North Umpqua, occasionally opens into fertile terraces and lush meadows.

Near Canyonville, the South Umpqua heads north to Myrtle Creek and Roseburg. It is a shallow, sometimes placid stream, bordered by open forests of ponderosa pine and black oak, its wooded margins painted blue by ceanothus blossoms in spring. Its water level drops considerably in summer, while its main tributary, Cow Creek, may almost dry up. Cow Creek also rises in the high Cascades in a parallel valley but swings far to the west through oak-clad hills before joining the South Umpqua near Riddle.

The North and South Umpqua join west of Roseburg, in a flat, fertile valley. The united waters of the Umpqua flow smoothly through the oak-studded meadows and hillsides of the Coast Range at a level of only 400 feet above the sea. The river is interrupted in its leisurely course by gentle rapids until it becomes a placid lowland stream at Scottsburg, a few miles above tidewater. Its lower course is a calm estuary, reaching deeply into the forested hills of the Coast Range. It flows into the Pacific at Winchester Bay.

West of Scottsburg, the Umpqua flows, at sea level, through the steep-sided, wooded canyon of a "sunken" riverbed that looks much like a glaciated fjord. A few miles east of Reedsport, where the valley widens, the **Dean Creek Elk Viewing Area** (south of Route 38) is home to 100 to 150 majestic Roosevelt elk. The elk roam freely year-round within the 1,000-acre preserve, which is also home to beavers, nutrias, and waterfowl. At times bald eagles visit these marshes.

■ ROSEBURG *map page 313, A-3*

This former lumber and cattle town is as popular with fly fishermen who have come to match their wits with the wily fish of the North Umpqua, as it is with hikers and lovers of fine wines. Roseburg has maintained the small-town feel of its business district, with galleries, cafes, and bookstores lining rather narrow, tree-shaded streets.

Nearby are the narrows, where the Molalla, a band of the Umpqua Indians, once speared and netted salmon and steelhead in a narrow, steep canyon of the North Umpqua. Today, the narrows is a popular place for salmon and steelhead fishermen. Farther east, in the Cascade Mountains, miles of secluded hiking trails and pristine Diamond Lake beckon the explorer.

The **Douglas County Museum** not only has splendid natural history displays about the Umpqua River Valley, but it also has a grand collection of local artifacts—including ones that predate the eruption that created Crater Lake. There is also an excellent little bookstore. *I-5 south of Roseburg, Exit 123; 541-957-7007.*

If you're traveling during the spring and fall, produce stands along the back roads sell fresh local fruits and vegetables. A picnic area at **River Forks Park**, at the confluence of the North and South Umpqua Rivers, marks the spot where pioneers on the Applegate Trail traveled "across the waters" in the mid-1800s. The park is at the north shore of North Umpqua; accessible via River Parks Road off Garden Valley Road.

The opulence of the 88-year-old **Roseburg Station Pub & Brewery** reflects the fact that Roseburg was once a major stopover on the north-south railway. *700 Sheridan Street, off Route 99 downtown; 541-672-1934.*

The **Wildlife Safari** is a surprisingly cozy, woodsy preserve where lions, giraffes, rhinos, grizzly bears, bison, elk, and other wild things roam freely on 600 wooded acres of oaks, madronas, and firs. You can drive through the reserve, which is located 6 miles south of Roseburg in Winston. *800-355-4848 or 541-679-6761.*

■ UMPQUA VALLEY WINE COUNTRY *map page 313, A-3*

A few miles west of Roseburg, in the lower part of the South Umpqua Valley, is Oregon's Umpqua Valley wine country. Unlike other wine valleys of the Pacific Northwest, the Umpqua Valley is not shaped like an open bowl, but is a maze of low, wooded hills and secluded, pastoral valleys.

Richard Sommer is the modern pioneer of Oregon wine-making. He first planted grapes on the western slopes of the valley in 1961 and made his first wines at **Hillcrest Vineyards** in 1963. Sommer believes the region is ideal for producing great Rieslings, and so far he's been right. But he also makes cabernet sauvignon and pinot noir. To get to the winery, take Garden Valley Road from I-5 in Roseburg west to Melrose, turn left and follow Melrose to Doerner (a fork in the road) and keep right. Another right turn on Elgarose will bring you to the winery. Driving distance is about 10 miles from I-5. *240 Vineyard Lane; 541-673-3709.*

Scott and Sylvia Henry's **Henry Estate Winery**, downriver from the junctions of the two forks of the Umpqua, was established in 1978 on the old family ranch, after they planted their first grapes in 1972. Henry Estate's pinot noirs and chardonnays have been consistently excellent—and have just as consistently been underrated and underpriced. To reach the winery, take Route 138 west from I-5 and bear left at Fort McKay Road/Sutherlin Umpqua Road, which turns into Hubbard Creek Road in the hamlet of Umpqua. *687 Hubbard Creek Road; 541-459-5120.*

Other wineries include **Champagne Creek Cellars** (340 Busenbark Lane; 541-673-7901), **La Garza Cellars & Gourmet Kitchen** (491 Winery Lane; 541-679-9654), **Abacela Vineyards and Winery** (12500 Lookingglass Road; 541-679-6642), and **Umpqua River Vineyards** (451 Hess Lane; 541-673-1975).

■ ROGUE RIVER   *map page 313, A-4*

Grants Pass, a lumber town in the Siskiyou Mountains, caters to travelers lured to the Rogue River's white water. The town is scrappy and partly malled, but historic homes converted into bed-and-breakfasts and antique shops can be found in the venerable downtown. On Saturday mornings, downtown streets take on extra color, fragrance, and bustle at the **Farmers Market.**

The main attraction is the Rogue, described by Western writer Zane Grey as:

> …Deep and dark green, swift and clear, and as pure as the snows from which it springs…. It is a river at its birth, gliding away through the Oregon forest with hurrying momentum, as if eager to begin the long leap down through the Siskiyous. The river tumbles off the mountain in mellow thundering music, racing between its timbered banks down the miles to the sheltered valley.

(opposite) Rafters and kayakers in Hellgate Canyon along the Rogue River in Southern Oregon.

Congress declared the Rogue "Wild and Scenic" in 1968, a classification that limits development. A permit is necessary to raft protected stretches of the Rogue. Permits are parceled out by lottery each February and are sometimes available throughout the summer at the Rand Visitors Center, just downstream from the town of Galice. To enter the permit lottery, call 541-479-3735. Rafting outfitters in Grants Pass and neighboring communities get a good share of the permits. They offer everything from rides on guided rafts to inflatable kayak rentals.

Jet boats are a common way to see the river's unprotected stretches. **Jerry's Rogue River Jet Boats** (U.S. 101, Gold Beach; 541-247-4571 or 800-451-3645) claims to be the original Rogue River jet boat trip and the first jet boat tour in America (since 1958). **Rogue River Mail Boats** (541-247-7033 or 800-458-3511) claims to have Oregon's only "mail boat hydro-jets." Besides taking passengers, the boats deliver the U.S. mail to the remote village of Agness, as they have for over 100 years. Passengers have a choice of 64-, 80-, or 104-mile round-trips.

The highest stretches of the Rogue River aren't far from Crater Lake. Less well-known but no less lovely than the upper section of the river, this area is well worth exploring. Stop off at the **Rogue River Gorge,** on Route 62 near Union Creek. Turn north to glacier-scoured **Diamond Lake,** popular year-round with southern Oregon families. In the winter it's possible to cross-country ski here and in the summer to boat and hike.

■ OREGON CAVES *map page 313, A-5*

From Grants Pass, I-5 heads off east and south through Medford and Ashland on its way to California. A two-lane, forest-shaded road, U.S. 199, runs to Crescent City, California. It crosses and runs up the valley of the Illinois River, a pleasant stream that flows north to the Rogue in convoluted meanders, before brushing the northern limit of redwood forests. En route, it passes a few wineries and many old mining sites.

A 45-minute, winding drive climbs from Cave Junction to the 4,000-foot-high cave entrance to **Oregon Caves National Monument** (541-592-2100). The cedar-shake **Caves Chateau** (20000 Cave Highway; 541-592-3400), a huge rustic inn, snugs in against the waterfall-streaked hillside. The caves are a subterranean wonderland of limestone formations. Three miles of trails are mapped, but the networks may be far more extensive. Tickets for cave tours are sold next to the gift shop. The tour is strenuous, and the air in the cave is cold. Dress warmly.

(opposite) Oregon Caves Chateau is a National Historic Monument.

■ JACKSONVILLE *map page 313, A-5*

Jacksonville, 5 miles west of Medford, had a gold boom in 1852. After gold ran out, Jacksonville almost became a ghost town, but it is now a paean to historic preservation with antique shops, pear trees, and the Britt Festival, a summer-long outdoor music festival.

Peter Britt, Jacksonville's most revered pioneer, was a Swiss-born photographer and painter. Back in the days when photography meant heavy cameras and glass-plate negatives, Britt lugged his equipment all over the wilds of southern Oregon. (He was the first to photograph Crater Lake.) He was also an amateur horticulturist, and his gardens are still a quiet, lovely grove. He was a pioneer Oregon vintner and is also remembered for introducing fruit trees. Like Ashland's Shakespeare Festival, the **Britt Festival** (541-773-6077) is hugely popular, and for good reason. The hillside setting lends itself to a relaxed, picnic-like atmosphere, and the performers run the gamut from bluegrass to classical musicians.

Also of interest is the town's **Jacksonville Museum.** Exhibits tell the story of the Applegate Trail and Jacksonville's gold rush days. Other exhibits give a glimpse into the life of Peter Britt. Located next door in the former Jackson County Jail, the Children's Museum has some 20 hands-on exhibits for the young-at-heart. The life-like scenes include an American Indian dwelling, an 1850s cabin, a one-room schoolhouse, and a 1920s gas station. *206 North Fifth Street; 541-773-6536.*

■ ASHLAND *map page 313, B-5*

A cultural hub, the charming theater town of Ashland is home to good bookstores and excellent restaurants. The half-timbered Elizabethan Theatre was being torn apart when Shakespeare aficionado Angus Bowmer noticed that, without the domed roof, the building bore an amazing resemblance to Shakespeare's Globe Theatre. Ashland residents built a 16th-century-style stage, dug through attics for costumes, and put on a show. The first **Oregon Shakespeare Festival** (541-482-4331) was staged in 1935.

Since then, it's been unstoppable. Three theaters now run 11 plays in repertory from mid-February through October. Shakespeare is always represented in the festival's outdoor Elizabethan Theatre, but most of the plays staged in the large Angus Bowmer Theatre or the smaller New Theatre are by other playwrights. Backstage tours and in-depth lectures are always worth your time. Book in advance, and call the box office for the schedule; *541-482-4331.*

Lithia Park was developed with 8 acres in 1892 as a place where the Chautauqua Association could bring entertainment and culture to southern Oregon. Since then, it has grown to 93 acres, and is now of one of the Northwest's premier urban parks. (The original Shakespeare theater began here in 1935.) Much of the park landscape was laid out in 1914 by John McLaren, who designed San Francisco's Golden Gate Park.

McLaren's landscape plan for Lithia Park was organic, following the natural canyon of Ashland Creek. Native alders, oaks, conifers, and madronas were offset by introduced willows, maples, sycamores, and ornamental varieties. A trail on the east side of Ashland Creek leads to the park headquarters, where visitors can pick up a trail guide to the park's features. Trails lead from here into the wild mountains west of town. *59 Winburn Way, off the Plaza; 541-488-5340.*

During the off season, room rates plummet, and locals head south to Mount Ashland's ski slopes. In summer, the top of Mount Ashland has one of the most beautiful displays of wildflowers in the region.

■ KLAMATH FALLS   *map page 313, C-5*

Once known for its bars and fist fights, Klamath Falls now attracts people perky enough to be up at dawn to scout the marshes for eagles, snow geese, and tundra swans. Klamath Falls leaders are working hard to change the city's rough and tumble image. Only one of the once-busy lakeside mills remains, and the town is on its way to becoming a telecommunications and recreation center.

It's worth taking a stroll downtown, where the buildings are adorned with terracotta busts of Nefertiti and animal heads peering over doorframes. The **Ross Ragland Theater** (888-627-5484) is a multi-disciplinary performing arts center.

The **Favell Museum** (125 West Main Street; 541-882-9996) has a remarkably good collection of Western and Indian art. It's hard to imagine a weapon more luminescent than the Favell's prized pink-and-blue fire-opal arrowhead, or a display quirkier than the miniature gun collection housed in a walk-in vault. This museum showcases the best of Klamath Falls. Teddy Roosevelt once stayed at the nearby Baldwin Hotel. Now it's the cherished **Baldwin Hotel Museum** (31 Main Street; 541-883-4207).

Klamath Lake is Oregon's largest natural lake, but it covers only a small part of its former expanse. Shallow lakes and marshlands that attracted birds to the Klamath Basin have been tapped and diverted for irrigation since 1902. Today, in an effort to keep salmon and suckers alive, canals and reservoirs are tightly managed. The tenuous balance is particularly difficult to maintain during drought years, when fishery biologists and farmers narrow their eyes at one another.

Every year, 20,000 acres in the Klamath Basin are flooded, then drained, to provide habitat for waterfowl. The basin's six refuges still attract incredible numbers of migrating waterbirds and, even in dry years, the basin seems awash with blue water lazing through perpetually spring-green flats. White pelicans nest in the Klamath Basin in March and stick around until late fall. During spring and fall, fields are carpeted with Canadian geese, snow geese, and swans.

Hundreds of eagles spend the winter in the Klamath Basin, roosting on sturdy old growth trees southwest of town. Every morning at sunrise they fly out for breakfast in a huge flock, with smaller hawks tagging along. Bird-watchers, wrapped tight in longjohns and puffy jackets, fumble between binoculars and thermoses of hot coffee.

When the first bird passes, unmistakable by its huge wingspan, there's a flurry of excited chatter. Soon the birds are coming in an almost steady stream, and the birders fall quiet, transfixed. In the late afternoon, the eagles straggle back to their roosts. Also on the wing at sunset, tundra swans who have flown thousands of miles come in great V formations looking for a place to rest.

Oregon Department of Fish and Wildlife (541-883-5734) can give details about viewing the fly-out. The local Audubon chapter sponsors a popular mid-February Bald Eagle Conference.

■ CRATER LAKE *map page 313, C-3*

Gold miners stumbled across Crater Lake in 1853. It was formed after the eruption of Mount Mazama 7,700 years ago. A violent explosion emptied the magma chamber of 10,000-foot-high Mount Mazama and blasted fiery ash beyond Bend. The mountain top collapsed into a 2,000-foot-deep pit. Lava continued to pulse up from the bottom of the basin, building smallish cones, including Wizard Island, which now breaks the surface of the lake.

A thousand years later, the caldera filled to within 1,000 feet of its rim with rainwater. No streams flow into or out of Crater Lake; it gains and loses water from precipitation and evaporation. Crater Lake is Oregon's only national park and the country's deepest lake.

The road to the lake from Klamath Falls climbs past big ponderosa pines until it reaches the crater's rim. There you can park, walk across the road past historic **Crater Lake Lodge** (400 Rim Village Drive at Crater Lake; 541-830-8700), and look down into the lake, where blue sky is reflected. Its water is 1,932 feet deep, a constant 39 degrees F, and so clear you can read the face of a (hopefully waterproof) watch 6 feet below the surface.

From the north rim, you can take a steep trail down to the water and catch the lake tour boat. A boat leaves every hour; tickets are available at the dock. Winter is incredible at Crater Lake. The southern entrance is plowed year-round, but the rim road is closed to all but cross-country skiers (the lakeside concession rents skis). Within yards of the rim parking lot, the only sounds beyond the chatter of Clark's nutcrackers and gray jays is the whoosh of snow falling from tree branches.

■ TRAVEL AND CLIMATE

■ GETTING THERE AND AROUND
This is a region of tall mountains, broad and beautiful valleys, and deeply cut, swift-flowing rivers, a place to take your time, drive slowly (a car is the best way to get around), and enjoy the scenery.

By Car
Interstate 5 is quite curvy south of Eugene. Watch for ice in spring, fall, and winter. Carry chains because several of the mountain passes are above 1,500 feet, and 4,310-foot Siskiyou Summit, just north of the California state line, can be a nightmare to drive even in pleasant weather. In winter, snow can pile up in prodigious quantities. Several times each winter, snow falls in the valleys, too. U.S. 199, a two-lane highway, is the main road to the coast. It, too, can be slick and icy and may be temporarily closed if winter snowfall is too heavy. Inquire in Grants Pass if you're in doubt about road conditions.

■ CLIMATE
The weather of this mountain wonderland can be very cold in winter and hot in summer. Spring and autumn are balmy and sunny, providing almost ideal conditions for hiking, fishing, or boating.

(following pages) On the rim of the crater surrounding Crater Lake. Wizard Island can be seen rising as a perfect cone from the middle of the lake.

OREGON COAST

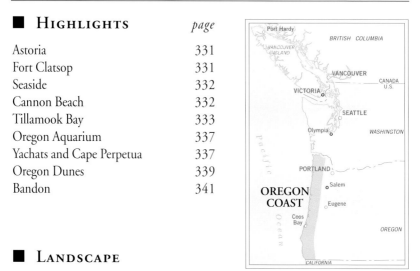

■ LANDSCAPE

ON THE OREGON COAST cold, green waves thunder toward evergreen headlands and craggy shorelines. Sea foam cold as shaved ice rolls up onto beachcombers' bare feet and curls around the fantastic forms of gray driftwood. Offshore lie fog-shrouded rocky islands filled with nesting seabirds. In winter, storms thunder in off the Pacific; during the summer, fog hovers over the coast. The ocean spray is so refreshing that even sedentary people seem game for long walks. Cliffside houses range from the palatial to weathered shacks, and the generally uncrowded beaches belong to the people.

Rocky headlands and cliffs alternate with sandy beaches that shelter estuaries and marshes—home of birds and other wildlife—from the ocean's fury. Oregon's beaches are public. In 1967, a bill was enacted that provided public access to the dry sand areas above the high-tide mark.

State parks, many with campsites, stipple the Oregon coast. Even on summer weekends, when Portlanders flock to Lincoln City and Cannon Beach, the long, broad beaches don't seem crowded. For real solitude, head to the south coast, pick a remote wayside, walk a hundred yards from the parking lot, and it'll be you and the sandpipers, investigating wave-tossed logs and huge hanks of kelp.

■ COASTAL INDIANS

Up and down the coast, indigenous people shared certain customs, though rarely did they speak the language of their neighbors. Over thousands of years, migrations down the coast from Alaska and across from the state's interior left a patchwork of languages, encouraging many people to become multilingual. In more than just place names can traces of the native peoples who passed through here be found.

It would be a stretch to say life was easy for coastal Indians, but the ocean, the estuaries, and the coastal forests supplied abundant food. Wealth was important, and poor people often ended up slaves of the rich. The well-born members of northern coastal tribes secured a board to a new baby's skull, gently molding it to a flat slope that was the signature head shape of the upper class. Southern tribes rarely flattened their heads, but women were often tattooed with three vertical lines on the chin.

A view of Astoria and its harbor in the 1880s. (Columbia River Maritime Museum)

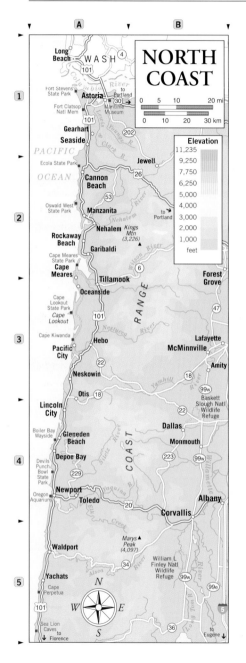

NORTH COAST

0 5 10   20 mi

0 10 20 30 km

Elevation

11,235
9,250
7,750
6,250
5,000
4,000
3,000
2,000
1,000
feet

Winter villages, usually located on a coastal river estuary, were the main bases. People harvested shellfish from the beaches and trapped salmon and other fish in elaborate weirs. Though they traveled by canoe, they weren't really seafarers. Trips from headland to headland were the extent of ocean travel. Indian women along the coast wove spruce roots into baskets, which were used as hats, baby cradles, and storage containers.

In the 1850s, white settlers and the territorial government wanted all Indians removed from western Oregon. The Indians were unwilling to leave and in 1855 two reservations were established for coastal tribes: the long narrow Coast Reservation on the central coast and the Grande Ronde Reservation in the Willamette Valley. The Coast Reservation was whittled away at the middle when whites took over the area around Yaquina Bay (the site of present-day Newport), creating the Siletz Reservation to the north and the Alsea Reservation to the south. Tensions between tribes on the Alsea Reservation led some Coos, Umpqua, and Siuslaw people to purchase a 6-acre reservation in Coos Bay. The tribes on these reservations had their relationships with the U.S. government severed in 1956 by an act that essentially dissolved all tribal entities in western Oregon. In 1977, the Confederated Tribes of the Siletz regained federal recognition and, eventually, a small, forested reservation northeast of Newport. The Confederated Tribes of the Coos, Lower Umpqua, and Siuslaw, federally reinstated in 1984, have a tribal hall in Coos Bay.

■ ASTORIA AND THE LOWER COLUMBIA RIVER
map page 330, A-1

The high surf of the Columbia River bar long obscured the river from early navigators, but in May 1792, Boston sea captain Robert Gray took a chance and sailed toward the bar and into the river he named after his ship. American explorers Lewis and Clark spent a wet winter at Fort Clatsop near the mouth of the Columbia in 1805, and half a dozen years later, John Jacob Astor set up a busy fur-trading post in what is now Astoria. (It was sold to the British during the War of 1812 to keep them from seizing it.)

Driving to the coast on U.S. 30 from Portland, you'll be tracing the route Lewis and Clark took, recalling the rainy-day passages of the journals describing "wet, cold, and miserable" weather, which hasn't changed one bit.

The Columbia River ushers travelers into **Astoria,** a gritty fishing and lumber port with many Victorian houses. From a hillside vantage point, or from a seat on a wharf, it's easy to imagine days long gone by, when Scandinavian fishermen ran gill-net boats, and Chinese laborers skinned fish in the riverside salmon canneries. Mammoth logs from the coastal mountains were, and still are, hoisted onto ships. Now they're sent, uncut, to Asia.

You might want to set aside an hour or two for a visit to the first-rate **Maritime Museum** (1792 Marine Drive; 503-325-2323) on the river. The museum is on the south side of U.S. 30 as you drive into town from the east. You can't miss it because there's a lightship moored right outside.

If you have the time, you might also want to drive up the hill and climb the 125-foot-high **Astoria Column**, a monument with a spiral frieze depicting much of Astoria's early history. From the top of the tower, the topography of rivers, bays, and estuaries becomes clear.

Fort Clatsop (503-861-2471, ext. 214), where Lewis and Clark spent the winter of 1805, is located southwest of Astoria on the banks of the Lewis and Clark River. The reconstructed quarters of Lewis and Clark's winter camp seem quite cramped for 33 people and a Newfoundland dog. In summer, park staff presents historical re-enactments, but a damp, chilly winter visit on a day when the sun never really shines, and then sets at 4 P.M., will etch the experience deeper.

Before heading south on U.S. 101, drive west to **Fort Stevens State Park**, near the town of Hammond, where a road leads to the end of Clatsop Spit, where the Columbia flows into the Pacific. Pilots from neon-orange boats guide freighters over the bar. Fishing boats take it on their own, sometimes with a few knocks.

■ RESORT COAST *map page 330, A-1/2*

Back on U.S. 101, in **Seaside**, Oregon's northernmost full-fledged beach town, be prepared for high-camp tourism. Ben Holladay, a Portland transportation mogul, built a resort here in the 1870s, and it became a Victorian-era hotspot. This is the coast's only town with a boardwalk (called "The Prom"). There's also a cruising street (Broadway), with a beachside loop ("The Turnaround").

Cannon Beach, 9 miles down U.S. 101 from Seaside, has long been labeled "artsy." The streets are jammed on summer weekends as people shop and enjoy

Sunset behind the sea stacks of Cannon Beach.

Cannon Beach Book Company or **Bill's Tavern**. You can escape the crowds by walking or flying a kite on the broad, sandy beach. Thousands of seabirds crowd onto **Haystack Rock**, and tide pools cradle anemones that look like peppermint candies. There's **Summer Theater** (108 North Hemlock; 503-436-1242), but the social event of the year is the **Sandcastle Contest** (503-436-2623), held in late May or early June, when teams build shell- and seaweed-trimmed fantasies.

Oswald West State Park rises above Short Sands Beach, a sheltered cove at the foot of Neahkanie Mountain 10 miles south of Cannon Beach with waves big enough to draw surfers and kayakers. The coast's best campground is in an old-growth grove nestling 36 walk-in campsites. A trail from the campground leads through big trees and a thick understory out to the tip of Cape Falcon, which affords views south to Manzanita. A second trail begins across the highway from the campground and winds up Neahkanie Mountain.

Some of the north coast's best views are from U.S. 101 between the park and the town of **Manzanita**. Manzanita is small and unhurried, "what Cannon Beach used to be," people lament. For local sagas or surfing tips, stop by **Manzanita News and Espresso** (500 Laneda Avenue) or enjoy a great meal at Jarboe's. Spring and fall storms bring good beachcombing.

Nehalem, just southeast of Manzanita, on the eastern edge of tiny Nehalem Bay, is even smaller and less rushed than its neighbor.

■ TILLAMOOK BAY AND VICINITY *map page 330, A-2*

Tillamook Bay's main fishing port is **Garibaldi,** near the bay's northern edge. Fish merchants line U.S. 101. Travelers can make an easy picnic of Dungeness crab, which come cleaned, cooked, and ready to eat. Or drop by Smith's Pacific Shrimp Company, out on the docks, for freshly caught and cooked shrimp.

East of Garibaldi, the bay is often filled with seabirds: cormorants, oystercatchers, grebes, harlequin ducks, and an assortment of gulls.

Tillamook is known for its lushly green pastureland. Local dairy farmers co-operatively own the Tillamook County Creamery Association, which supplies the **Tillamook Cheese Factory** (4175 U.S. 101 North; 503-842-4481). More people stop at the cheese factory, on the northern edge of Tillamook, than at any other spot on the coast. There's a self-guided tour of the factory, an exhibit extolling the virtues of butterfat, and an excellent gift shop selling Oregon products.

■ A SPIT, THREE CAPES, AND A HEAD *map page 330, A-2/4*

Three storm-tossed Pacific capes south of Tillamook are worth a detour. To reach them follow U.S. 101 to Route 6, then swing back west from U.S. 101 (this "Three Capes Loop" is well marked), and then continue south on U.S. 101 near Pacific City. If you're coming up from the south, look for signs directing you to the Three Capes Loop, where U.S. 101 swings away from the coast east of Pacific City. From the Three Capes Loop Road west of Tillamook, Bayocean Road runs north along the edge of Tillamook Bay. Bird-watchers walk or bike out on the 7-mile-long spit coming up from the south end of the bay. In late summer, thousands of sandpipers run across the mudflats. (You can also reach the spit by way of the Cape Meares Loop road, which runs north from Netarts through Oceanside and connects with Bayocean Road at the junction with Bayocean Dike Road.)

At **Cape Meares State Park,** parrot-billed puffins nest in the cliff, and sea lions, harbor seals, and murres frequent the surf-washed rocks.

(preceding page) Tidal pools with mussels, starfish, and sea anemones dot the shoreline, as do lighthouses on many of the headlands. (above) Heceta Head Lighthouse, about 12 miles north of Florence.

Harbor seals lounging on the rocks near Strawberry Hill State Wayside.

Cape Lookout, the next cape south, sticks out into the Pacific like a finger. A well-marked trail here twists from the campground through big old spruce, hemlock, and cedar trees to the cape, offering long views north to Cape Meares and south to **Cascade Head.** Whales migrate south to Baja from December to February; then they go into reverse and head north to Alaska from March to May, with April the peak of migration. **Depoe Bay,** south of here, is the best place to join a whale-watching charter boat.

Cape Kiwanda, the southernmost cape on the Three Capes Loop, is a fine place to pit your leg muscles against sand. The trail leads up the high sandy cape to its windy head and, from a sheltered spot, affords a view of waves crashing far below. This is a place to feel as big as king of the hill, or as small as a speck of blowing sand. Hang gliders take off from Kiwanda for circuitous trips to sea level. In the mid-1960s, the Nature Conservancy acquired **Cascade Head,** between Neskowin and Lincoln City, preserving the Sitka spruce, hemlock, and alder forests and the native prairie on the headland. Access to the 2-mile trail is from Three Rocks Road; the parking area is just beyond the Sitka Center.

Five small towns between Cascade Head and the Siletz River grew together in 1965 to become **Lincoln City.** From the north end of town, Route 18 takes off toward McMinnville and Portland. Minutes from the coast, in the hamlet of **Otis,** is the Otis Cafe, which serves some of the state's best pie.

■ NEWPORT AND VICINITY *map page 330, A-4*

Newport is enlivened by its active bayfront fishing port. It's certainly given a boost by the bustle at Nye Beach, an old-time beach resort gone derelict until the Sylvia Beach Hotel launched a neighborhood renaissance in the mid-1980s. The Sylvia Beach, a "hotel for booklovers," is as good as they come.

Newport's big draw is the **Oregon Aquarium,** where jellyfish swim through a room-sized cylindrical aquarium that glows like a beautiful lava lamp. A giant octopus lives outside in a rock crevice surrounded by an aviary, where puffins and other seabirds fly. For the last several years, the aquarium's main attraction was Keiko, an orca (killer whale) who starred in the movie *Free Willie*. Keiko has been returned to her native Icelandic waters, but her absence does not make the aquarium a less appealing place. To the contrary. Visitors no longer have to fight long lines and can spend their time viewing the excellent marine life. *2820 East Ferry Slip Road; 541-867-3474.*

Visit Newport's old-town bayfront fishing village for a bowl of clam chowder and watch boats sail in and out of the harbor while sea lions bob in the waves.

■ YACHATS AND CAPE PERPETUA *map page 330, A-5*

South of Newport, the Coast Range presses closer to the sea, and commercial hustle gives way to tidepools, sea lions, and whales. **Yachats** [YAH-HOTS] may be the perfect coast town. It's close to the water, nearly buried in salal and huckleberry. From April until October, sea-run smelt hurl themselves up the Yachats River, aiming straight toward clever, triangular smelt nets. **Cape Perpetua,** the epitome of the rocky, wild Oregon coast, is just a few miles south of Yachats. The picture window at the **Cape Perpetua Visitor Center** (541-547-3289) is a good place to watch for whales. Even if it's raining, it's worth taking the short walk to the **Devil's Churn,** where the ocean cleaves a thick basalt flow into a narrow chasm. Starfish keep a stubborn suction-grip on the sides of the wave-battered basalt cliffs. Chartreuse rock-top slime grows a stone's throw from a damp dark-green forest. An oceanside trail continues south from Devil's Churn, and it's easy to spend a morning staring at the waves and poking into tide pools.

If, along the beaches, you notice small sand dunes that seem to be made of shells, they're middens formed by the Alsea Indians, who used these beaches regularly and left behind the refuse of their meals: clam, oyster, crab, and mussel shells.

The area around Yachats and Cape Perpetua has stretches of coastal temperate rain forest. Two small wilderness areas, Cummins Creek and Rock Creek, are enveloped in a canopy of Sitka spruce, Douglas fir, western hemlock, and western red cedar. A trail up **Cummins Creek** leads to a damp rain forest with 9-foot-diameter spruce trees growing among decomposing nurse logs. Almost all the ground is covered by a dense green mat of salal and ferns.

■ FLORENCE AND VICINITY *map page 338, A-1*

An elevator drops 208 feet to **Sea Lion Caves** (91560 U.S. 101 North; 541-547-3111), tucked under the cliffs between Cape Perpetua and Florence. At the bottom are great close-up views of the 800-pound behemoths lounging and playing in the cave. Sea lions are usually visible in the ocean

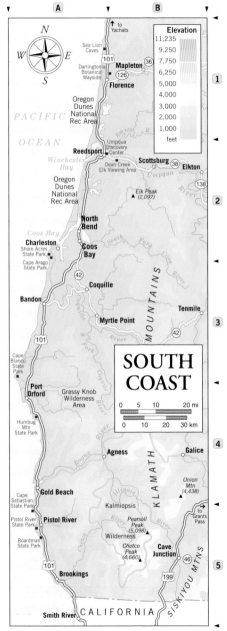

near the cave's entrance from the cliff-top parking lot. It's pretty easy to tell Oregon coast pinnipeds apart: sea lions tend to be larger than seals, and, unlike their smaller brethren, they have ears and can get up onto all fours.

Darlingtonia Botanical Wayside, 4 miles north of Florence, is home to fragrant cedars, Oregon grape, salal, kinnikinnick, and delicate ferns surrounding a sphagnum bog filled with the coast's most fascinating plant, *Darlingtonia californica,* also known as cobra lily or pitcher plant. This is a flesh-eating plant, and while *Darlingtonias* rarely eat anything bigger than a bug, they grow a foot or two tall, they stand close together, and they look weird—as you look at them you feel like you're staring down into a snake pit. Trails and wooden boardwalks lead on through the bog.

All the original bridges on U.S. 101 are distinctive, but the **bridge spanning the Siuslaw River** at Florence is particularly charming. It beckons one to leave the car and walk across, inspect the dark green river, and explore the old town beneath the bridge, a charming place to linger.

■ **OREGON DUNES** *map page 338, A-1/2*

The dense forests and seaside basalt cliffs of the northern coast are replaced by giant sand dunes from the mouth of the Siuslaw south to Coos Bay. Here ocean sands blow inland, forming vast shifting hills. In some places, these sand hills reach a couple of miles inland.

To get a sense of their scale, walk toward the ocean. There's an observation wayside halfway between Florence and Reedsport (10 miles from either town) where blue-topped posts guide hikers. On a sunny day, you can find warm spots in the lee of dunes—take an hour or two to read and nap in the sand. Or, if the giant dunes make you feel more fiesty than contemplative, stop at one of the many dune buggy rental shops on U.S. 101 between Reedsport and Florence.

This is an enchanted landscape, where the lines between the land and the sea, between rivers, creeks, and dunes, are smudged and shift their positions ever so slightly. Beach and surf, bog and lake, dune and forest create a kaleidoscope of wildness as they blend together. In springtime, the heady scent of flowers is accented by the crisp tang of salt spray and the resinous aroma of the pines.

While in the town of Reedsport, walk along the boardwalk on the Umpqua riverfront and visit the **Umpqua Discovery Center** to learn about the natural and human history of this region. *409 Riverfront Way; 541-271-4816.*

■ SOUTH COAST *map page 338, A-2*

Coos Bay, with its Siamese twin, **North Bend,** is the coast's largest city. It's the only place on the coast where buildings rise to five or six stories. Coos Bay exports more timber than any other port in the world, and it's the best natural harbor between San Francisco and Puget Sound. Local craftsmen are known for fashioning fragrant and durable myrtlewood into highly polished clocks, coffee tables, and salad bowls.

Charleston, 8 miles southwest, is a fishing town, where you may wander around the docks. Seafood markets sell fresh local catch, and Qualman's Oyster Company, across the slough from town, offers (you guessed it) fresh oysters.

South on Seven Devils Road is **South Slough,** a broad estuary extending half a dozen miles inland. Hiking trails touch different habitats. The best trail takes two hours to hike and passes through coastal forest and 19th-century logging sites down to a boardwalk built across a swamp and a salt marsh (where sharp-edged grasses brush bare legs, and the humidity is broken by wisps of ocean breeze).

U.S. 101 snakes along the southern coastline between Cape Sebastian and Pistol River State Park.

Coos County was once strewn with such marshes (the city of Coos Bay was originally named Marshfield).

A few miles south of town, **Shore Acres State Park** (541-888-3732 or 800-551-6949) near Cape Alava, is a bit unusual for a coastal Oregon state park. Unlike the other parks, which highlight the rugged beauty of the natural setting, this one also pays tribute to the horticultural achievements of man, with beautiful gardens. Perched on rugged sandstone cliffs high above the ocean, Shore Acres has a formal garden, an oriental-style pond, and two rose gardens, which include an all-American rose selection display.

Once owned by pioneer timber baron Louis Simpson, founder of the nearby lumber town of North Bend, the estate was sold to Oregon State Parks in 1942. During World War II, soldiers who were stationed here used the viewpoint as a lookout to spot potential foreign invaders. After the war, the decaying mansion was razed, and the gardens were replaced by lawns. They were fully restored in 1973, with the help of the original plans and old photos.

To visit the gardens, which are 3 miles southwest of Coos Bay, take U.S. 101 to Coos Bay, then take Route 14 south through Charleston. Follow signs to Shore Acres State Park.

■ SMALL TOWNS OF THE SOUTHERN COAST
map page 338, A-3/5

Artists and craftspeople liven up the town of **Bandon**. Across the mouth of the Coquille River from Bandon, a restored stucco lighthouse marks the bar. Though fishing boats tie up in downtown Bandon, summer winds make the bar crossing hazardous. In recent years, much of Bandon's business center has moved to U.S. 101, and Old Town, the former business hub, has become a pleasant, laid-back quarter of restaurants, galleries, boutiques, and bookstores. West of downtown Bandon, at the end of First Street, is a parking area at the breakwater with good waves, surf, and bird-watching. There's a truly spectacular cliff-top walk south of downtown off Beach Loop Drive.

Some of the coast's most spectacular views are from the bluff at **Port Orford** when Humbug Mountain, south of town, is shrouded in misty clouds. To get a feel for the town, head down to the port. There are no boat slips or rampways—a hoist plucks boats from the water and lifts them onto the dock. Sport fishers go after rockfish, lingcod, and other bottomfish. Stacks of crab traps and mesh-net traps suspended inside chicken wire cubes crowd one end of the dock—the latter are used to catch sablefish ("black cod").

Port Orford is famous for its straight-grained and durable Port Orford cedar. Much of the harvest goes to Japan, where one tree may fetch up to $10,000. A virulent root fungus has destroyed entire drainages of cedars, but you can still see and smell these exquisitely fragrant trees at the **Grassy Knob Wilderness Area,** 7 miles east of the Cape Blanco turnoff.

Gold Beach first attracted settlers in the 1850s, when gold was found in its sands. After floods swept the beach clean of gold in 1861, the town survived on the timber harvest in the Coast Range and on the fishery in offshore waters. Mail boats started making the upstream trip to Agness in 1895, when it took several days of rowing to travel the 32 miles from Gold Beach; now, jet boats shoot upriver in two hours.

Boardman State Park, north of Brookings, is a long strip with many waysides, where trails lead down steep cliffs to sheltered coves. These beaches are rarely crowded; a hundred yards past the parking lot your only companions will be birds and waves and rocks.

Brookings is, all winter long, the warmest spot in the state. The fishing port of **Harbor,** on the south side of the **Chetco River,** is a good place to hang out and chat with the locals. In season, fields are white with flowers, as Brookings grows most of the nation's Easter lilies.

The banks of the broad, shallow Chetco River are lined with myrtlewood trees. Their bay-like leaves are used to season food. **Loeb Park,** off North Bank Road, is flush with salmonberries and myrtlewood trees. From Quail Prairie on the edge of the Kalmiopsis Wilderness Area, it's a short 1.4-mile hike to **Vulcan Lake,** which nests in a glaciated red peridotite basin, a favorite swimming hole for Brookings residents. Here, you're far from coastal fog and into the hot, dry zone of the Kalmiopsis. To get to the trailhead for Vulcan Lake involves a bit of driving: You head east from Brookings on Northbank Chetco River Road/CR 784 (the last road north of the Chetco River Bridge, on the east side of the road). The road turns into a well-maintained gravel road after a few miles; and the trailhead is at mile 31.5.

■ TRAVEL AND CLIMATE

■ GETTING THERE AND AROUND

U.S. 101, a slow, winding, two-lane road, is the one north-south highway. Route 126 runs inland from Florence to Eugene; U.S. 20 takes you inland from Newport; Route 18 runs from north of Lincoln City to the Yamhill wine country and Portland.

■ BICYCLING THE COAST

A bike route, essentially along the wide shoulder of U.S. 101, with a few detours, runs the entire length of the coast. A weeklong ride is one of the best ways to really get into the scenery. After you pump up the steep hills you'll feel entitled to stop at beaches, bakeries, and ice cream shops.

Coastal bicycle trips are best from north to south, because they take advantage of the prevailing winds and the ocean views. Cycling about 50 miles a day is a reasonable goal. State park campgrounds have hiker/biker areas with hot showers. If the weather is good, this is a great and inexpensive way to go. But there are plenty of motels if that suits you better.

Anyone who is not used to this will want to think twice before starting off on a loaded bicycle. Coastal hills are steep, and can be long—don't expect momentum to do all the work. For the inexperienced cyclist, an organized tour with a sag wagon or a credit card ride (every night in a motel) may be a more enjoyable way to go.

Cyclists who make the 367-mile trip from Astoria to Brookings can leave their cars at the Visitors Center in Astoria and have bikes boxed for bus travel at the Escape Hatch (541-469-2914) in Brookings. (Call when you're a day or two away and they'll save a box for you.) Greyhound runs buses along U.S. 101, but doesn't cover the entire coast in one trip. To ride the full length of the coast, it's necessary to transfer in Portland to another Greyhound or to an Amtrak Thruway motor coach.

■ CLIMATE

Better bring a sweater. And a windbreaker. And warm socks. In July? You bet! Summer fogs can keep the coast cool and damp while the rest of the state broils. But it's just as likely that the clouds will burn off early in the day and by midmorning you'll be strolling the beach in shorts. Winters are generally mild and wet on the coast, though the roads over the Coast Range frequently become ice-glazed.

R E G I O N A L
T R A V E L   I N F O R M A T I O N

■ AREA CODES AND TIME ZONE

The area codes in Vancouver are 604 and 778. The area code in Victoria is 250; Whistler and the lower mainland is 604. The area codes in the Seattle area are 206 for the city proper, 425 for Everett and south Snohomish County, Bellevue and east King County, and 360 for the San Juan Islands. Other area codes in Washington include 253 for Tacoma, Puyallup, and the south Puget Sound area (excluding Olympia, which is 360); and 564, which is supposed to "overlay" (run parallel to and in the same area as) 360; and 509 for Spokane and eastern Washington. Central, southern, and eastern Oregon use 541; Portland and coastal Oregon use 503 and 971.

The entire Pacific Northwest is in the Pacific time zone.

■ METRIC CONVERSIONS

Canada officially uses the metric system, although most people are still comfortable with the English system. Conversions follow:

1 foot = .305 meters
1 mile = 1.6 kilometers
Centigrade = Fahrenheit temperature minus 32, divided by 1.8
(Thus a warm day in Vancouver at 21 degrees is a nice 70 in Seattle.)

■ CLIMATE

A brief description of the climate relevant to the area described in each chapter can be found in the chapter's "Travel and Climate." It rains a lot in the Pacific Northwest west of the Cascade and Coast Ranges. But east of the Cascades, it seldom rains. And even west of the Cascades, summers tend to be dry. (That dryness may be why western Washington is covered with conifers instead of deciduous trees; deciduous trees couldn't survive the summer droughts.) Even when it rains, however, it seldom rains hard. Seattle has many more cloudy and drizzly days than New York, but it has less annual precipitation. Real downpours are rare. Locals rarely carry umbrellas.

TEMPS (F°) North to South	AVG. JAN. HIGH/LOW	AVG. APRIL HIGH/LOW	AVG. JULY HIGH/LOW	AVG. OCT. HIGH/LOW	RECORD HIGH	RECORD LOW
Vancouver	41/32	58/40	74/54	57/44	92	2
Victoria	43/35	55/43	68/52	56/46	95	4
Seattle	45/36	58/43	72/54	59/47	100	3
Olympic Coast	46/34	55/37	68/49	59/41	97	5
Mt. Rainier	33/21	44/27	64/44	48/33	92	-20
Yakima	38/20	63/35	87/53	64/35	111	-25
Portland	44/34	61/43	77/56	62/47	107	-3
Astoria	49/38	56/40	68/53	60/44	101	6
Eugene	45/32	60/39	81/50	64/40	108	-12
Crater Lake	35/18	45/24	70/42	52/31	100	-21
Medford	45/30	65/39	90/54	70/40	115	-10

PRECIPITATION (INCHES)	AVG. JAN.	AVG. APRIL	AVG. JULY	AVG. OCT.	ANNUAL RAIN	SNOW
Vancouver	8.6	3.3	1.2	5.8	57	21
Victoria	4.3	1.4	0.5	3.0	26	13
Seattle	4.8	2.3	0.6	2.9	38	7
Olympic Coast	13.8	7.4	2.6	10.4	105	15
Mt. Rainier	14.5	6.7	1.7	12.0	114	578
Yakima	1.3	0.5	0.1	0.5	8	24
Portland	6.1	2.8	0.5	3.3	37	7
Astoria	10.3	4.6	1.1	6.1	68	5
Eugene	7.8	2.8	0.3	3.7	47	7
Crater Lake	10.9	4.3	0.6	6.4	67	541
Medford	3.0	1.0	0.3	1.7	19	8

Victoria, western and southern Vancouver Island, Vancouver, and the lower mainland have a maritime climate and rarely receive snow in winter. But when it snows, watch out! The first flakes often signal instant traffic gridlock. The rest of the province gets heavy snowfall each winter. Mountain roads and passes are treacherous at such times.

A note of caution: According to the British Columbia Insurance Company, B.C. drivers are the worst in Canada. Drive extra cautiously and be sure to have sufficient insurance. Recently B.C. drivers have taken to running stop signs and red stoplights, resulting in a dramatic increase of collisions.

Location and season must both be considered when packing for a trip to Oregon and Washington. Generally speaking, the Cascades, which run north to south through the western part of the states, block moist Pacific air, leaving wet weather on the western side of the mountains, while the east side remains drier. The coast is the rainiest part of the state. It's typically stormy in the winter and foggy in the summer, though warm, sunny summer days are certainly not unheard of. It rarely gets below freezing here, but those who drive over the Coast Range or the I-5 pass near the California border in winter should check on conditions. For road conditions in Oregon, call 800-977-6368 (Oregon only) or 503-588-2941 (elsewhere). Western Oregon valleys are slightly less rainy than the coast and typically enjoy dry summers. Snow falls occasionally.

The Cascades get cold weather and snow in the winter, with generally cool summer weather. Year-round, there are distinct west-slope and east-slope climates; if it's cloudy west of a pass, the sun may be shining to the east.

Central and eastern Oregon and Washington get less rain and more extreme temperatures than the west. The mountainous areas do catch more moisture, especially as snow, and summer thunderstorms are no rarity here (as they are west of the Cascades).

Every year brings some unusual weather—sometimes it's a wet and cold summer, other years a sun-drenched Portland winter. It's never a mistake to pack a wool sweater and an umbrella, and it's also smart to include sunglasses.

■ TRANSPORTATION

■ BRITISH COLUMBIA

By Air

Most major airlines fly into Vancouver International Airport (YVR) and Victoria International Airport (YYJ). Smaller carriers, such as Horizon Air (800-547-9308), Air Canada (604-688-5515 or 800-776-3000) in the U.S., and Harbour Air (604-688-1277 or 800-665-0212) in Vancouver, serve smaller cities throughout the province, using floatplanes to reach remote communities. Harbour Air in British Columbia has a marine terminal on the downtown waterfront. Seaplanes fly from here to Victoria (250-385-2203), the Gulf Islands, and Vancouver International Airport (604-688-1277, www.harbour-air.com). Helijet Airways helicopters fly from a pad near the SeaBus terminal to downtown: in Vancouver (604-273-1414); in Victoria (250-382-6222); general (800-665-4354).

By Car

Major roads and most secondary roads are paved; back-country roads are gravel. The Trans-Canada Highway (TCH) Route 1 runs from Victoria (via ferry) and Vancouver to eastern Canada.

By Train

Amtrak (800-872-7245) links Vancouver to Seattle. Via Rail (800-561-8630) is the Canadian equivalent of Amtrak. B.C. Rail (604-631-3500) runs daily trains to Whistler from the B.C. train station at 1311 West First Street, North Vancouver. Sky-Train runs from Vancouver south to New Westminster and Surrey between 5 A.M. and 1 A.M. For route assistance, call B.C. Transit (604-521-0400). All of these trains are wheelchair accessible.

By Bus

Greyhound Lines (800-231-2222) has scheduled runs between Vancouver and other British Columbia cities and Seattle.

By Ferry

B.C. Ferries in Vancouver has year-round passenger service between Vancouver and Tsawwassen (south of Vancouver), and to Swartz Bay (30 minutes by car north of Victoria). Ferries also run between Tsawwassen and Nanaimo, and between Nanaimo and Horseshoe Bay (north of Vancouver). B.C. ferries also provide service to the Gulf Islands (reserve ahead), to the Sunshine Coast north of Howe Sound, from Port Hardy through the Inside Passage to Prince Rupert, from Port Hardy to Ocean Falls, Bella Coola, and other remote settlements on the central coast, and from Prince Rupert to the Queen Charlotte Islands. For information, call 888-223-3779 (B.C. only); for reservations, 888-724-5223 (B.C. only) or 250-386-3431 (in U.S.)

■ WASHINGTON

By Air

Most major airlines fly into Sea-Tac International (Seattle-Tacoma; SEA). Horizon Air (not always dependable) and San Juan Airlines serve the smaller cities throughout the state.

By Train

Amtrak (800-872-7245) links Seattle to most major American cities, and from Seattle, Amtrak's *Mount Rainier* has frequent service to Tacoma, Olympia, and Portland, Oregon.

By Bus

Greyhound Lines (800-231-2222) has many scheduled bus routes in the state but runs mainly along I-5 and I-90. Call the local chamber of commerce for phone numbers of other companies that service towns not along these two highways.

By Ferry

Washington operates the largest ferry system in the United States. Most of the ferries carry cars, although some smaller boats that run between Seattle and Bremerton or Bainbridge and Vashon Islands carry passengers only. All ferries carry bikes. At commuting hours and on summer weekends, cars line up well in advance of the scheduled departure time.

A daily Washington State Ferry carries cars and passengers between Anacortes (west of Mount Vernon) and Sidney, British Columbia (north of Victoria). Be sure to call ahead as there has been talk of cancelling this run.

Contact Washington State Ferries at 206-464-6400.

■ OREGON

By Air

The major airport in Oregon is Portland International Airport (PDX). From there service is available to the state's smaller cities. Horizon Air is the main carrier (and not always dependable) for these short hops. Other airports are in Eugene, Medford, Bend, Klamath Falls, Pendleton, and North Bend.

By Train

Amtrak's route from southern California into Canada runs through Klamath Falls, Eugene, and Portland. The train from Salt Lake City comes in through Baker City, La Grande, Pendleton, The Dalles, and Hood River before it reaches Portland.

■ CANADIAN–U.S. BORDER

Crossing the border in either direction is easy if you follow common sense.

Passports

Bring a passport with you. Border guards are more likely than in times past to ask to see your identification. If they do, and you don't have any, you may not be able to reenter the country. Depending on the traffic, crossing the border may take as little as 5 minutes or as much as an hour or more. The best times are early on weekday mornings or in the late evening.

Smuggling

Don't even think about smuggling. If you're caught, you may not only have to pay a fine or go to jail, but your car may be confiscated. Declare all weapons. Handguns are not allowed in Canada. If you carry one in your car, check it at the border and pick it up on your return.

Fruits, Vegetables, and Alcoholic Beverages

All three are subject to special laws. You're better off buying them where you consume them. Do not bring any into the U.S. (Or stop at the U.S. border station on your trip north and ask for a list of current exceptions.)

Gasoline

Gasoline is highly taxed and expensive in British Columbia, about 25 to 50 percent more than it is in the United States.

Money

U.S. money is accepted as legal tender in southern British Columbia, but at a discount charged by businesses to offset their cost of converting the money. You get the best exchange rates if you pay with a credit card or take out money at a cash machine. Canadian banks give a better exchange rate than U.S. ones, making exchanging money before you leave home not so hot an idea. The money changer next to the visitors center just north of the border may seem convenient, but be prepared for the highest fees and the worst exchange rate.

Goods and Services Tax

Non-Canadian visitors can have Canada's 7-percent Goods and Services Tax (GST) refunded on goods they buy for use outside Canada and on short-term accommodation costs paid by visitors leaving Canada. Application forms are available at duty-free shops located at land crossings and airports. Claims must total $7 or more (the tax paid on goods worth $100 Canadian or more).

Visitors must show all receipts to prove they paid GST. No rebate for gifts left in Canada, meals, cleaning and repair bills, camping and trailer park fees, alcoholic beverages, and tobacco. For more information, please call (in Canada) 800-668-4748.

■ NORTHWEST CUISINE

The Northwest is truly a food paradise. Its waters produce some of North America's best oysters, crabs, clams, shrimp, and prawns. Apples, pears, peaches, apricots, plums, raspberries, blueberries, strawberries, and cherries grow plump in orchards on both sides of the Cascade Mountains. Yakima Valley farmers grow succulent asparagus and hotly flavorful peppers. Willamette Valley farmers are known for vegetables, wine grapes, and hazelnuts. This is dairy country and fine local cheeses are being made, including Oregon blue. Mountain and coastal forests provide chanterelle and morel mushrooms, and cooks are learning to create more and better mushroom recipes.

The cooking is evolving from an old-time American style of cuisine to an original Northwestern style of light, delectable dishes containing the freshest local ingredients. The wine grapes and vineyards are coming into their own, as growers learn what this region can produce best. (Oregon is growing and producing varietals such as pinot gris, chardonnay, and zinfandel, but pinot noir is the local favorite.) Microbreweries create handcrafted beers, ales, and stouts from locally grown barley and hops.

As the reputation of Northwest cuisine has spread, many people now travel here just to eat. Vancouver, Seattle, and Portland all have great restaurants, as has the countryside—often in unexpected places. Vancouver, with its huge influx of residents from Hong Kong, now abounds in excellent Chinese restaurants. The orchards of the Columbia Gorge produce apples, pears, and peaches. As for coffee, a real Northwest coffeehouse will make some of the best to be found anywhere.

Northwest wines complement Northwest foods, though not everyone agrees about what goes best with what. For every aficionado who claims that (white) Oregon pinot gris goes best with sockeye salmon, there's one who maintains that (red) pinot noir brings out the best flavor in the fish. Chefs in the "red meat country" east of the Cascades have been known to serve a big, rich Yakima Valley chardonnay with lamb. Westsiders enjoy their oysters best with Walla Walla cabernet sauvignon or sangiovese instead of the more traditional sauvignon blanc, semillon, or chardonnay. Just think about all the exciting wines you can serve with locally raised chicken, clams, and mussels—from Riesling through gewürztraminer to merlot.

But that's what makes dining in the Northwest so much fun. Both the Northwest food revolution and the rise of local wineries are less than 40 years old, and they grew up together in a tasty pas de deux. As local chefs further hone their skills, and as winemakers learn to turn their grapes into liquid perfection, all sorts of exciting things are going to happen. I get hungry just thinking about it.

■ ACCOMMODATIONS

Even though you are dealing with two currencies in the Pacific Northwest—U.S. and Canadian dollars—the dollar amounts charged per night are similar. If you're a U.S. citizen, just figure that each time you are quoted a rate in Canadian dollars, you get an automatic 25 to 30 percent discount (depending on the day's exchange rate); and if you're Canadian, unhappily, it's vice versa. Paying by credit card generally gets you the best exchange rate.

■ RESERVATIONS SERVICES
Karen Brown's Guides. *www.karenbrown.com/pnw*
A Pacific Reservation Service. *206-439-7677 or 800-684-2932*; *www.seattlebedandbreakfast.com*
Unique Northwest Inns. *877-286-4783; www.uniqueinns.com*

■ CHAIN HOTELS AND MOTELS
Best Western. *800-528-1234; www.bestwestern.com*
Choice Hotels. *800-424-6423; www.choicehotels.com*
Days Inn. *800-329-7466; www.daysinn.com*
Delta. *800-268-1133; www.deltahotels.com*
Doubletree. *800-222-8733; www.doubletree.com*
Embassy Suites. *800-362-2779; www.embassysuites.com*
Four Seasons. *800-332-3442; www.fourseasons.com*
Holiday Inn. *800-465-4329; www.6c.com*
Hyatt. *800-233-1234; www.hyatt.com*
La Quinta. *800-531-5900; www.laquinta.com*
Marriott. *800-228-9290; www.marriott.com*
Radisson. *800-333-3333; www.radisson.com*
Ramada. *800-272-6232; www.ramada.com*
Renaissance. *888-236-2427; www.marriott.com*
Sheraton. *800-325-3535; www.sheraton.com*
Travelodge. *800-835-2424; www.travelodge.com*
W Hotels. *877-946-8357; www.whotels.com*
WestCoast. *800-325-4000; www.westcoasthotels.com*
Westin. *800-228-3000; www.westin.com*

■ CAMPING

Camping is one of the best ways to get a feel for some of the region's wilder areas. Most state and provincial park campgrounds are fairly developed and on well-beaten paths. Many Pacific Northwest campgrounds have wooden picnic shelters adjacent to the campsites (some with electrical outlets and fireplaces), allowing you to stay dry even on the wettest night. Due to budget cuts, several popular Oregon state parks have been closed in the off-season. National Forest and Bureau of Land Management sites are generally more primitive (pit toilets), more remote, and less expensive.

Bureau of Land Management. *www.blm.org*
Ministry of Parks in British Columbia. *604-387-5002; www.gov.bc.ca/wlap*
National Parks and Forests Outdoor Recreation Information. *206-220-7450.*
Oregon State Parks. *800-551-6949; www.sova.org or www.oregonstateparks.org*
U.S. Forest Service/U.S. Army Corps of Engineers. *www.reserveusa.com*
U.S. National Parks. *800-365-2267; reservations.nps.gov*
Washington State Parks and Recreation. *206-874-1283; www.parks.wa.gov*

■ OFFICIAL TOURISM INFORMATION

British Columbia. *800-663-6000; www.hellobc.com*
Washington. *800-544-1800; www.tourism.wa.gov*
Seattle. *206-386-1234; www.ci.seattle.wa.us*
Vancouver. *604-682-2222; www.tourism-vancouver.org*
Oregon. *800-547-7842; www.traveloregon.com*
Portland. *877-678-5263; www.pova.com*

■ TOURS

■ BRITISH COLUMBIA
Harbour Cruises Boat-Train Daytrip. From Vancouver (604-688-7246).
Fraser River Canyon. Fraser River Raft Expeditions (250-863-2336).
Okanagan Valley, Kelowna. Okanagan Canoe Holidays (604-762-8156) offers inland canoe trips.
Vancouver Island, Nanaimo. Call Wild Heart Adventures (250-722-3683) for guided kayak trips. **Telegraph Cove** (north island), Stubbs Island Whale Watching tours (250-928-3117).

■ **WASHINGTON**

Fidalgo and Whidbey Islands. Velocity Bikes (5603½ South Bayview Road, Langley; 360-321-5040) rents bikes.

Long Beach Peninsula. Washington Coast: Pacific Salmon Charters (Ilwaco; 360-642-3466) offers year-round fishing charters.

Mount Rainier. Rainier Mountaineering, Inc. (Tacoma; 253-627-6242 or Paradise; 360-569-2227) leads expeditions up Mount Rainier and rents equipment.

Mount St. Helens. Mount St. Helens Adventure Tours (Castle Rock; 360-274-6542) offers van tours and overnight camping trips in the blast zone.

North Cascades. Northwest Interior: American Alpine Institute (1515 12th Street, Bellingham; 360-671-1505) rents gear for rock climbing, mountain climbing, and ice climbing and leads expeditions in the North Cascades.

Olympic Peninsula. Olympic Raft and Guide Service (8 miles west of Port Angeles; 360-452-1443) leads rafting trips. Fairholm General Store (U.S. 101, 26 miles west of Port Angeles; 360-928-3020) has boat and fishing rentals and supplies.

San Juan Islands. San Juan Island Bicycles (Friday Harbor; 360-378-4941) rents bikes, or go with San Juan Kayak Expeditions (Friday Harbor; 360-378-4436).

Seattle. Northwest Outdoor Center (2100 Westlake Avenue North; 206-281-9694) rents kayaks for expeditions around Lake Union, Lake Washington, and Elliott Bay. Instruction provided. Emerald City Charters (206-624-3931) departs from Pier 56 on Puget Sound sailboat excursions.

■ **OREGON**

Deschutes River. High Desert Drifter (541-389-0607) has fishing float trips on the Deschutes. Lacy's Whitewater and Wild Fish (541-389-2434) offers float and fish trips as well as trips to the Cascade Lakes.

John Day River. Lacy's Whitewater and Wild Fish (541-389-2434). Go on float and fish trips.

Mount Hood. Timberline Mountain Guides (Portland; 800-464-7704).

North Umpqua, Southern Oregon. North Umpqua Outfitters (Roseburg; 541-673-4599) offers rafting services.

Oregon Coast, Cannon Beach. Cleanline Surf (171 Sunset Boulevard; 503-436-9726) rents surfboards and wetsuits.

Rogue River. Noah's River Adventure Float Trips (Ashland; 541-476-6493) has a variety of trips. River Trips Unlimited (Medford; 541-779-3798) also does trips.

■ Useful Web Sites

Go Northwest. All about outdoor activities; *www.gonorthwest.com*

■ British Columbia

City of Vancouver. Excellent city information; *www.city.vancouver.bc.ca*
City of Victoria. Basic trip planning, and more; *www.city.victoria.bc.ca*
Greater Victoria Visitors and Convention Bureau. Great information on Victoria, Vancouver Island, and the Gulf Islands; *www.tourismvictoria.com*
Thompson Okanagan Tourism Association. What to do when visiting southern British Columbia's sunny valleys; *www.thompsonokanagan.com*

■ Washington

Long Beach Peninsula Visitors Bureau. An accessible site about Washington's Long Beach Peninsula and lower Columbia River; *www.funbeach.com*

Seattle Convention and Visitors Bureau. A good site that gives an overview of what Seattle has to offer; *www.seeseattle.org*

University of Washington Libraries Digital Collections. Photos and documents about politics, industry, history, and other topics; *content.lib.washington.edu*

Washington Wine Country. Everything you need to know about the state's wineries; *www.washingtonwine.org*

Yakima Valley Visitors and Convention Bureau. User-friendly site with info on the Yakima Valley, local wineries, and nearby mountains; *www.visityakima.com*

■ Oregon

Medford Visitors and Convention Bureau. Good information on southern Oregon attractions, dining, lodging—even the weather; *www.visitmedford.org*

Oregon Wine Advisory Board. All about wines and wineries; *www.oregonwine.org*

■ BEST SKI AREAS OF THE NORTHWEST

Apex Alpine
Located near Penticton, Okanagan Valley, B.C., Apex has great powder snow and full resort facilities. *Information 250-292-8111; accommodations 800-387-2739.*

Mission Ridge
Great powder snow and cross-country skiing abound at Mission Ridge located near Wenatchee, Washington. *509-663-7631.*

Mount Bachelor
The mountain has great powder snow and cross-country trails. Overnight lodging is not available, but the resort is close to Bend, Oregon. *General information 800-829-2442; ski report 541-382-7888.*

Mount Baker
East of Bellingham, Washington, Baker has the most snow of any ski area in North America. It is often the earliest resort to open and the last to close (October to June). There are basic facilities and no overnight lodging, but great ski runs make it worth the trip. Cross-country skiing is available on lower slopes of mountain. *360-734-6771.*

Mount Hood
Located east of Portland, Oregon, this mountain has great snow, downhill and cross-country skiing, and the fabulous Timberline Lodge. *Timberline Lodge 503-222-2211; Mount Hood Meadows 503-227-7669.*

Whistler/Blackcomb
Whistler was voted the continent's best resort for five years in a row. Located north of Vancouver, B.C., the mountain receives great snow. Heli-skiing, cross-country skiing, tobogganing, and dog-sledding are popular activities in this inspiring, beautiful setting. Facilities range from the plain and affordable to the most luxurious. Its restaurants are of uncommonly high quality for a ski resort. *800-944-7853 or 604-685-3650.*

Festivals and Events

January
Bald Eagle Count. *San Juan Island, WA.*
Fire and Ice Winterfest. Chili cook-off, ice fishing, cross-country skiing. *Chelan, WA; 800-424-3526 or 509-682-2381.*

January or February
Chinese New Year Celebration. *Seattle, WA; 206-323-2700.*

February
Fat Tuesday. Parade, pub run, and Spam-carving. *Seattle, WA; 206-622-2563.*
Northwest Flower and Garden Show. *Washington State Convention Center, Seattle, WA;* 206-789-5333.
Shakespeare Festival. Eleven plays, until October. *Ashland, OR; 541-482-4331.*
Upper Skagit Bald Eagle Festival. Celebration of eagle migration; *360-853-7009.*

March
Gray Whale Migration. *Westport, WA.*

April
Cherry Blossom Festival. Hood River celebrates the season with pancake breakfasts, barbeques, arts and crafts shows, and antique sales. *Hood River, OR; 800-366-3530.*
Skagit Valley Tulip Festival. Spring blooms, exhibits, picnics, and fireworks. *Mount Vernon, WA; 360-428-5959.*
Washington State Apple Blossom Festival. Parades, arts and crafts, and a carnival. *Wenatchee, WA; 509-662-3616.*
Yakima Valley Spring Barrel Tasting. Late April. *Yakima County, WA; 509-829-6029.*

May
All-Indian Rodeo. *Tygh Valley, OR.*
Match Made in Heaven. Food and wine matching at local wineries. Yamhill County Wineries Association; Memorial Day weekend. *Yamhill County, OR; 503-434-5814.*
Rhododendron Festival. A popular event. *Port Townsend, WA; 360-385-1456.*

■ **MAY TO JUNE**

Northwest Folklife Festival. Immensely popular music festival. Crafts, clothing, and incense vendors. Memorial Day weekend. *Seattle, WA; 206-684-7300.*

Pi-Ume-Sha. Powwow and celebration of the heritage of three tribes sharing the Warm Springs Reservation. *Warm Springs, OR; 541-553-3468.*

Ski-to-Sea Festival. Street fair and relay race from Mount Baker to salt water. Memorial Day weekend. *Bellingham, WA; 360-671-3990.*

■ **JUNE**

Fiddle Tunes Festival. *Port Townsend, WA; 800-733-3608 or 360-385-3102.*

Rose Festival. Two parades, a waterfront carnival, and the roses blooming in Washington Park are the main attractions at the Rose Festival, which takes place in early June. Contact the Portland Visitors Association. *Portland, OR; 503-222-2223.*

Sandcastle Contest. *Cannon Beach, OR; 503-436-2623.*

Wildflower Festival. Second weekend in June. *Darrington, WA.*

■ **JULY**

Darrington Bluegrass Festival. Music festival celebrating the town's early settlers from North Carolina. *Darrington, WA; 360-436-1177.*

Dixieland Jazz Festival. *Friday Harbor, San Juan Island, WA; 360-378-5509.*

Fort Vancouver Fourth of July Fireworks. *Vancouver, WA; 360-693-5481.*

Loganberry Festival. Whidbey's Greenbank Berry Farm, Greenbank. *Whidbey Island, WA; 360-678-3005.*

Seafair. Parades, hydro races, and crowds. *Seattle, WA; 206-728-0123.*

■ **JULY TO AUGUST**

Bluegrass Festival. Third weekend of July. *Darrington, WA; 360-436-1006.*

Victoria International Festival. Classical music performances and recitals, and ballet. Free concert by Victoria Symphony from a band-shell barge in the Inner Harbour. *Victoria, B.C.; 604-736-2119.*

■ **AUGUST**

Makah Days. Traditional dancing and singing, salmon bakes, and canoe races. *Olympic Peninsula, Neah Bay, WA; 360-645-2711.*

Omak Stampede and Suicide Run. The largest rodeo in northeastern Washington. *Omak, WA; 800-933-6625 or 509-826-1002.*

Shakespeare Festival. *Olympia, WA; 360-943-9492.*

Washington State International Kite Festival. *Long Beach, WA; 800-451-2542.*

■ SEPTEMBER

Bumbershoot. Music and arts festival. Labor Day weekend. *Seattle, WA; 206-684-7337.*

Western Washington State Fair. *Puyallup, WA; 206-845-1771.*

Wooden Boat Festival. Races, rides, and craft shows. *Port Townsend, WA; 360-385-3628.*

■ OCTOBER

Cranberry Festival. Food booths, musical entertainment, and tours through the cranberry bogs. *Ilwaco, WA; 800-451-2542.*

Okanagan Wine Festival, B.C. Call the B.C. Wine Institute for information. *604-986-0440.*

West Coast Oyster Shucking Championship and Seafood Fest. *Shelton, WA; 360-426-2021.*

■ NOVEMBER

Winery Open Houses. Over 20 wineries serve samplings of their wine, paired with the right food. *Yakima Valley, WA.*

Winery Open Houses. Thanksgiving Day Weekend. County Wineries Association. *Yamhill, OR; 503-434-5814.*

■ DECEMBER

Eagles Return to the Skagit River. *Marblemount, WA.*

Harbor Christmas Carol Ship Parade. Carolers cruise the waterfront on boats decorated with Christmas lights. *Vancouver. B.C.; 604-682-2007.*

Lighted Boat Parade. Children's activities and music. *Bellingham, WA; 360-671-3990.*

New Year's Powwow. Traditional Indian food, dancing, and games beginning December 30 and lasting until New Year's Day. *White Swan, WA; 509-865-5121.*

Victorian Tea and Home Tour. Self-guided tours of homes throughout the Sequim and Dungeness Valleys. Begins at the Old Dungeness Schoolhouse. *Sequim, WA; 360-683-8110.*

INDEX

COMPASS AMERICAN GUIDES

Alaska (3rd Edition)
376 pages; 0-679-00838-1

American Southwest (3rd Edition)
368 pages; 0-679-00646-X

Arizona (5th Edition)
292 pages; 0-679-00432-7

Boston (3rd Edition)
328 pages; 0-676-90132-8

Chicago (3rd Edition)
288 pages; 0-679-00841-1

Coastal California (2nd Edition)
400 pages; 0-679-00439-4

Colorado (6th Edition)
304 pages; 1-4000-1204-X

Florida (2nd Edition)
336 pages; 0-676-90494-7

Georgia (2nd Edition)
312 pages; 0-676-90137-9

Gulf South: Louisiana, Alabama,
Mississippi (1st Edition)
352 pages; 0-679-00533-1

Hawaii (5th Edition)
368 pages; 0-679-00839-X

Idaho (2nd Edition)
288 pages; 0-679-00231-6

Kentucky (1st Edition)
324 pages; 0-679-00537-4

Las Vegas (7th Edition)
304 pages; 0-676-90138-7

Maine (3rd Edition)
320 pages; 0-679-00436-X

Manhattan (4th Edition)
336 pages; 0-676-90495-5

Michigan (1st Edition)
320 pages; 0-679-00534-X

Minnesota (2nd Edition)
352 pages; 0-679-00437-8

Montana (5th Edition)
304 pages; 0-676-90133-6

Nevada (1st Edition)
344 pages; 0-679-00535-8

New Hampshire (1st Edition)
304 pages; 0-676-90151-4

New Mexico (4th Edition)
336 pages; 0-679-00438-6

New Orleans (4th Edition)
304 pages; 0-679-00647-8

North Carolina (3rd Edition)
352 pages; 0-676-90498-X

Oregon (4th Edition)
304 pages; 0-676-90140-9

Pennsylvania (1st Edition)
336 pages; 0-679-00182-4

San Francisco (5th Edition)
336 pages; 0-679-00229-4

Santa Fe (3rd Edition)
272 pages; 0-679-00286-3

South Carolina (3rd Edition)
328 pages; 0-679-00509-9

South Dakota (2nd Edition)
312 pages; 1-878867-47-4

Southern New England (1st Edition)
384 pages; 0-679-00184-0

Tennessee (1st Edition)
320 pages; 0-679-00536-6

Texas (2nd Edition)
336 pages; 1-878867-98-9

Utah (5th Edition)
352 pages; 0-679-00645-1

Vermont (2nd Edition)
336 pages; 0-676-90139-5

Virginia (3rd Edition)
312 pages; 0-679-00282-0

Washington (3rd Edition)
320 pages; 0-676-90497-1

Wine Country (3rd Edition)
312 pages; 0-679-00434-3

Wisconsin (3rd Edition)
308 pages; 0-679-00433-5

Wyoming (4th Edition)
368 pages; 0-676-90499-8

■ AUTHOR

John Doerper is the publisher and editor of *Pacific Epicure: A Quarterly Journal of Gastronomic Literature* and has worked as a food and wine columnist and editor for numerous publications. His articles about food, wine, and travel have appeared in *Travel & Leisure* and *Pacific Northwest Magazine,* among others. He is also the author of several books, including *Shellfish Cookery: Absolutely Delicious Recipes from the West Coast* and the Compass American Guides *Wine Country, Pacific Northwest,* and *Coastal California.* John lives in Bellingham, Washington.

PENELOPE JONES VAUGHN

■ PHOTOGRAPHER

Greg Vaughn's award-winning imagery has appeared in *National Geographic, Outside, National Wildlife, Sierra, Natural History,* and *Travel & Leisure,* and he was the principal photographer for two books about Hawaii and the Compass American Guides *Oregon* and *Washington.*